# Applied XML Solutions

Benoît Marchal

**SAMS**

A Division of Macmillan

201 West 103rd Street, Ir

# Applied XML Solutions

Benoît Marchal

**Copyright © 2000 by Sams**

International Standard Book Number: 0-672-32054-1

Library of Congress Catalog Card Number: 00-104353

Printed in the United States of America

First Printing: September 2000

02   01   00        4   3   2   1

## Trademarks

## Warning and Disclaimer

**Associate Publisher**
Tracy Dunkelberger

**Acquisitions Editor**
Todd Green

**Development Editor**
Sean Dixon

**Managing Editor**
Thomas F. Hayes

**Project Editor**
Tricia Sterling

**Copy Editor**
Megan Wade

**Indexer**
Mary SeRine

**Proofreader**
Jeanne Clark

**Technical Editors**
Claude Chiaramonti
Bryan Scattergood

**Team Coordinator**
Cindy Teeters

**Media Developer**
Michael Hunter

**Interior Designer**
Gary Adair

**Cover Designer**
Jay Corpus

**Production**
Darin Crone

# Contents

# About the Author

**Benoît Marchal** runs the consulting company Pineapplesoft, which specializes in Internet applications, particularly e-commerce, XML, and Java. He has worked with major players in Internet development, such as Netscape and EarthWeb, and is a regular contributor to Gamelan and other Internet publications.

In 1997, he co-founded the XML/EDI Group, a think tank that promotes the use of XML in e-commerce applications. Benoît frequently leads corporate training on XML and other Internet technologies.

Benoît also publishes a free email magazine, Pineapplesoft Link. Each month it provides technologies, trends, and facts of interest to Web developers. You can subscribe at www.marchal.com.

# Dedication

*To Pascale*

# Acknowledgments

I want to thank the readers of *XML by Example*, Pineapplesoft Link, and my technical articles. You are the motivation and inspiration to explore new topics. I am particularly grateful to readers who emailed me or otherwise commented on my work. Your opinions are always instructive.

# Tell Us What You Think!

As the reader of this book, *you* are our most important critic and commentator. We value your opinion and want to know what we're doing right, what we could do better, what areas you'd like to see us publish in, and any other words of wisdom you're willing to pass our way.

As an Associate Publisher for Sams, I welcome your comments. You can fax, email, or write me directly to let me know what you did or didn't like about this book—as well as what we can do to make our books stronger.

*Please note that I cannot help you with technical problems related to the topic of this book, and that due to the high volume of mail I receive, I might not be able to reply to every message.*

When you write, please be sure to include this book's title and author as well as your name and phone or fax number. I will carefully review your comments and share them with the author and editors who worked on the book.

| | |
|---|---|
| Fax: | 317-581-4770 |
| Email: | consumer@mcp.com |
| Mail: | Associate Publisher |
| | Sams |
| | 201 West 103rd Street |
| | Indianapolis, IN 46290 USA |

# Introduction

## Why a Solution Book?

This book teaches you how to solve common problems in development, how to impress your boss (or your customer if you're a freelancer), and how to use XML in your projects.

Through my experience lecturing and consulting, I know that the main problem for developers trying to leverage XML in their applications is not a lack of information but too much of it! There is an almost endless flow of announcements from standardization bodies and vendors and no shortage of conferences, books, and magazines.

All this information is useful—it can solve real problems for some people—but it is not always easy for the developer to decide whether the information applies to him or his problem.

I meet many developers, like you, who have learned the basics of XML (elements, tags, attributes, DTDs, and more) and the most popular XML vocabularies (RSS, WML, SOAP, XSL, and so on). But what these developers are missing is information on how it all works in real projects.

When I started discussing this book with my editor, we worked hard to develop a book that would address your concerns as a developer. We deliberately decided not to try to cover every XML vocabulary or every technology but to concentrate on the few tools every programmer needs to know to succeed in his or her project.

Furthermore, the feedback we received on my tutorial book, *XML by Example*, convinced us that a practical book—a book that teaches by using carefully chosen examples and a lot of code—would be useful. In that respect, *Applied XML Solutions* grew out of the readers' feedback, out of *your* feedback.

We selected eight projects that are representative of real applications of XML. The eight projects became nine chapters, with each chapter demonstrating how to build one project with XML (one project required two chapters).

The eight projects we selected are as follows:

- Linking an object data structure with XML. Most applications have an internal data structure that might be close, but is seldom identical, to the XML format. A few simple patterns can help bridge the differences.

- Preparing advanced configuration files. Many applications benefit from a solid configuration file format, and XML is a great solution for this. XML offers enormous flexibility. It also can be used as a true scripting solution.

- Using electronic forms and XML editors. A good XML editor is a powerful addition to any programmer's toolbox because it makes it easy to create an efficient user interface on XML applications.

- Using multi-format publishing. With the advent of mobile phones, PDAs, and other devices, the PC might not remain the dominant platform for Internet browsing. Web sites will need increased flexibility to work with these multiple formats.

- Integrating with legacy format. Even the most fanatic XML developer must recognize that many non-XML formats exist. Few applications leave in isolation, therefore it is crucial to integrate with legacy formats.

- Conducting business-to-business e-commerce. XML profiles itself as the HTML of business-to-business e-commerce. This is an important topic that deserved a project of its own.

- Using XML to organize the work of a team. Web development requires many talents, and organizing them is not always easy. Furthermore, Web sites increasingly need to be multi-lingual. This project addresses these two issues.

- Integrating with an ERP. As organizations strive to streamline their operations, they will increasingly need to place information from their ERPs online. SOAP is an interesting approach in that arena.

As you can see, this is not a list of technologies but of solutions to problems. However, in building these solutions, we will explore many useful technologies, such as SAX2 parsing, patterns, DOM and JavaScript, CSS, XSLT, non-XML formatters, non-XML parsers, XSLT extensions, automatic posting, servlets, SOAP, and more.

# Who Should Read This Book

*Applied XML Solutions* will be helpful to programmers, analysts, Web developers, and consultants who need to use XML in their work. Developers will benefit directly from exposure to practical solutions and a lot of code. However, analysts and consultants will also benefit from new ideas and new solutions to problems.

*Applied XML Solutions* will be particularly valuable if you are currently working on XML projects or if you will soon join such a team. It provides sample solutions to problems and plenty of code you can reuse, teaches you new tools, and explains how to better use your current set of tools.

If you are not actively involved in an XML project, *Applied XML Solutions* will be a source of inspiration for the future. As you read through the solutions, I am sure you will find several examples that would work well for you.

*Applied XML Solutions* assumes that you know the XML syntax, how an XML parser works, and how to write an XSLT style sheet. If this is your first XML book, you might want to turn to a tutorial first. I think my previous book, *XML by Example*, is a good introduction to the material in *Applied XML Solutions*.

Most of the code (the only exception is Chapter 3, "Electronic Forms") is written in Java. Most of the solutions will port easily to C++, Delphi, Perl, Python, and other languages (I have included pointers where appropriate), so you will benefit from reading this book even if you are not a Java developer. However, you must be able to read and understand Java code.

Flip through the book and you will see several commented listings. As I have already indicated, I listened to reader feedback in preparing *Applied XML Solutions*, so I tried to include as many listings and examples as possible. This is clearly a hands-on book. The only persons who should not read this book are developers who hate studying listings. Only a few such developers exist, but if you are one of them, I hope I catch you in the bookstore, before you've bought the book.

# How to Read This Book

This book can be read in any order. If you are working on a project, you might want to jump to one of the chapters to learn about that particular solution. In some cases, I have made references to earlier chapters, so you might need to backtrack for a section or two.

However, this book can also be read from cover to cover. The chapters follow a logical progression from simple to more complex.

Whenever possible, I have included refreshers that summarize the essential aspects of technology and point you to more resources, as appropriate.

Finally, each chapter concludes with an "Additional Resources" section. This section points to Web sites and other resources where you can learn more information on the topic.

# Conventions Used in This Book

Tips on how to take advantage of XML are identified as follows:

**Tip**
Tips appear here.

When a risk of error exists, special warning notes are identified as follows:

**Warning**
Warnings appear here.

Additional information about a topic is marked as follows:

**Note**
Notes appear here.

**Refreshers**
Refreshers appear here.

Listings, code, and class names appear in a monospace font, such as the following:

```
<?xml version="1.0"?>
```

# Additional Resources

To save you some typing, all the listings are available on the enclosed CD-ROM. You also should visit the Que Web site and my own site for updates and additional information.

The Que Web site is at www.macmillanusa.com. If required, we will post code updates, bug fixes, and general updates there.

My site is at www.marchal.com. Here you will find links to articles and other useful information on XML. You can also subscribe to my free email magazine, Pineapplesoft Link—your source for technology news, trends, and facts of interest to Web developers.

If you use this book to solve an interesting problem or if you develop your own solutions, I'd like to hear from you. Write to me at bmarchal@pineapplesoft.com.

I wish you a lot of success in your XML projects.

# Lightweight Data Storage

IN THIS CHAPTER, YOU BUILD your first solution based on XML. The solution demonstrates XML as an alternative to databases and proprietary file formats. Many applications benefit from this solution and it is particularly valuable for the following:

- Applications downloaded from the Internet, when it is not possible to ship a database at runtime
- CD-ROMs and DVDs where the files are read-only
- Applications that work on a subset of a database, where it must be easy to unload the data from the database
- Applications running on multiple platforms or written in different languages, where it should be possible to exchange files between, for example, the Windows (C++), UNIX (Java), and Macintosh (Java) versions of the product

More importantly, this chapter will concentrate on how to structure the application, using two simple patterns, for optimum flexibility.

## Why Lightweight Data Storage?

Applications must perform many duties, including taking care of the user interface (for example, painting screens, opening dialog boxes, or responding to menu selections), providing help and assistance, and increasingly being network savvy (such as sending and receiving emails or connecting to the Web). Not to be forgotten is the capability to save work and later reload it, which is our current topic of interest.

Java, similar to other programming languages, supports these functions through libraries. Two libraries exist for the user interface: AWT (Abstract Window Toolkit) and Swing. In addition, JavaHelp exists for documentation. Also, no less than four options are available for networking: the java.net package, RMI (Remote Method Invocation), Jini, and CORBA.

Finally, Java supports permanent storage through the java.io package and JDBC (Java Database Connectivity). However, for a number of applications, java.io is too limited and JDBC is too complex. This chapter introduces a solution that sits somewhere in between. It is more powerful than raw I/O but not as costly as full-blown SQL databases.

Databases are convenient because they store large amounts of data and access it rapidly. Furthermore, they are well supported by third-party vendors. A typical Java development environment offers wizards and other tools to help you build database-driven applications. Figure 1.1 demonstrates database support in JBuilder.

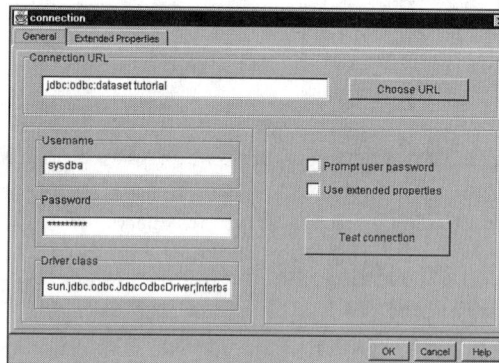

**Figure 1.1** A dialog box helps configure and test the database connections in JBuilder.

Databases are also open, which means one application can share data easily with other applications. This enables you, the developer, to quickly and inexpensively extend the application. For example, if the user wants new reports, a report writer such as Crystal Report (www.seagatesoftware.com) or Enterprise Report (www.enterprisesoft.com) is handy.

On the downside, databases tend to be costly. Database licenses can run in the tens of thousands of dollars and they can require dedicated servers, which further adds to the cost.

I am reminded of one project in which a company installed a new sales system. It worked brilliantly until they decided to give a laptop to each of their salespeople. The cost of the licenses (and in particular, the database licenses) skyrocketed to the point where the laptops would have cost ten times more than the central system in licenses only!

In addition, they needed high-end laptops to run the database and the sales software concurrently. Worse, it was obvious to everybody involved that a full-blown database was overkill in this setup because a salesperson managed only a few dozen customers and worked with a limited set of about a thousand references.

Therefore, the developers needed to downscale from a full-blown database to a simpler file format. Java is very convenient in this respect because it offers serialization (`java.io.ObjectInputStream` and `java.io.ObjectOutputStream`).

However, while serialization makes it easy to save complex data structures to disk, it is a closed format. It works only with the original application and no third-party tools are available, such as report writers for serialized files.

In this chapter, we'll develop a solution, based on XML, that offers the following benefits:

- XML keeps growing so no lack of third-party tools exists. For example, style sheets make it easy to produce reports.

- Most databases have an XML interface (either available now or in the making) that makes loading and unloading a database in XML easy.

- The data model behind XML is a tree of elements, which is a natural match for an object-oriented data structure.

- XML support is available to most programming languages on the major platforms, so it is possible to share data between different applications (for example, a UNIX server and a PC client).

**Caution**

This solution is appropriate for small to medium sets of data only because it loads the file in memory. In other words, it is limited by the amount of memory available.

Yet, this is not a limitation of XML. XML databases, such as eXcelon (www.exceloncorp.com), can manipulate documents of any size. However, the cost of these databases is comparable to SQL databases, so it's no longer a solution to our present problem.

# Meeting the Catalog Viewer

The example I'll use in this chapter is a catalog viewer. Assume that you have been asked to develop a catalog viewer. The specifications are as follows:

- Customers and prospective customers receive a new version of the catalog viewer every month. The monthly update presents the latest offerings (such as new products and promotions).

- The list of products is managed in the company's central database, and a file with the month's offering will be automatically extracted from the database.

- Product descriptions include the product name and either a picture of the product or a textual description. The management expects to enhance product descriptions with video and HTML in the future.

- Customers browse through the catalog and mark those products they are interested in buying.

- The catalog viewer creates a file with the customer's selection. Customers can submit their selections by email and receive more information on those products relevant to them.

The catalog viewer looks similar to Figure 1.2.

**Note**

A catalog can be as simple or as complex as one likes. In its simplest form it is just a list of product names; in the most complex form it can include videos. It also can compute the correct price (including any discounts) and even support online ordering.

In this chapter, I strove for the middle ground with a set of data rich enough to explore all the problems you are likely to face in a real catalog application. However, I used a limited user interface and a limited set of features so as not to bury the XML techniques in a lot of Java programming.

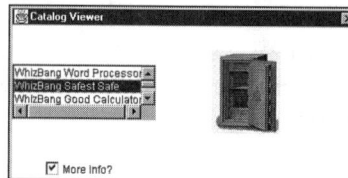

**Figure 1.2** The catalog viewer.

The catalog viewer needs a simple, inexpensive file format to store the list of products and the prospective buyers' selections. Because the list of products is stored in a central database, you need a format recognized by the database.

Figure 1.3 is the class model (in UML [Unified Modeling Language]) for the catalog. This model abstracts product descriptions: The Product class holds only basic information about products (such as the name). Descendants of Product implement more complete descriptions (in this case, through an image or through text).

In particular, each product object is responsible for drawing its own description onscreen. Therefore, if a future version of the catalog includes video, it suffices to add descendants to the Product class.

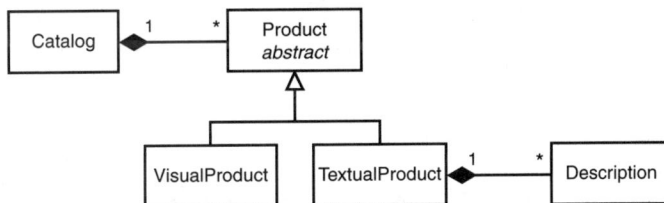

**Figure 1.3** The catalog class model.

## Building the Catalog

Listings 1.1–1.6 implement this class model in Java. Listing 1.1 is the Catalog class. And as you can see, Catalog is simply a list of Product objects.

### Warning

Ignore the reference to the CatalogElement and CatalogVisitor interfaces as well as the accept() method for the time being. These will be introduced in subsequent sections.

Listing 1.1 *Catalog.java*

```java
package com.psol.catalog;

import java.util.Vector;
import java.io.IOException;

public class Catalog
    implements CatalogElement
{
    protected Product[] products;

    public Catalog(Vector products)
    {
        this.products = new Product[products.size()];
        products.copyInto(this.products);
    }
```

Listing 1.1 **Continued**

```
    public Product productAt(int i)
    {
       return products[i];
    }

    public int getSize()
    {
       return products.length;
    }

    public void accept(CatalogVisitor visitor)
       throws IOException
    {
       visitor.visitCatalog(this);
    }
}
```

The `Product` class is declared in Listing 1.2. `Product` is an abstract class that implements properties shared by all descendants, namely the product's name and whether the product was selected (checked) by a customer.

`Product` also defines the abstract method `getComponent()`. Descendants of `Product` implement this method and return an AWT component that knows how to draw the product description.

For example, `VisualProduct` objects return a component that draws the image of the product. `TextualProduct` objects return text labels.

If a `VideoProduct` class is introduced in the future, it will return components that play the product's video.

Listing 1.2 *Product.java*

```
package com.psol.catalog;

import java.io.IOException;
import java.awt.Component;

public abstract class Product
   implements CatalogElement
{
   protected String text,
                    id;
   protected boolean checked;

   public Product(String text,
                  String id,
                  boolean checked)
```

Listing 1.2 **Continued**

```
    {
        this.text = text;
        this.id = id;
        this.checked = checked;
    }

    public String getText()
    {
        return text;
    }

    public String getId()
    {
        return id;
    }

    public void setChecked(boolean checked)
    {
        this.checked = checked;
    }

    public boolean isChecked()
    {
        return checked;
    }

    public abstract Component getComponent();
}
```

## Browsing the Catalog

The abstract method `getComponent()` is responsible for painting the product description, which greatly simplifies the user interface. Listing 1.3 is the `CatalogPanel` class, a simple graphical interface to the catalog.

`CatalogPanel` accepts a catalog in its constructor, builds a list of products on the right side of the screen, and paints the appropriate product on the left side, as the customer browses through the list. It also provides a checkbox for the customer to select the product.

`itemStateChanged` events are generated as the customer browses the list of products. Then the event handler calls `getComponent()` to draw the appropriate product. Note that the event handler does not know whether a given product is a `VisualProduct` or a `TextualProduct`, but it doesn't need to know:

```
public void itemStateChanged(ItemEvent evt)
{
    if(evt.getStateChange() == ItemEvent.SELECTED)
    {
```

```java
            viewer.removeAll();
            int idx = list.getSelectedIndex();
            Product product = catalog.productAt(idx);
            viewer.add(product.getComponent());
            checkbox.setState(product.isChecked());
            checkbox.setEnabled(true);
            validate();
        }
    }
```

Listing 1.3  ***CatalogPanel.java***

```java
package com.psol.catalog;

import java.awt.*;
import java.awt.event.*;

public class CatalogPanel
    extends Panel
{
    protected List list;
    protected Checkbox checkbox;
    protected Container viewer;
    protected Catalog catalog;

    public CatalogPanel(Catalog _catalog)
    {
        catalog = _catalog;
        setLayout(new GridBagLayout());

        list = new List();
        GridBagConstraints constraints = new GridBagConstraints();
        add(list,constraints);
        for(int i = 0;i < catalog.getSize();i++)
            list.add(catalog.productAt(i).getText());
        list.addItemListener(new ItemListener()
        {
            public void itemStateChanged(ItemEvent evt)
            {
                if(evt.getStateChange() == ItemEvent.SELECTED)
                {
                    viewer.removeAll();
                    int idx = list.getSelectedIndex();
                    Product product = catalog.productAt(idx);
                    viewer.add(product.getComponent());
                    checkbox.setState(product.isChecked());
                    checkbox.setEnabled(true);
                    validate();
                }
            }
        });
```

Listing 1.3 **Continued**

```
        viewer = new Panel();
        constraints.gridwidth = GridBagConstraints.REMAINDER;
        constraints.weightx = 1.0;
        constraints.weighty = 1.0;
        add(viewer,constraints);

        checkbox = new Checkbox("More info?",false);
        constraints.gridwidth = 1;
        constraints.weightx = 0.0;
        constraints.weighty = 0.0;
        add(checkbox,constraints);
        checkbox.setEnabled(false);
        checkbox.addItemListener(new ItemListener()
        {
            public void itemStateChanged(ItemEvent evt)
            {
                int stateChange = evt.getStateChange();
                if(ItemEvent.SELECTED == stateChange ||
                    ItemEvent.DESELECTED == stateChange)
                {
                    int idx = list.getSelectedIndex();
                    Product product = catalog.productAt(idx);
                    product.setChecked(
                        ItemEvent.SELECTED == stateChange);
                }
            }
        });
    }
}
```

## Extending the Product

Listing 1.4 is a TextualProduct. A TextualProduct is a collection of Description objects. To render itself onscreen, the TextualProduct creates a component with as many labels as there are Description objects:

```
public Component getComponent()
{
    LayoutManager layout =
        new GridLayout(descriptions.length + 1,1);
    Panel panel = new Panel(layout);
    panel.add(new Label("Description:"));
    for(int i = 0;i < descriptions.length;i++)
    {
        String language = descriptions[i].getLanguage(),
                text = descriptions[i].getText();
        Label label = new Label(language + ": " + text);
        panel.add(label);
    }
    return panel;
}
```

Listing 1.4   *TextualProduct.java*

```java
package com.psol.catalog;

import java.awt.*;
import java.util.Vector;
import java.io.IOException;

public class TextualProduct
    extends Product
{
   protected Description[] descriptions;

   public TextualProduct(String text,
                         String id,
                         boolean checked,
                         Vector descriptions)
   {
      super(text,id,checked);
      this.descriptions = new Description[descriptions.size()];
      descriptions.copyInto(this.descriptions);
   }

   public Component getComponent()
   {
      LayoutManager layout =
         new GridLayout(descriptions.length + 1,1);
      Panel panel = new Panel(layout);
      panel.add(new Label("Description:"));
      for(int i = 0;i < descriptions.length;i++)
      {
         String language = descriptions[i].getLanguage(),
                text = descriptions[i].getText();
         Label label = new Label(language + ": " + text);
         panel.add(label);
      }
      return panel;
   }

   public Description descriptionAt(int i)
   {
      return descriptions[i];
   }

   public int getSize()
   {
      return descriptions.length;
   }

   public void accept(CatalogVisitor visitor)
      throws IOException
   {
      visitor.visitTextualProduct(this);
   }
}
```

Listing 1.5 is `Description`, which is simply a description and the description's language. We can have multilingual catalogs!

Listing 1.5 *Description.java*

```java
package com.psol.catalog;

import java.io.IOException;
import java.awt.Component;

public class Description
    implements CatalogElement
{
    protected String language,
                     text;

    public Description(String language,
                       String text)
    {
        this.language = language;
        this.text = text;
    }

    public String getLanguage()
    {
        return language;
    }

    public String getText()
    {
        return text;
    }

    public void accept(CatalogVisitor visitor)
        throws IOException
    {
        visitor.visitDescription(this);
    }
}
```

Compare Listing 1.4 with Listing 1.6, the `VisualProduct`. Both are similar, but a `VisualProduct` is rendered as an image onscreen.

Listing 1.6 *VisualProduct.java*

```java
package com.psol.catalog;

import java.awt.*;
import java.io.IOException;
```

Listing 1.6 **Continued**

```java
public class VisualProduct
    extends Product
{
    protected String image;

    protected class ImageCanvas
        extends Component
    {
        protected Image image = null;
        public ImageCanvas(String filename)
        {
            Toolkit toolkit = getToolkit();
            image = toolkit.getImage(filename);
        }
        public void paint(Graphics g)
        {
            if(null != image)
                g.drawImage(image,0,0,this);
        }
        public Dimension getPreferredSize()
        {
            int width = image.getWidth(this),
                height = image.getHeight(this);
            if(width == -1)
                width = 100;
            if(height == -1)
                height = 100;
            return new Dimension(width,height);
        }
    }

    public VisualProduct(String text,
                         String id,
                         boolean checked,
                         String image)
    {
        super(text,id,checked);
        this.image = image;
    }

    public String getImage()
    {
        return image;
    }

    public Component getComponent()
    {
        return new ImageCanvas(image);
    }
```

Listing 1.6 **Continued**

```
    public void accept(CatalogVisitor visitor)
        throws IOException
    {
        visitor.visitVisualProduct(this);
    }
}
```

# The XML Side

The object model is one side of the equation; the other side is the XML file. In an ideal world, the XML file would match your object structure exactly and would be similar to the following:

```
<?xml version='1.0' encoding='ISO-8859-1'?>
<Catalog>
    <VisualProduct>
        <Id>wp01</Id>
        <Checked>false</Checked>
        <Name>WhizBang Word Processor</Name>
        <Image>images/wordprocessor.jpg</Image>
    </VisualProduct>
    <TextualProduct>
        <Id>li04</Id>
        <Checked>false</Checked>
        <Title>WhizBang Bright Light</Title>
        <Descriptions>
            <Description>
                <Language>EN</Language>
                <Text>With power saving.</Text>
            </Description>
            <Description>
                <Language>FR</Language>
                <Text>Avec gestion d'énergie.</Text>
            </Description>
        </Descriptions>
    </TextualProduct>
</Catalog>
```

**Crash Course on XML**

*XML* stands for eXtensible Markup Language. Similar to HTML, it is a markup language developed by the World Wide Web Consortium (W3C).

The syntax for XML is similar to HTML syntax, so it looks familiar. However, the X in XML means that, unlike HTML, the language is not fixed.

Indeed, HTML has a fixed set of tags (<BODY>, <TITLE>, <P>, <IMG>, and so on); the list of acceptable tags was published by the W3C.

XML has no built-in tags and it is up to you, the developer, to create the tags you need.

Therefore, whereas HTML tags carry presentation instructions (for example, <FONT>, <CENTER>, and <PRE>), XML tags tend to be related to the structure of the information. For example, an address book will have tags such as <Name>, <Street>, and <Phone>.

In other words, XML tags don't tell you how the information should be presented onscreen (bold, italics, or centered) but rather what the information is. For example, the tag

```
<Name>John Doe</Name>
```

means that the person's name is John Doe.

The second major difference between XML and HTML is that XML enforces a very strict syntax. Without going in the details, note the following:

- Elements must be enclosed in a start tag and an end tag. It is no longer possible to ignore the end tag. The following is an example:

```
<Phone>513-744-7098</Phone>
```

- Empty elements (elements with no content) follow a special syntax, which looks similar to the following:

```
<Email href="mailto:jdoe@emailaholic.com"/>
```

- Attribute values must be enclosed in double or single quotes.

For a comprehensive introduction to XML, I recommend you read my other book, *XML by Example*, published by Que.

However, that is the ideal case. In practice, the product information comes from the central database, so chances are the XML file will be closer to the database organization than to your object model. It is not unlikely that the file will look similar to Listing 1.7.

Obviously, because it is based on the same list of products, Listing 1.7 is not completely alien to your object model either. The major difference is that it doesn't have a VisualProduct or TextualProduct. In Listing 1.7, every entry is a product. Listing 1.7's structure is illustrated in Figure 1.4.

Listing 1.7 *catalog.xml*

```
<?xml version='1.0' encoding='ISO-8859-1'?>
<Catalog>
   <Product id='wp01' checked='false'>
      <Text>WhizBang Word Processor</Text>
      <Image>images/wordprocessor.jpg</Image>
   </Product>
```

Listing 1.7 **Continued**

```
    <Product id='sf02' checked='false'>
        <Text>WhizBang Safest Safe</Text>
        <Image>images/safe.jpg</Image>
    </Product>
    <Product id='ca03' checked='false'>
        <Text>WhizBang Good Calculator</Text>
        <Image>images/calculator.jpg</Image>
    </Product>
    <Product id='li04' checked='false'>
        <Text>WhizBang Bright Light</Text>
        <Descriptions>
            <Text xml:lang='EN'>With power saving.</Text>
            <Text xml:lang='FR'>Avec gestion d'énergie.</Text>
        </Descriptions>
    </Product>
</Catalog>
```

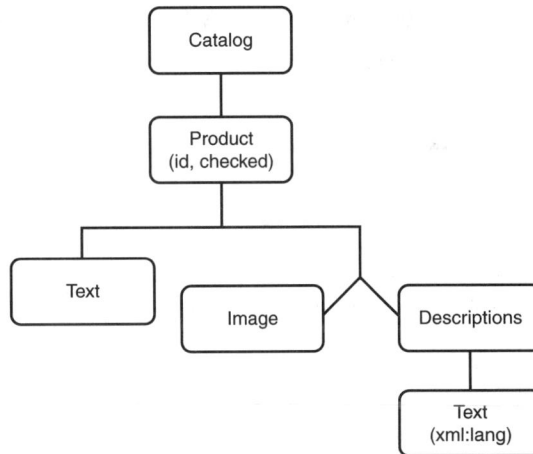

Figure 1.4  XML document structure.

## Designing with Patterns

This is where the interesting part begins. Your goal is to read the XML file in Listing 1.7 in the object structure outlined in Figure 1.3.

The simplest solution is to add methods to the various classes to read and write the XML document. A method to read a Description might look similar to

```
public static Description readXML(Element element)
{
```

```
    if(element.getTagName().equals("Text"))
    {
        String text = null;
        Node child = element.getFirstChild();
        if(child != null &&
            child.getNodeType() == Node.TEXT_NODE)
        {
            Text t = (Text)child;
            text = t.getData();
        }
        String language = element.getAttribute("xml:lang");
        return new Description(language,text);
    }
    else
        return null;
}
```

Note that this method relies on a DOM (Document Object Model) parser to handle the XML syntax. So, the `Element` parameter is a DOM `Element` object.

The method to write a `Description` object in XML would be as follows:

```
public void writeXML(PrintWriter pw)
    throws IOException
{
    pw.print("<Text xml:lang='" + language + "'>");
    pw.print(text);
    pw.println("</Text>");
}
```

This is simple, but it is also limited. First, it mixes the XML into the data structure, which greatly limits your ability to evolve one independently from the other. It also spreads the XML code over the entire object hierarchy, which makes it more difficult to maintain.

We can do better using two patterns, the builder pattern and the visitor pattern, as described in *Design Patterns* by Gamma, et al. (Addison-Wesley).

Use these patterns to separate the XML-related code from the object structure so that you can change the file format without having to change your objects…or vice versa.

# Meeting the Builder Pattern

Let's start with reading. To read the XML document and create the corresponding object structure, use the builder pattern on top of the XML parser. Figure 1.5 illustrates the generic builder pattern.

The various components of the pattern are as follows:

- A builder interface and one (or more) concrete builders, which create the object structure.

- A director that interacts with the builder to create the object structure. The director is driven by the parser.
- Product, which is a placeholder in the pattern for the object structure being created.

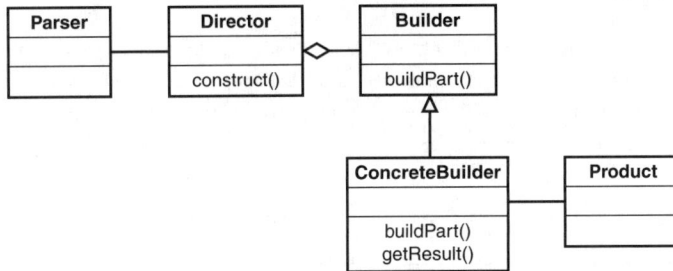

**Figure 1.5** The builder pattern.

## Applying the Builder Pattern

Figure 1.6 illustrates how to apply the pattern to your object structure. In addition to the Catalog, Product, and Description classes introduced previously, this diagram has the following:

- A CatalogBuilder interface that defines methods to create the various objects in the structure (such as buildCatalog(), buildVisualProduct(), and so on)
- A DefaultCatalogBuilder class that implements the CatalogBuilder interface
- An XMLDirector class that drives the CatalogBuilder and is the class that implements the SAX-defined DocumentHandler interface

In effect, XMLDirector convert SAX's events into calls to CatalogBuilder. The CatalogBuilder is responsible for creating the various catalog objects.

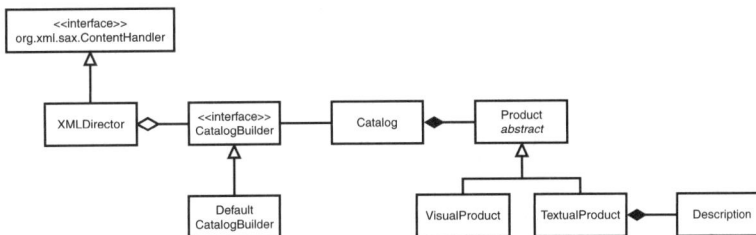

**Figure 1.6** Applying the builder pattern.

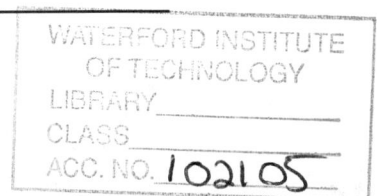

### A Simple API for XML

*SAX* stands for the Simple API for XML. It declares an interface to an XML parser, and in this respect, SAX is similar to W3C's Document Object Model (DOM). However, the way SAX works is different the way DOM does. An XML parser is a library to read XML documents. The parser enforces the XML syntax, decodes the elements, resolves the entities, and more. In a nutshell, it takes care of low-level work for the programmer.

SAX is an event-based interface. Similar to AWT, your application must register for events of interest. However, unlike AWT, SAX events are not related to buttons and menus. SAX events relate to the XML document instead. Events exists for the beginning and the end of the document, for the beginning and the end of an element, for character data, for processing instructions, and more (see Figure 1.7).

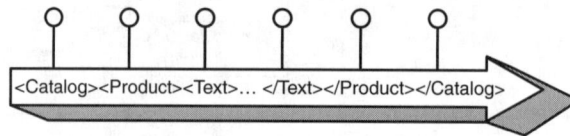

**Figure 1.7** A SAX parser generates events as it reads the XML document.

Because it is event based, SAX does not explicitly build the document tree in memory. It is therefore more efficient than DOM and, in particular, it can process documents larger than the available memory.

You can learn more about SAX at www.meggison.com/SAX.

In practice, `CatalogBuilder` is implemented in Listing 1.8. It declares one build method for each object in the data structure: `buildCatalog()`, `buildVisualProduct()`, and so on.

Notice that it does not declare a `buildProduct()` because `Product` is an abstract class. It is therefore impossible to instantiate it.

Listing 1.8 *CatalogBuilder.java*

```
package com.psol.catalog;

public interface CatalogBuilder
{
   public void buildCatalog();
   public void buildVisualProduct(String text,
                                  String id,
                                  boolean checked,
                                  String image);
   public void buildTextualProduct(String text,
                                   String id,
                                   boolean checked);
   public void buildDescription(String language,
                                String text);
   public Catalog getCatalog();
}
```

XMLDirector and DefaultCatalogBuilder are more interesting classes. XMLDirector is demonstrated in Listing 1.9; let's walk through it step by step.

First, XMLDirector implements the SAX's DocumentHandler interface, which declares SAX events related to the document:

```
public class XMLDirector
   implements ContentHandler
```

The constructor accepts an object that implements the CatalogBuilder interface. As XMLDirector progresses through the XML document, it collects information on the various objects and calls the Catalogbuilder to create the Product objects:

```
public XMLDirector(CatalogBuilder builder)
{
   this.builder = builder;
}
```

The meat of XMLDirector is in startElement() and endElement(). These two event handlers track where the reader is in the document using the state variable. startElement() also initializes various buffers, depending on the current element. For the <Product> and <Text> elements, it collects the value of their attributes:

```
public void startElement(String namespaceURI,
                         String localName,
                         String tag,
                         Attributes atts)
{
   if(tag.equals("Catalog") && ROOT == state)
      state = CATALOG;
   else if(tag.equals("Product") && CATALOG == state)
   {
      state = PRODUCT;
      id = atts.getValue("id");
      String st = atts.getValue("checked");
      checked = Boolean.valueOf(st).booleanValue();
      text = null;
      image = null;
   }
   else if(tag.equals("Text") && PRODUCT == state)
   {
      state = PRODUCT_TEXT;
      buffer = new StringBuffer();
   }
   else if(tag.equals("Image") && PRODUCT == state)
   {
      state = IMAGE;
      buffer = new StringBuffer();
   }
   else if(tag.equals("Descriptions") && PRODUCT == state)
      state = DESCRIPTIONS;
   else if(tag.equals("Text") && DESCRIPTIONS == state)
   {
```

```
        state = DESCRIPTIONS_TEXT;
        language = atts.getValue("xml:lang");
        buffer = new StringBuffer();
    }
}
```

When an XML element corresponds to a Java object, endElement() calls the builder, passing it the appropriate information.

This illustrates how the builder pattern works. The director accumulates just enough information to construct one object and calls the builder to do the actual work:

```
public void endElement(String namespaceURI,
                       String localName,
                       String tag)
{
    if(tag.equals("Catalog") && CATALOG == state)
    {
        state = ROOT;
        builder.buildCatalog();
    }
    else if(tag.equals("Product") && PRODUCT == state)
    {
        state = CATALOG;
        if(null == image)
            builder.buildTextualProduct(text,id,checked);
        else
            builder.buildVisualProduct(text,id,checked,image);
    }
    else if(tag.equals("Text") && PRODUCT_TEXT == state)
    {
        state = PRODUCT;
        text = buffer.toString();
    }
    else if(tag.equals("Image") && IMAGE == state)
    {
        state = PRODUCT;
        image = buffer.toString();
    }
    else if(tag.equals("Descriptions") &&
            DESCRIPTIONS == state)
        state = PRODUCT;
    else if(tag.equals("Text") && DESCRIPTIONS_TEXT == state)
    {
        state = DESCRIPTIONS;
        builder.buildDescription(language,buffer.toString());
    }
}
```

**Tip**

XMLDirector does not validate the structure of the XML document—for example, it does not test whether the attributes or the elements exist.

If your applications need to validate the structure of the document, you should consider using a validating parser.

As promised, the code for XMLDirector is in Listing 1.9.

Listing 1.9 *XMLDirector.java*

```java
package com.psol.catalog;

import org.xml.sax.*;

public class XMLDirector
   implements DocumentHandler
{
   protected CatalogBuilder builder;
   protected static final int ROOT = 0,
                              CATALOG = 1,
                              PRODUCT = 2,
                              PRODUCT_TEXT = 3,
                              IMAGE = 4,
                              DESCRIPTIONS = 5,
                              DESCRIPTIONS_TEXT = 6;
   protected int state;
   protected StringBuffer buffer;
   protected String text,
                    id,
                    image,
                    language;
   protected boolean checked;

   public XMLDirector(CatalogBuilder builder)
   {
      this.builder = builder;
   }

   public void setDocumentLocator (Locator locator)
      {}

   public void startDocument()
   {
      state = ROOT;
   }

   public void endDocument()
      {}
```

Listing 1.9 **Continued**

```java
public void startElement(String tag,AttributeList atts)
{
   if(tag.equals("Catalog") && ROOT == state)
      state = CATALOG;
   else if(tag.equals("Product") && CATALOG == state)
   {
      state = PRODUCT;
      id = atts.getValue("id");
      String st = atts.getValue("checked");
      checked = Boolean.valueOf(st).booleanValue();
      text = null;
      image = null;
   }
   else if(tag.equals("Text") && PRODUCT == state)
   {
      state = PRODUCT_TEXT;
      buffer = new StringBuffer();
   }
   else if(tag.equals("Image") && PRODUCT == state)
   {
      state = IMAGE;
      buffer = new StringBuffer();
   }
   else if(tag.equals("Descriptions") && PRODUCT == state)
      state = DESCRIPTIONS;
   else if(tag.equals("Text") && DESCRIPTIONS == state)
   {
      state = DESCRIPTIONS_TEXT;
      language = atts.getValue("xml:lang");
      buffer = new StringBuffer();
   }
}

public void endElement(String tag)
{
   if(tag.equals("Catalog") && CATALOG == state)
   {
      state = ROOT;
      builder.buildCatalog();
   }
   else if(tag.equals("Product") && PRODUCT == state)
   {
      state = CATALOG;
      if(null == image)
         builder.buildTextualProduct(text,id,checked);
      else
         builder.buildVisualProduct(text,id,checked,image);
   }
   else if(tag.equals("Text") && PRODUCT_TEXT == state)
   {
```

Listing 1.9 **Continued**

```
            state = PRODUCT;
            text = buffer.toString();
        }
        else if(tag.equals("Image") && IMAGE == state)
        {
            state = PRODUCT;
            image = buffer.toString();
        }
        else if(tag.equals("Descriptions") &&
                DESCRIPTIONS == state)
            state = PRODUCT;
        else if(tag.equals("Text") && DESCRIPTIONS_TEXT == state)
        {
            state = DESCRIPTIONS;
            builder.buildDescription(language,buffer.toString());
        }
    }

    public void characters(char ch[],int start,int len)
    {
        if(PRODUCT_TEXT == state ||
           IMAGE == state ||
           DESCRIPTIONS_TEXT == state)
           buffer.append(ch,start,len);
    }

    public void ignorableWhitespace(char ch[],
                                    int start,
                                    int length)
        {}

    public void processingInstruction(String target,String data)
        {}
}
```

The builder pattern cleanly separates the work between the director (responsible for collecting the information from the XML file) and the builder (responsible for creating and maintaining the object structure).

Listing 1.10 is DefaultCatalogBuilder. Again, let's first review the salient points.

DefaultCatalogBuilder provides storage for the catalog in the making. It stores a list of descriptions because it is being built through calls to buildDescription(). It also stores a list of products because it's being built through calls to buildTextualProduct() and buildVisualProduct():

```
protected Catalog catalog = null;
protected Vector products = new Vector(),
               descriptions = new Vector();
```

buildCatalog() is a very simple method. It simply creates a catalog object:

```
public void buildCatalog()
{
   catalog = new Catalog(products);
}
```

buildVisualProduct() creates new product objects and stores them in the products vector. buildTextualProduct() and buildDescription() are very similar:

```
public void buildVisualProduct(String text,
                               String id,
                               boolean checked,
                               String image)
{
   Product product = new VisualProduct(text,
                                        id,
                                        checked,
                                        image);
   products.addElement(product);
}
```

As promised, the code for DefaultCatalogBuilder is in Listing 1.10.

Listing 1.10  *DefaultCatalogBuilder.java*

```
package com.psol.catalog;

import java.util.Vector;

public class DefaultCatalogBuilder
   implements CatalogBuilder
{
   protected Catalog catalog = null;
   protected Vector products = new Vector(),
                    descriptions = new Vector();

   public void buildCatalog()
   {
      catalog = new Catalog(products);
   }

   public void buildVisualProduct(String text,
                                  String id,
                                  boolean checked,
                                  String image)
   {
      Product product = new VisualProduct(text,
                                           id,
                                           checked,
                                           image);
      products.addElement(product);
   }
```

Listing 1.10 **Continued**

```
    public void buildTextualProduct(String text,
                                    String id,
                                    boolean checked)
    {
       Product product = new TextualProduct(text,
                                             id,
                                             checked,
                                             descriptions);
       products.addElement(product);
       descriptions = new Vector();
    }

    public void buildDescription(String language,
                                 String text)
    {
       Description description = new Description(language,text);
       descriptions.addElement(description);
    }

    public Catalog getCatalog()
    {
       return catalog;
    }
}
```

To start the pattern, it suffices to create an XMLDirector and register it, as a
DocumentHandler, with a SAX parser:

```
XMLReader xmlReader =
   XMLReaderFactory.createXMLReader(PARSER_NAME);
CatalogBuilder builder = new DefaultCatalogBuilder();
xmlReader.setContentHandler(new XMLDirector(builder));
xmlReader.parse("catalog.xml");
Catalog catalog = builder.getCatalog();
```

# Meeting the Visitor Pattern

The visitor pattern is a sort of mirror of the builder pattern. Again, our goal will be to
separate the object structure from the writing of the XML document.

Figure 1.8 illustrates the generic visitor pattern. The various components are as
follows:

- The Element class and its descendants, which represent the object structure
- The Structure class, which is the root of the structure

- The Visitor and its descendant, which walk through the object structure, writing the XML document as they progress
- The client, which is the class that sends the visitor on to the data structure

**Warning**

Don't confuse the class Element with an XML element. In the visitor pattern, Element stands for an element in the data structure.

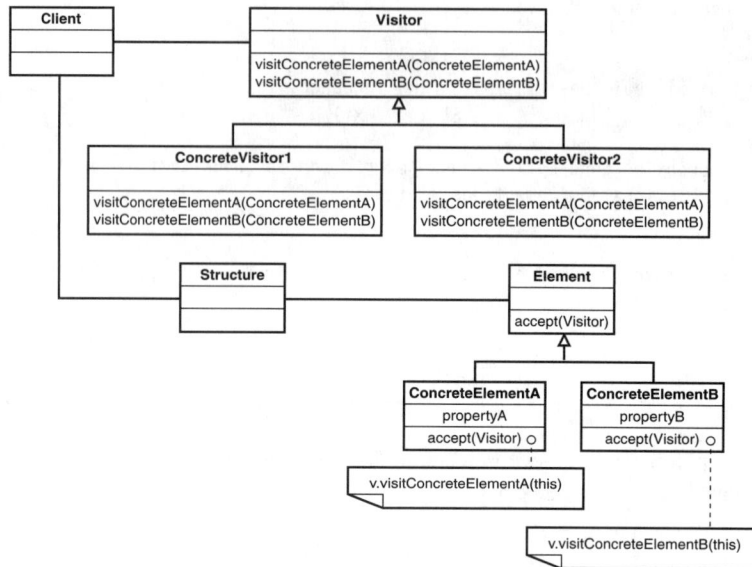

**Figure 1.8** Visitor pattern.

One of the remarkable aspects of this pattern is how a Visitor object recognizes a concrete element. It would have been possible to explicitly test the various options, such as in the following:

```
if(element instanceof Catalog)
    visitCatalog((Catalog)element);
else if(element instanceof VisualProduct)
    visitVisualProduct((VisualProduct)element);
// and more
```

However, this method is error prone. It is particularly easy to forget to update this list of tests when new classes are added to the structure.

Instead, Element and Visitor use a two-step protocol to recognize each other. Element implements the accept() method, which takes a Visitor as a parameter. When an Element accepts a Visitor, it calls the appropriate visitConcreteElement() method, passing a reference to itself, to the Visitor object.

## Applying the Visitor Pattern

Figure 1.9 applies the visitor pattern to our object structure. It introduces two new interfaces and two new classes:

- The `CatalogElement` interface from which the various classes in the data structure inherit. It declares the `accept()` method.
- The `CatalogVisitor` interface declares various methods for visiting the object structure.
- The `XMLVisitor` class is one visitor that writes the object structure in XML.
- The `CatalogViewer` class implements the `main()` method for the application. It starts the visitor pattern.

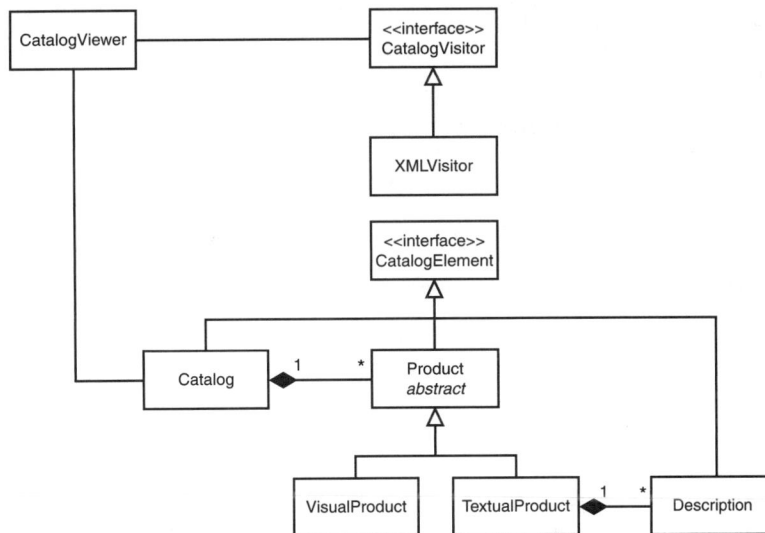

**Figure 1.9** Applying the visitor pattern.

The `CatalogElement` interface is shown in Listing 1.11. It declares only one method: `accept()`.

Listing 1.11 *CatalogElement.java*

```
package com.psol.catalog;

import java.io.IOException;

public interface CatalogElement
{
    public void accept(CatalogVisitor visitor)
        throws IOException;
}
```

The accept() method is implemented in CatalogElement's descendants, such as the Catalog class (refer to Listing 1.1):

```
public void accept(CatalogVisitor visitor)
   throws IOException
{
   visitor.visitCatalog(this);
}
```

Listing 1.12 is the CatalogVisitor. It declares one method for each element in the object structure.

Listing 1.12  *CatalogVisitor.jar*

```
package com.psol.catalog;

import java.io.IOException;

public interface CatalogVisitor
{
   public void visitCatalog(Catalog catalog)
      throws IOException;
   public void visitVisualProduct(VisualProduct product)
      throws IOException;
   public void visitTextualProduct(TextualProduct product)
      throws IOException;
   public void visitDescription(Description description)
      throws IOException;
}
```

XMLVisitor, as seen in Listing 1.13, is one implementation of CatalogVisitor that writes the XML document.

For each object, it writes the corresponding XML code. If the object contains other objects, it calls their accept() method, which causes these objects to be written as well:

```
public void visitTextualProduct(TextualProduct product)
   throws IOException
{
   pw.print("<Product");
   printAttribute("id",product.getId());
   Boolean bool = new Boolean(product.isChecked());
   printAttribute("checked",bool.toString());
   pw.println('>');
   printElement("Text",product.getText());
   pw.println("<Descriptions>");
   for(int i = 0;i < product.getSize();i++)
      product.descriptionAt(i).accept(this);
   pw.println("</Descriptions>");
   pw.println("</Product>");
}
```

Listing 1.13  *XMLVisitor.java*

```java
package com.psol.catalog;

import java.io.*;

public class XMLVisitor
   implements CatalogVisitor
{
   protected PrintWriter pw;

   public XMLVisitor(PrintWriter pw)
   {
      this.pw = pw;
   }

   public void visitCatalog(Catalog catalog)
      throws IOException
   {
      pw.println("<?xml version='1.0'?>");
      pw.println("<Catalog>");
      for(int i = 0;i < catalog.getSize();i++)
         catalog.productAt(i).accept(this);
      pw.print("</Catalog>");
      pw.flush();
   }

   public void visitVisualProduct(VisualProduct product)
      throws IOException
   {
      pw.print("<Product");
      printAttribute("id",product.getId());
      Boolean bool = new Boolean(product.isChecked());
      printAttribute("checked",bool.toString());
      pw.println('>');
      printElement("Text",product.getText());
      printElement("Image",product.getImage());
      pw.println("</Product>");
   }

   public void visitTextualProduct(TextualProduct product)
      throws IOException
   {
      pw.print("<Product");
      printAttribute("id",product.getId());
      Boolean bool = new Boolean(product.isChecked());
      printAttribute("checked",bool.toString());
      pw.println('>');
      printElement("Text",product.getText());
      pw.println("<Descriptions>");
      for(int i = 0;i < product.getSize();i++)
         product.descriptionAt(i).accept(this);
```

Listing 1.13 **Continued**

```java
      pw.println("</Descriptions>");
      pw.println("</Product>");
   }

   public void visitDescription(Description description)
      throws IOException
   {
      pw.print("<Text");
      printAttribute("xml:lang",description.getLanguage());
      pw.print('>');
      printContent(description.getText());
      pw.println("</Text>");
   }

   public void printElement(String tag,String content)
      throws IOException
   {
      pw.print('<'); pw.print(tag); pw.print('>');
      printContent(content);
      pw.print("</"); pw.print(tag); pw.println('>');
   }

   public void printContent(String content)
      throws IOException
   {
      // works with any Writer encoding but EBCDIC
      for(int i = 0;i < content.length();i++)
      {
         char c = content.charAt(i);
         if(c == '<')
            pw.print("&lt;");
         else if(c == '&')
            pw.print("&amp;");
         else if(c > '\u007f')
         {
            pw.print("&#");
            pw.print(Integer.toString(c));
            pw.print(';');
         }
         else
            pw.print(c);
      }
   }

   public void printAttribute(String name,String value)
      throws IOException
   {
      pw.print(' '); pw.print(name); pw.print("='");
      // works with any Writer encoding but EBCDIC
      for(int i = 0;i < value.length();i++)
```

Listing 1.13 **Continued**

```
        {
            char c = value.charAt(i);
            if(c == '\'')
                pw.print("&apos;");
            else if(c == '&')
                pw.print("&amp;");
            else if(c > '\u007f')
            {
                pw.print("&#");
                pw.print(Integer.toString(c));
                pw.print(';');
            }
            else
                pw.print(c);
        }
        pw.print('\'');
    }
}
```

The application's main class is shown in Listing 1.14, `CatalogViewer`. `CatalogViewer` creates a frame on which it places an instance of `CatalogPanel` (refer to Listing 1.3). At startup, it uses the builder pattern to read the `catalog.xml` file.

When the window is closed, it uses the visitor pattern to overwrite `catalog.xml`. This saves any changes by the customer, such as selecting or deselecting a product:

```
Writer writer = new FileWriter("catalog.xml");
CatalogVisitor visitor =
    new XMLVisitor(new PrintWriter(writer));
catalog.accept(visitor);
```

▶ **Tip**

It would not be difficult to use JavaMail (the standard Java API for emailing) in conjunction with the visitor pattern to automatically email the product selection. This is left as an exercise for the reader.

Listing 1.14 *CatalogViewer.java*

```
package com.psol.catalog;

import java.io.*;
import java.awt.*;
import org.xml.sax.*;
import java.awt.event.*;
import org.xml.sax.helpers.XMLReaderFactory;

public class CatalogViewer
{
```

Listing 1.14 **Continued**

```java
public static final String PARSER_NAME =
    "org.apache.xerces.parsers.SAXParser";

protected static class SaveOnClose
    extends WindowAdapter
{
    protected Catalog catalog;
    public SaveOnClose(Catalog catalog)
    {
        this.catalog = catalog;
    }
    public void windowClosing(WindowEvent evt)
    {
        try
        {
            Writer writer = new FileWriter("catalog.xml");
            CatalogVisitor visitor =
                new XMLVisitor(new PrintWriter(writer));
            catalog.accept(visitor);
        }
        catch(IOException e)
            {}
        System.exit(0);
    }
}

public static void main(String[] args)
    throws Exception
{
    XMLReader xmlReader =
        XMLReaderFactory.createXMLReader(PARSER_NAME);
    CatalogBuilder builder = new DefaultCatalogBuilder();
    xmlReader.setContentHandler(new XMLDirector(builder));
    xmlReader.parse("catalog.xml");
    Catalog catalog = builder.getCatalog();

    Panel panel = new CatalogPanel(catalog);
    Frame frame = new Frame("Catalog Viewer");
    frame.add(panel);
    frame.setResizable(false);
    frame.setSize(400,200);
    frame.addWindowListener(new SaveOnClose(catalog));
    frame.show();
}
}
```

# Building and Running the Project

The catalog viewer project is available on the CD that accompanies this book. Copy the project directory from the CD to your hard disk and then go to the command line and change to the root of the project. You can run the catalog viewer with the `catalog` command (see Figure 1.10).

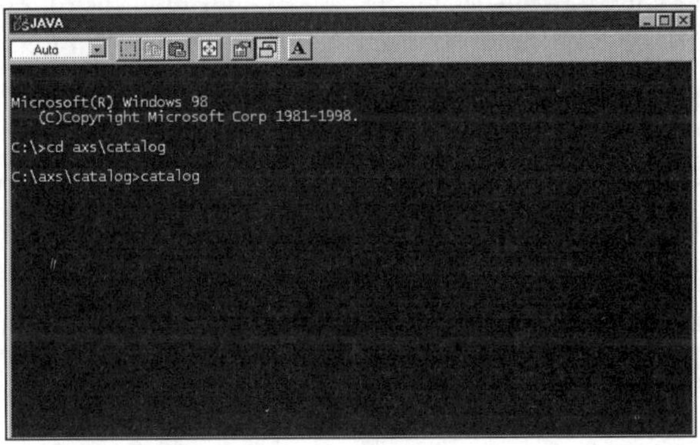

**Figure 1.10** Running the catalog viewer.

**Caution**

You need a version of Java 2 (JDK 1.2 or above) installed on your machine to run this project. The project should run on JDK 1.1, but you will need to adapt the `catalog.bat` file.

You also need a SAX 2.0–compliant XML parser to run this project. The project on the accompanying CD uses Xerces, which is available on the CD and from `xml.apache.org`.

If you switch to another parser, you will need to update `PARSER_NAME` in `CatalogViewer`.

## Pattern Benefits

The major benefits of the builder and visitor patterns are as follows:

- They separate reading and writing XML documents from the object structure.
- They centralize the XML-related code in a few classes that simplify maintenance. This is particularly valuable in large projects where one developer is responsible for the object structure and another one is in charge of XML-related aspects.

## Replacing the Director

The benefit of adopting a flexible design is that it is simple to change the application. For example, you can

- Change the structure of the XML document by adapting the director (and the visitor) with no changes whatsoever to the object structure.
- Only load a subset of the catalog, to save memory, by adapting the builder to discard those objects you don't need. Again, changes are limited to one class.
- Replace the SAX parser with a DOM parser or even a database by adapting the director. Again, changes do not impact other classes.

Listing 1.15 demonstrates the last advantage. As the name implies, the DOMDirector is a director built on a DOM parser. This director makes exactly the same calls to the builder, so changes are really limited to one class!

Although a DOM parser is less efficient, because it uses more memory, it might be the only parser available to you.

Listing 1.15  **DOMDirector.java**

```
package com.psol.catalog;

import org.w3c.dom.*;

public class DOMDirector
{
    protected CatalogBuilder builder;

    public DOMDirector(CatalogBuilder builder)
    {
        this.builder = builder;
    }

    public void walkDocument(Document document)
    {
        Element el = document.getDocumentElement();
        if(el.getTagName().equals("Catalog"))
            walkCatalog(el);
    }

    public void walkCatalog(Element element)
    {
        NodeList children = element.getChildNodes();
        for(int i = 0;i < children.getLength();i++)
        {
            Node node = children.item(i);
            if(node.getNodeType() == Node.ELEMENT_NODE)
            {
                Element el = (Element)node;
```

Listing 1.15 **Continued**

```
            if(el.getTagName().equals("Product"))
                walkProduct(el);
        }
    }
    builder.buildCatalog();
}

public void walkProduct(Element element)
{
    NodeList children = element.getChildNodes();
    String text = null,
           image = null;
    for(int i = 0;i < children.getLength();i++)
    {
        Node node = children.item(i);
        if(node.getNodeType() == Node.ELEMENT_NODE)
        {
            Element el = (Element)node;
            if(el.getTagName().equals("Text"))
                text = extractContent(el);
            else if(el.getTagName().equals("Image"))
                image = extractContent(el);
            else if(el.getTagName().equals("Descriptions"))
                walkDescriptions(el);
        }
    }
    String id = element.getAttribute("id"),
           st = element.getAttribute("checked");
    boolean checked = Boolean.valueOf(st).booleanValue();
    if(null == image)
        builder.buildTextualProduct(text,id,checked);
    else
        builder.buildVisualProduct(text,id,checked,image);
}

public void walkDescriptions(Element element)
{
    NodeList children = element.getChildNodes();
    for(int i = 0;i < children.getLength();i++)
    {
        Node node = children.item(i);
        if(node.getNodeType() == Node.ELEMENT_NODE)
        {
            Element el = (Element)node;
            if(el.getTagName().equals("Text"))
            {
                String text = extractContent(el),
                       lang = el.getAttribute("xml:lang");
                builder.buildDescription(lang,text);
            }
```

Listing 1.15 **Continued**

```
            }
        }
    }

    public String extractContent(Element element)
    {
        // currently ignores entities, CDATA section, etc.
        element.normalize();
        Node child = element.getFirstChild();
        if(child != null && child.getNodeType() == Node.TEXT_NODE)
        {
            Text text = (Text)child;
            return text.getData();
        }
        else
            return null;
    }
}
```

## Replacing the Visitor

The catalog viewer saves the complete catalog so the customer must email a file that is larger than required. However, it would be more efficient to save a smaller file with the list of products the customer selected.

This is easy to accomplish by writing a new visitor class, such as the XMLRequestVisitor shown in Listing 1.16.

Listing 1.16 *XMLRequestVisitor.java*

```
package com.psol.catalog;

import java.io.*;

public class XMLRequestVisitor
    implements CatalogVisitor
{
    protected PrintWriter pw;

    public XMLRequestVisitor(PrintWriter pw)
    {
        this.pw = pw;
    }

    public void visitCatalog(Catalog catalog)
        throws IOException
    {
        pw.println("<?xml version='1.0'?>");
```

Listing 1.16 **Continued**

```java
      pw.println("<Request>");
      for(int i = 0;i < catalog.getSize();i++)
         catalog.productAt(i).accept(this);
      pw.print("</Request>");
      pw.flush();
   }

   public void visitVisualProduct(VisualProduct product)
      throws IOException
   {
      visitProduct(product);
   }

   public void visitTextualProduct(TextualProduct product)
      throws IOException
   {
      visitProduct(product);
   }

   public void visitProduct(Product product)
      throws IOException
   {
      if(product.isChecked())
      {
         pw.print("<Product id='");
         // works with any Writer encoding but EBCDIC
         String value = product.getId();
         for(int i = 0;i < value.length();i++)
         {
            char c = value.charAt(i);
            if(c == '\'')
               pw.print("&apos;");
            else if(c == '&')
               pw.print("&amp;");
            else if(c > '\u007f')
            {
               pw.print("&#");
               pw.print(Integer.toString(c));
               pw.print(';');
            }
            else
               pw.print(c);
         }
         pw.println("\'/>");
      }
   }

   public void visitDescription(Description description)
      throws IOException
      {}
}
```

# Additional Resources

The patterns and tools introduced in this chapter are not limited to the catalog viewer written in Java.

## Other Applications

Many applications will benefit from using XML as lightweight data storage. In addition, XML is such a versatile format that it can be applied in any industry.

Many reasons exist to choose XML as a file format. The following are some of the most popular reasons:

- XML works well with object-oriented languages such as Java.

- By choosing XML, your application has the backing of some of the biggest names in the industry: Microsoft, IBM, Sun, Oracle, and Netscape. In practice, this means your files interface more easily into their systems.

- XML is easy to use and easy to learn. Plus, more professionals are learning XML, which means even more support exists for it.

- XML has good press. I saved this one for the end. Please note that I didn't write "there's a lot of hype around XML." A few of my customers have adopted XML because it looks good on their press release but more have adopted it because they want to benefit from the growing XML industry.

## Parsers in Other Languages

SAX parsers are available to most programming languages, including

- **C++**—The C++ version of the Xerces parser also is available from `xml.apache.org`.

- **Python**—SAX for Python is available from `www.stud.ifi.uio.no/~lmariusg/download/python/xml/saxlib.html`.

- **Perl**—XML::Parser::PerlSAX is available from `www.bitsko.slc.ut.us/libxml-perl`.

- **Eiffel**—eXML is available from `exml.sourceforge.net`.

- **And most languages on the Windows platform (Visual Basic, Delphi) through ActiveSAX**—ActiveSAX is a commercial COM component available from `www.vivid-creations.com`.

# 2

# Scripted Configuration Files

IN THE PREVIOUS CHAPTER, you saw how effective a file format XML is. This chapter addresses similar issues but from a different angle. More specifically, you will concentrate on special files: the configuration files.

You will see why XML is intrinsically a good replacement for most configuration files but, also, you will see how XML makes it easy to extend the classical configuration file in scripted configuration files.

## Configuration Files

Most applications use some sort of configuration files to store information such as paths, window sizes, user preferences, and network addresses.

Because configuration files are so important, most programming languages, including Java, have built-in support for them. In Java, this support takes the form of the `java.util.Properties` class. Windows and other platforms use the `ini` files. Windows also has the Registry.

With the exception of the Windows Registry (which has other problems of its own), most configuration files are flat text files. They store a list of properties similar to the following:

```
#  @(#)flavormap.properties    1.5
```

```
TEXT=text/plain;charset=ascii
UNICODE\ TEXT=text/plain;charset=unicode
HTML\ Format=text/html;charset=unicode
Rich\ Text\ Format=text/enriched;charset=ascii
HDROP=application/x-java-file-list;class=java.util.List
```

In practice, many applications would benefit from a richer structure. Consider the following extract from a Web server configuration file:

```
SERVERS : main

main.CLASS : com.mortbay.HTTP.HttpServer
main.STACKS : root
main.PROPERTY.SessionMaxInactiveInterval : 3600
main.PROPERTY.MinListenerThreads : 10
main.PROPERTY.MaxListenerThreads : 0
main.PROPERTY.MaxListenerThreadIdleMs : 0
main.LISTENER.all.CLASS : com.mortbay.HTTP.HttpListener
main.LISTENER.all.ADDRS : 0.0.0.0:8080

main.root.PATHS : /
main.root.HANDLERS : file

main.root.file.CLASS : com.mortbay.HTTP.Handler.FileHandler
main.root.file.PROPERTY.FILES.FileBase.PATHS : /
main.root.file.PROPERTY.FILES.FileBase.DIRECTORY : ./docs
```

Obviously, these properties are organized in a hierarchical format. For example, `main.root.file.CLASS` and `main.root.file.PROPERTY` are related to the same process within the server.

This chapter is a manifesto to encourage you to use XML as the preferred format for serious configuration files. But it won't stop there. You will also explore how (and when) XML lends itself to building a mini-script language.

## Scripted Configuration Files

Take the example of an online survey application. Online surveys are popular, and Web sites are struggling to come up with imaginative surveys. The survey in this example measures interest in books on XML.

Imagine a survey engine. It presents questions to visitors and collects the answers. Most questions are simple, simply requiring the visitor to pick the answer from a list of choices. However, some questions can be open-ended, requiring the visitor to type his choice.

The list of questions will typically end up in a configuration file to make it easy to edit. Obviously, XML is a good choice because it will support the relationship between the questions and their choices, as in the following:

```
<?xml version="1.0"?>
<survey>
   <question>
      <label>Do you use XML?</label>
      <choice>
         <option>
            <label>I do</label>
            <value>yes</value>
         </option>
         <option>
            <label>No but I plan to use it</label>
            <value>planning</value>
         </option>
         <option>
            <label>No and I don't plan to use it</label>
            <value>no</value>
         </option>
      </choice>
   </question>
   <question>
      <label>Do you need more XML books?</label>
      <choice>
         <option>
            <label>Yes, I would like more XML books</label>
            <value>yes</value>
         </option>
         <option>
            <label>No, I have all the books I need</label>
            <value>no</value>
         </option>
      </choice>
   </question>
   <!-- more questions deleted -->
</survey>
```

In all but the simplest survey, questions are linked to each other and the answer to one might determine which question is asked next. For example, if the visitor has no plan to use XML, it does not make a lot of sense to inquire whether that visitor would be interested in an XML book. Move to another part of the survey instead.

How should you represent this linking in the configuration file? Again, traditional configuration files are ill-equipped for this, but, with XML, you can build a nice answer: a scripted configuration file.

A *scripted configuration file* can store some of the logic, such as how to decide on the next question, in the configuration file. It takes the form of a simple script, such as

```
<if>
   <eq>
      <answer>usingxml</answer>
      <text>no</text>
   </eq>
```

```
    <text>done</text>
    <text>morebook</text>
  </if>
```

If the visitor replies that he is not using XML, the survey is complete. Otherwise, you inquire about more books.

## Why Not a Real Scripting Language?

Why ponder on this hybrid, the scripted configuration file; why not adopt a real scripting language? After all, ready-made interpreters are available for the most popular scripting languages, such as VBScript, JavaScript, Tcl, Perl, and Python.

Scripted configuration files are a middle ground between a full-blown scripting language, which is intimidating for many users, and a non-scripted configuration file, which is often too limited.

Furthermore, interpreters tend to be large. Because they support a full-blown language, they offer many options at the cost of being larger and more complicated to use.

In other words, scripted configuration files strike the right balance between complexity and usefulness for many projects. As you will see, building them in XML is not difficult.

Finally, users can take advantage of many XML tools, including editors, to help them prepare the configuration files—and it does not require more work from you.

For completeness, I must stress that this does not replace your favorite scripting language. For heavy-duty programming, adopting a real scripting language makes more sense, if only because you will benefit from standard libraries and other facilities.

# Meeting Survex

In the rest of this chapter, you'll build the Survex. Survex is a generic survey application. It is configured for a specific survey through an XML file, such as Listing 2.1.

Listing 2.1  *survey.xml*

```
<?xml version="1.0"?>
<survey>
   <question>
      <name>email</name>
      <title>Welcome to our XML book survey</title>
      <label>Thank you for participating in our survey.</label>
      <input>Enter your email address</input>
      <next><text>usingxml</text></next>
   </question>
```

Listing 2.1 **Continued**

```xml
<question>
   <name>usingxml</name>
   <title>XML and You</title>
   <label>Do you use XML?</label>
   <choice>
      <option>
         <label>I do</label>
         <value>yes</value>
      </option>
      <option>
         <label>No but I plan to use it</label>
         <value>planning</value>
      </option>
      <option>
         <label>No and I don't plan to use it</label>
         <value>no</value>
      </option>
   </choice>
   <next>
      <if>
         <eq>
            <answer>usingxml</answer>
            <text>no</text>
         </eq>
         <block>
            <save><answer>email</answer></save>
            <text>done</text>
         </block>
         <text>booktraining</text>
      </if>
   </next>
</question>
<question>
   <name>booktraining</name>
   <title>XML Books</title>
   <label>Do you need more XML books?</label>
   <choice>
      <option>
         <label>Yes, I would like more XML books</label>
         <value>yes</value>
      </option>
      <option>
         <label>No, I have all the books I need</label>
         <value>no</value>
      </option>
   </choice>
   <next>
      <if>
         <eq>
            <answer>booktraining</answer>
```

Listing 2.1 **Continued**

```xml
                    <text>yes</text>
                </eq>
                <text>timeframe</text>
                <block>
                    <save><answer>email</answer></save>
                    <text>done</text>
                </block>
            </if>
        </next>
    </question>
    <question>
        <name>timeframe</name>
        <title>Timeframe</title>
        <label>When do you plan to buy new XML books?</label>
        <choice>
            <option>
                <label>Now</label>
                <value>now</value>
            </option>
            <option>
                <label>Within 3 months</label>
                <value>months</value>
            </option>
            <option>
                <label>Within a year</label>
                <value>year</value>
            </option>
            <option>
                <label>I don't know yet</label>
                <value>unknown</value>
            </option>
        </choice>
        <next>
            <block>
                <save><answer>email</answer></save>
                <text>done</text>
            </block>
        </next>
    </question>
    <question>
        <name>done</name>
        <title>Thank you</title>
        <label>Thank you for your time!</label>
        <next><text>done</text></next>
    </question>
</survey>
```

The survey is a list of question in which each question has the following:

- A name, which uniquely identifies a section
- A title, which is presented to the visitor

- A label or the text of the question itself
- Either a list of options from which the visitor can choose an answer (for closed questions) or an input field (for open questions)
- A small script to decide on the next question

The first question in the listing will be rendered as in Figure 2.1. Note that the script could not be simpler; it unconditionally moves to the next question:

```
<question>
    <name>email</name>
    <title>Welcome to our XML book survey</title>
    <label>Thank you for participating in our survey.</label>
<input>Enter your email address</input>
    <next><text>usingxml</text></next>
</question>
```

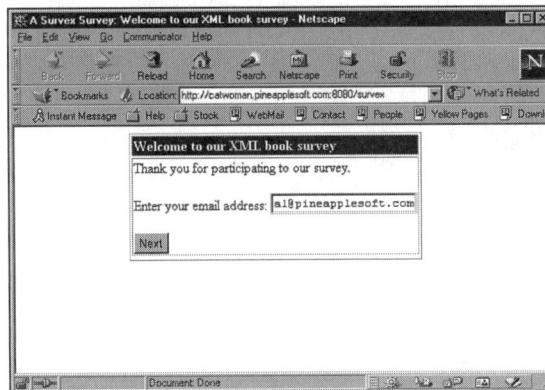

**Figure 2.1**  The survey first asks for your email address.

## Designing Survex

The model behind Survex is shown in Figure 2.2. The main classes are

- `Survex`—The servlet that runs it all.
- `Survey`—The list of questions in the current survey.
- `Question`—Stores information on one question.
- `Option`—Stores information on an option in a list of options.
- `Statement`—It and its descendants are used for scripting.
- `SurveyReader`—Parses the XML file and builds the corresponding `Survey` object.

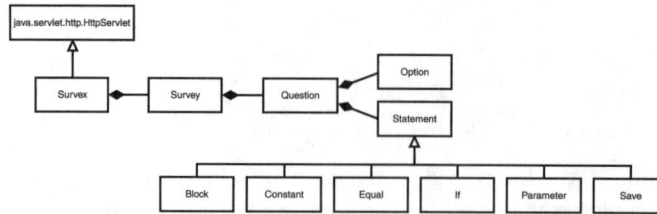

**Figure 2.2** The script is modeled as Statement descendants.

## The Data Structure

At the heart of the data structure is the Question class (see Listing 2.2). The Question defines a number of properties: the name, title, and label, as well as the input or the list of options. Note that the code enforces an exclusive on the input and the list of options. Finally, the script is used.

Listing 2.2 *Question.java*

```
package com.psol.survex;

import java.io.*;
import java.util.*;

public class Question
{
    protected String name,
                     title,
                     label,
                     input;
    protected Option[] options;
    protected Statement script;

    public String getName()
    {
        return name;
    }

    public void setName(String name)
    {
        this.name = name;
    }

    public String getTitle()
    {
        return title;
    }

    public void setTitle(String title)
```

Listing 2.2 **Continued**

```
    {
        this.title = title;
    }

    public String getLabel()
    {
        return label;
    }

    public void setLabel(String label)
    {
        this.label = label;
    }

    public Option[] getOptions()
    {
        return options;
    }

    public void setOptions(Option[] options)
    {
        this.options = options;
        input = null;
    }

    public String getInput()
    {
        return input;
    }

    public void setInput(String input)
    {
        this.input = input;
        options = null;
    }

    public void setScript(Statement script)
    {
        this.script = script;
    }

    public Statement getScript()
    {
        return script;
    }
}
```

Question uses the Option class, in Listing 2.3, to store the properties for the various options. Each option has a label and a value.

Listing 2.3 *Option.java*

```java
package com.psol.survex;

import java.io.*;

public class Option
{
   protected String label,
                    value;

   public void setLabel(String label)
   {
      this.label = label;
   }

   public String getLabel()
   {
      return label;
   }

   public void setValue(String value)
   {
      this.value = value;
   }

   public String getValue()
   {
      return value;
   }
}
```

At the root of the data structure is the Survey class (see Listing 2.4). It maintains the list of questions in a dictionary for fast retrieval.

Listing 2.4 *Survey.java*

```java
package com.psol.survex;

import java.io.*;
import java.util.*;

public class Survey
{
   protected String rootName;
   protected Dictionary questions = new Hashtable();

   public Enumeration getKeys()
   {
      return questions.keys();
   }
```

Listing 2.4 **Continued**

```
   public void addQuestion(Question question)
   {
      if(questions.isEmpty())
         rootName = question.getName();
      questions.put(question.getName(),question);
   }

   public Question getQuestion(String name)
   {
      return (Question)questions.get(name);
   }

   public Question getRootQuestion()
   {
      return (Question)questions.get(rootName);
   }
}
```

## Building a Script Interpreter

A *script* is an object that implements the `Statement` interface (see Listing 2.5). The interface is trivial, defining only one method, `apply()`, which executes the statement and returns a string. For simplicity, the string is the only data type. Also, no local variables exist, only global parameters.

Listing 2.5 *Statement.java*

```
package com.psol.survex;

import java.util.Dictionary;
import javax.servlet.ServletException;

public interface Statement
{
   public String apply(Dictionary parameters)
      throws ServletException;
}
```

Looking back at Listing 2.1, you can identify the following statements:

- `<text>`—Used for a text constant
- `<answer>`—Retrieves an answer chosen by the visitor
- `<eq>`—Tests for equality
- `<if>`—Is the classical if/then/else construct

- <save>—Saves the results to a file
- <block>—Combines several statements

The <text> statement is implemented in the class named Constant (see Listing 2.6). Constant has one property, text, and its apply() method returns the value of the text property.

Listing 2.6  *Constant.java*

```
package com.psol.survex;

import java.util.Dictionary;
import javax.servlet.ServletException;

public class Constant
   implements Statement
{
   protected String text;

   public void setText(String text)
   {
      this.text = text;
   }

   public String apply(Dictionary parameters)
      throws ServletException
   {
      return text;
   }
}
```

The <answer> XML element is implemented in the Parameter class in Listing 2.7. This class has one property, name, and its apply() method returns the parameter whose name matches the name property. As you will see, the servlet loads the parameters with the visitor's choices.

Listing 2.7  *Parameter.java*

```
package com.psol.survex;

import java.util.Dictionary;
import javax.servlet.ServletException;

public class Parameter
   implements Statement
{
   protected String name;

   public void setName(String name)
   {
```

Listing 2.7 **Continued**

```
        this.name = name;
    }

    public String apply(Dictionary parameters)
        throws ServletException
    {
        String st = (String)parameters.get(name);
        return null != st ? st : "";
    }
}
```

`Equal` (in Listing 2.8) supports the `<eq>` statement. `Equal` has two properties, `arg1` and `arg2`, both of which are `Statements` themselves. `Equal` executes the two `Statements` (by calling their `apply()` method) and compares the results.

> **Note**
>
> `Equal` illustrates how `Statements` are combined. The scripting language has a distinct functional style: Each `Statement` is a function (it takes one or more parameters and returns a value). Also, no global variables exist.
>
> A functional style is simpler to understand and, remember, you are looking for a simple-to-use scripting language. For more sophistication, you would have turned to an existing scripting language.

Listing 2.8 *Equal.java*

```
package com.psol.survex;

import java.util.Dictionary;
import javax.servlet.ServletException;

public class Equal
    implements Statement
{
    protected Statement arg1, arg2;

    public void setArgs(Statement arg1,Statement arg2)
    {
        this.arg1 = arg1;
        this.arg2 = arg2;
    }

    public String apply(Dictionary parameters)
        throws ServletException
    {
        String value1 = arg1.apply(parameters),
               value2 = arg2.apply(parameters);
        return value1.equals(value2) ? "true" : "false";
    }
}
```

If has three properties: cond, then, and _else. It executes the first statement: cond, the condition. Depending on the result, it next executes the then or _else statement (see Listing 2.9).

Listing 2.9  *If.java*

```
package com.psol.survex;

import java.util.Dictionary;
import javax.servlet.ServletException;

public class If
   implements Statement
{
   protected Statement cond,
                       then,
                       _else;

   public void setArgs(Statement cond,
                       Statement then,
                       Statement _else)
   {
      this.cond = cond;
      this.then = then;
      this._else = _else;
   }

   public String apply(Dictionary parameters)
      throws ServletException
   {
      if(cond.apply(parameters).equals("true"))
         return then.apply(parameters);
      else
         return _else.apply(parameters);
   }
}
```

Save is a special function because it has a side effect: It creates a file and writes the parameters. The script uses this before terminating the survey (see Listing 2.10).

### Tip

Listing 2.10 saves the survey results under the visitor's email address. Email addresses are a simple mechanism to identify visitors. Obviously, some people have several email addresses, whereas some families share email addresses, but it's accurate enough for our needs.

An added bonus is that when a visitor changes his mind and answers differently, the new answer overrides the older one.

Listing 2.10  *Save.java*

```java
package com.psol.survex;

import java.io.*;
import java.util.*;
import javax.servlet.ServletException;

public class Save
   implements Statement
{
   protected Statement filename;

   public void setFilename(Statement filename)
   {
      this.filename = filename;
   }

   public void escape(Writer w,String s)
      throws IOException
   {
      for(int i = 0;i < s.length();i++)
      {
         char c = s.charAt(i);
         if(c == '<')
            w.write("&lt;");
         else if(c == '&')
            w.write("&amp;");
         else if(c == '\'')
            w.write("&apos;");
         else if(c == '"')
            w.write("&quot;");
         else if(c > '\u007f')
         {
            w.write("&#");
            w.write(Integer.toString(c));
            w.write(';');
         }
         else
            w.write(c);
      }
   }

   public String apply(Dictionary parameters)
      throws ServletException
   {
      try
      {
         String fname = filename.apply(parameters);
         File file = new File("results",fname + ".xml");
         Writer writer = new FileWriter(file);
         writer.write("<?xml version='1.0'?><survex>");
```

Listing 2.10 **Continued**

```java
            Enumeration keys = parameters.keys();
            while(keys.hasMoreElements())
            {
                String name = (String)keys.nextElement();
                writer.write("<question><name>");
                escape(writer,name);
                writer.write("</name><answer>");
                escape(writer,(String)parameters.get(name));
                writer.write("</answer></question>");
            }
            writer.write("</survex>");
            writer.close();
            return fname;
        }
        catch(IOException e)
        {
            throw new ServletException(e);
        }
    }
}
```

**Block** offers a solution to combine several **Statements**. It executes each **Statement** and returns the result of the last one. In effect, this is similar to the {} construct in Java (see Listing 2.11).

Listing 2.11 *Block.java*

```java
package com.psol.survex;

import java.util.*;
import javax.servlet.ServletException;

public class Block
    implements Statement
{
    protected Statement[] statements;

    public void setStatements(Statement[] statements)
    {
        this.statements = statements;
    }

    public String apply(Dictionary parameters)
        throws ServletException
    {
        String result = "";
        // on the stack they are collected in reverse order
        for(int i = statements.length - 1;i >= 0;i--)
            result = statements[i].apply(parameters);
        return result;
    }
}
```

## Reading the Configuration File

The extensive data structure must be read from the XML configuration file. This is the role of SurveyReader, a class that implements the SAX's ContentHandler interface. SurveyReader is demonstrated in Listing 2.12.

Listing 2.12 *SurveyReader.java*

```java
package com.psol.survex;

import org.xml.sax.*;
import java.util.*;

public class SurveyReader
    implements ContentHandler
{
    protected Stack stack;
    protected StringBuffer buffer;

    public Survey getSurvey()
    {
        return (Survey)stack.pop();
    }

    public void setDocumentLocator(Locator locator)
        {}

    public void startDocument()
    {
        stack = new Stack();
    }

    public void endDocument()
        {}

    public void startElement(String namespaceURI,
                             String localName,
                             String tag,
                             Attributes atts)
    {
        if(tag.equals("survey"))
            stack.push(new Survey());
        else if(tag.equals("question"))
            stack.push(new Question());
        else if(tag.equals("choice"))
            stack.push(new Vector());
        else if(tag.equals("option"))
            stack.push(new Option());
        else if(tag.equals("input"))
            buffer = new StringBuffer();
        else if(tag.equals("text"))
        {
            stack.push(new Constant());
```

Listing 2.12 **Continued**

```
        buffer = new StringBuffer();
    }
    else if(tag.equals("answer"))
    {
        stack.push(new Parameter());
        buffer = new StringBuffer();
    }
    else if(tag.equals("if"))
        stack.push(new If());
    else if(tag.equals("eq"))
        stack.push(new Equal());
    else if(tag.equals("save"))
        stack.push(new Save());
    else if(tag.equals("block"))
        stack.push(new Block());
    else if(tag.equals("name") ||
            tag.equals("title") ||
            tag.equals("label") ||
            tag.equals("value"))
        buffer = new StringBuffer();
}

public void endElement(String namespaceURI,
                       String localName,
                       String tag)
{
    if(tag.equals("question"))
    {
        Question question = (Question)stack.pop();
        Survey survey = (Survey)stack.peek();
        survey.addQuestion(question);
    }
    else if(tag.equals("choice"))
    {
        Vector vector = (Vector)stack.pop();
        Option[] options = new Option[vector.size()];
        vector.copyInto(options);
        Question question = (Question)stack.peek();
        question.setOptions(options);
    }
    else if(tag.equals("option"))
    {
        Option option = (Option)stack.pop();
        Vector vector = (Vector)stack.peek();
        vector.addElement(option);
    }
    else if(tag.equals("input"))
    {
        Question question = (Question)stack.peek();
        question.setInput(buffer.toString());
        buffer = null;
    }
```

Listing 2.12 **Continued**

```java
    else if(tag.equals("text"))
    {
       Constant constant = (Constant)stack.peek();
       constant.setText(buffer.toString());
       buffer = null;
    }
    else if(tag.equals("answer"))
    {
       Parameter parameter = (Parameter)stack.peek();
       parameter.setName(buffer.toString());
       buffer = null;
    }
    else if(tag.equals("if"))
    {
       Statement _else = (Statement)stack.pop(),
                 then = (Statement)stack.pop(),
                 cond = (Statement)stack.pop();
       If _if = (If)stack.peek();
       _if.setArgs(cond,then,_else);
    }
    else if(tag.equals("eq"))
    {
       Statement arg1 = (Statement)stack.pop(),
                 arg2 = (Statement)stack.pop();
       Equal equal = (Equal)stack.peek();
       equal.setArgs(arg1,arg2);
    }
    else if(tag.equals("save"))
    {
       Statement filename = (Statement)stack.pop();
       Save save = (Save)stack.peek();
       save.setFilename(filename);
    }
    else if(tag.equals("block"))
    {
       Vector vector = new Vector();
       Statement s = (Statement)stack.pop();
       while(!(s instanceof Block))
       {
          vector.addElement(s);
          s = (Statement)stack.pop();
       }
       Statement[] statements = new Statement[vector.size()];
       vector.copyInto(statements);
       ((Block)s).setStatements(statements);
       stack.push(s);
    }
    else if(tag.equals("name"))
    {
       Question question = (Question)stack.peek();
       question.setName(buffer.toString());
       buffer = null;
```

Listing 2.12 **Continued**

```
      }
      else if(tag.equals("title"))
      {
         Question question = (Question)stack.peek();
         question.setTitle(buffer.toString());
         buffer = null;
      }
      else if(tag.equals("label"))
      {
         Object o = stack.peek();
         if(o instanceof Question)
            ((Question)o).setLabel(buffer.toString());
         else
            ((Option)o).setLabel(buffer.toString());
         buffer = null;
      }
      else if(tag.equals("value"))
      {
         Option option = (Option)stack.peek();
         option.setValue(buffer.toString());
         buffer = null;
      }
      else if(tag.equals("next"))
      {
         Statement script = (Statement)stack.pop();
         Question question = (Question)stack.peek();
         question.setScript(script);
      }
   }

   public void characters(char ch[],int start,int len)
   {
      if(null != buffer)
         buffer.append(ch,start,len);
   }

   public void ignorableWhitespace(char ch[],
                                   int start,
                                   int length)
      {}

   public void processingInstruction(String target,String data)
      {}

   public void skippedEntity(String name)
      {}

   public void startPrefixMapping(String prefix,String uri)
      {}

   public void endPrefixMapping(String prefix)
      {}
}
```

Notice that this class uses a different approach to tracking states than the `DocumentHandler` from Chapter 1, "Lightweight Data Storage." Specifically, instead of using constants, it uses a stack.

In `startElement()`, it pushes objects on the stack:

```
else if(tag.equals("option"))
   stack.push(new Option());
```

And in `endElement()`, it pops. In most cases, it will pass them (as properties) to their parents, which are also in the stack:

```
else if(tag.equals("option"))
{
   Option option = (Option)stack.pop();
   Vector vector = (Vector)stack.peek();
   vector.addElement(option);
}
```

## Putting It All Together in the Servlet

From these building blocks, building the servlet is not difficult. The servlet class, `Survex`, is shown in Listing 2.13.

Listing 2.13 *Survex.java*

```
package com.psol.survex;

import java.io.*;
import java.util.*;
import org.xml.sax.*;
import javax.servlet.*;
import javax.servlet.http.*;
import org.xml.sax.helpers.*;

public class Survex
   extends HttpServlet
{
   public static final String PARSER_NAME =
      "org.apache.xerces.parsers.SAXParser";

   protected Survey survey;

   public void init()
      throws ServletException
   {
      try
      {
         XMLReader xmlReader =
            XMLReaderFactory.createXMLReader(PARSER_NAME);
         SurveyReader sreader = new SurveyReader();
```

Listing 2.13 **Continued**

```
        xmlReader.setContentHandler(sreader);
        xmlReader.parse("survey.xml");
        survey = sreader.getSurvey();
    }
    catch(IOException e)
    {
        throw new ServletException(e);
    }
    catch(SAXException e)
    {
        throw new ServletException(e);
    }
}

public Dictionary getParameters(HttpServletRequest request)
{
    Dictionary parameters = new Hashtable();
    Enumeration keys = survey.getKeys();
    while(keys.hasMoreElements())
    {
        String name = (String)keys.nextElement(),
               value = request.getParameter(name);
        if(null != value)
            parameters.put(name,value);
    }
    return parameters;
}

public void writeHTML(Question question,
                      String servletpath,
                      Writer writer,
                      Dictionary parameters)
    throws IOException
{
    writer.write("<HTML><HEAD><TITLE>");
    writer.write("A Survex Survey: ");
    writer.write(question.getTitle());
    writer.write("</TITLE></HEAD><BODY>");
    writer.write("<FORM ACTION='");
    writer.write(servletpath);
    writer.write("' METHOD='POST'>");
    writer.write("<INPUT TYPE='HIDDEN' NAME='name' VALUE='");
    writer.write(question.getName());
    writer.write("'>");
    writer.write("<TABLE ALIGN='CENTER' BORDER='1'>");
    writer.write("<TR><TD BGCOLOR='black'><B>");
    writer.write("<FONT COLOR='white'>");
    writer.write(question.getTitle());
    writer.write("</B></FONT></TD></TR><TR><TD><P>");
    writer.write(question.getLabel());
    if(null != question.getOptions())
    {
```

Listing 2.13 **Continued**

```
            writer.write("<P>");
            Option[] options = question.getOptions();
            for(int i = 0;i < options.length;i++)
            {
               writer.write("<INPUT TYPE='RADIO' NAME='");
               writer.write(question.getName());
               writer.write("' VALUE='");
               writer.write(options[i].getValue());
               writer.write("'>");
               writer.write(options[i].getLabel());
               writer.write("<BR>");
            }
         }
         else if(null != question.getInput())
         {
            writer.write("<P>");
            writer.write(question.getInput());
            writer.write(": <INPUT TYPE='TEXT' NAME='");
            writer.write(question.getName());
            writer.write("'>");
         }
         if(null != question.getOptions() ||
            null != question.getInput())
            writer.write("<P><INPUT TYPE='SUBMIT' VALUE='Next'>");
         writer.write("</TD><TR></TABLE>");
         Enumeration keys = parameters.keys();
         while(keys.hasMoreElements())
         {
            String parameter = (String)keys.nextElement();
            writer.write("<INPUT TYPE='HIDDEN' NAME='");
            writer.write(parameter);
            writer.write("' VALUE='");
            writer.write((String)parameters.get(parameter));
            writer.write("'>");
         }
         writer.write("</FORM></BODY></HTML>");
         writer.flush();
      }

      public void doGet(HttpServletRequest request,
                        HttpServletResponse response)
         throws ServletException, IOException
      {
         Question question = survey.getRootQuestion();
         if(null != question)
            writeHTML(question,
                      request.getServletPath(),
                      response.getWriter(),
                      new Hashtable());
         else
```

Listing 2.13 **Continued**

```
            response.sendError(HttpServletResponse.SC_NOT_FOUND);
    }

    public void doPost(HttpServletRequest request,
                       HttpServletResponse response)
        throws ServletException, IOException
    {
        Dictionary parameters = getParameters(request);
        String name = request.getParameter("name");
        Question question = null;
        if(null == name)
            question = survey.getRootQuestion();
        else
        {
            question = survey.getQuestion(name);
            if(null != question)
            {
                Statement script = question.getScript();
                name = script.apply(parameters);
                question = survey.getQuestion(name);
            }
        }
        if(null != question)
            writeHTML(question,
                      request.getServletPath(),
                      response.getWriter(),
                      parameters);
        else
            response.sendError(HttpServletResponse.SC_NOT_FOUND);
    }
}
```

Review the following listing step by step. The first method is init(), which reads the XML configuration file upon loading.

Next, the class defines two helper methods: getParameters() and writeHTML(). getParameters() collects the answers for all the questions. As you will see, the browser always has the entire list of answers and passes them to the servlet with each request:

```
public Dictionary getParameters(HttpServletRequest request)
{
    Dictionary parameters = new Hashtable();
    Enumeration keys = survey.getKeys();
    while(keys.hasMoreElements())
    {
        String name = (String)keys.nextElement(),
               value = request.getParameter(name);
        if(null != value)
            parameters.put(name,value);
    }
    return parameters;
}
```

writeHTML() prints a Question as an HTML page. Notice that the page includes the various answers as hidden input fields. Another hidden field contains the name of the current question. These hidden fields are returned to the server by the browser with each request, as in the following:

```java
public void writeHTML(Question question,
                      String servletpath,
                      Writer writer,
                      Dictionary parameters)
    throws IOException
{
    writer.write("<HTML><HEAD><TITLE>");
    writer.write("A Survex Survey: ");
    writer.write(question.getTitle());
    writer.write("</TITLE></HEAD><BODY>");
    writer.write("<FORM ACTION='");
    writer.write(servletpath);
    writer.write("' METHOD='POST'>");
    writer.write("<INPUT TYPE='HIDDEN' NAME='name' VALUE='");
    writer.write(question.getName());
    writer.write("'>");
    writer.write("<TABLE ALIGN='CENTER' BORDER='1'>");
    writer.write("<TR><TD BGCOLOR='black'><B>");
    writer.write("<FONT COLOR='white'>");
    writer.write(question.getTitle());
    writer.write("</B></FONT></TD></TR><TR><TD><P>");
    writer.write(question.getLabel());
    if(null != question.getOptions())
    {
        writer.write("<P>");
        Option[] options = question.getOptions();
        for(int i = 0;i < options.length;i++)
        {
            writer.write("<INPUT TYPE='RADIO' NAME='");
            writer.write(question.getName());
            writer.write("' VALUE='");
            writer.write(options[i].getValue());
            writer.write("'>");
            writer.write(options[i].getLabel());
            writer.write("<BR>");
        }
    }
    else if(null != question.getInput())
    {
        writer.write("<P>");
        writer.write(question.getInput());
        writer.write(": <INPUT TYPE='TEXT' NAME='");
        writer.write(question.getName());
        writer.write("'>");
    }
    if(null != question.getOptions() ||
```

```
         null != question.getInput())
         writer.write("<P><INPUT TYPE='SUBMIT' VALUE='Next'>");
      writer.write("</TD><TR></TABLE>");
      Enumeration keys = parameters.keys();
      while(keys.hasMoreElements())
      {
         String parameter = (String)keys.nextElement();
         writer.write("<INPUT TYPE='HIDDEN' NAME='");
         writer.write(parameter);
         writer.write("' VALUE='");
         writer.write((String)parameters.get(parameter));
         writer.write("'>");
      }
      writer.write("</FORM></BODY></HTML>");
      writer.flush();
   }
```

doGet() outputs the first (or root) question to get the user started. doPost(), on the other hand, is where all the fun is because it uses the script to decide on which question to post.

doPost() first retrieves the name of the current question and the answers to the various questions. Next, it calls the script to compute the name of the next question. It couldn't be simpler! The following demonstrates this:

```
   public void doPost(HttpServletRequest request,
                      HttpServletResponse response)
      throws ServletException, IOException
   {
      Dictionary parameters = getParameters(request);
      String name = request.getParameter("name");
      Question question = null;
      if(null == name)
         question = survey.getRootQuestion();
      else
      {
         question = survey.getQuestion(name);
         if(null != question)
         {
            Statement script = question.getScript();
            name = script.apply(parameters);
            question = survey.getQuestion(name);
         }
      }
      if(null != question)
         writeHTML(question,
                   request.getServletPath(),
                   response.getWriter(),
                   parameters);
      else
         response.sendError(HttpServletResponse.SC_NOT_FOUND);
   }
```

# Building and Running the Project

The survey project is available on the CD that accompanies this book. Copy the project directory from the CD to your hard disk. Start the Web server with the survey command.

Next, open a browser and type the survey URL:

```
http://localhost:8080/survex
```

If everything works well, the result should look like Figure 2.3.

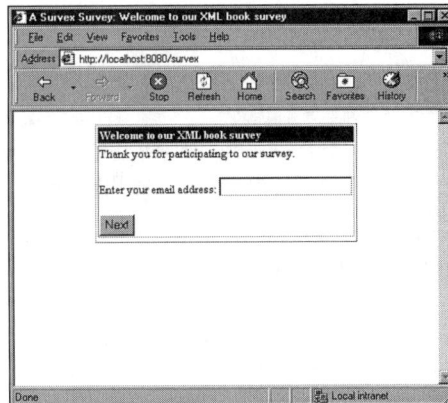

**Figure 2.3** Taking your first survey.

For your convenience, the project ships with its own Web server. It uses Jetty, an open-source Web server available from www.mortbay.com. Jetty is a very good Web server, but it is not as user-friendly as commercial offerings. For example, to terminate the server, you must kill the process (under Windows, Ctrl+C it).

However, Survex is a regular servlet, so you should be able to use it with any servlet-enabled Web server.

> **Tip**
>
> Using JRun, you can add servlet support to all the popular Web servers (including Apache, Netscape, and IIS). JRun is available from www.jrun.com.

> **Caution**
>
> You need a SAX 2.0–compliant XML parser to run this project. The project on the enclosed CD uses Xerces, which is available on the CD, or you can download the latest version from xml.apache.org.
>
> If you switch to another parser, you will need to update PARSER_NAME in Survex.

# Benefits

Scripted configuration files in XML have several benefits over the regular `java.util.Properties`:

- XML offers a hierarchical structure that matches the needs of all but the most trivial applications.
- XML files are text based, so they can be exchanged via email and are very readable. Furthermore, XML editors are plentiful.
- Building a simple scripting language in an XML file is easy. This can greatly enhance the usefulness of configuration files.

# Additional Resources

Although this chapter concentrates on configuration files, other applications use XML-based scripting language extensively. Some examples include

- XSL (the XML Stylesheet Language), which is a simple but powerful scripting language used to manipulate XML documents. With its roots firmly at the W3C, XSL is written in XML.
- WebMethods has developed at least two XML-based scripting languages: WIDL and Flow. Both extract information from Web sites. You can find more information about them at www.webmethods.com.
- Miva is an application server similar to ASP, except that it uses an XML scripting language instead of VBScript. You can find more information about it at www.miva.com.

# 3

# Electronic Forms

SHIFTING THROUGH THE MORNING MAIL, I cannot help but notice how our society relies on forms. There is a tax declaration form, the announcement for an e-commerce conference comes with a registration form, there are a couple of invoices, and there is a royalties statement (so it's not all bad news).

Companies and administrations stack forms in all their communications. We receive information on forms (bank statements, wages bill, invoices) and we are requested to fill out forms throughout the day: to buy goods (order form), to pay for them (check or card vouchers), to declare revenues (tax forms), to claim benefits (insurance forms), to borrow books at the library (reader forms), and so on.

The forms, of course, have found their way online. Many organizations make their forms available for download as PDF (Adobe Acrobat) or Word files. You can print them, fill them out, and mail or fax them. Other companies encourage you to fill in HTML forms to enter data directly in their databases.

In this chapter, you see how an XML editor can replace a word processor or a browser. This is advantageous because it produces an XML document (which can be parsed, read into a database, transformed through a style sheet, or generally manipulated through the myriad of XML tools available to us) in a familiar word processor–like environment.

# The Event Form

Imagine you are working for the local newspaper. The newspaper publishes much information, including articles, advertisements, classifieds, and local information such as the agenda of local events.

Event organizers call the newspaper and a clerk collects the data for the event. Obviously, he or she has a form to fill out.

Recently, the newspaper began taking steps toward electronic publishing. The ultimate goal is to make the newspaper available online. Therefore, the paper form must be replaced by an electronic form.

Let's see how you can take advantage of an XML editor to build a simple and familiar editing environment for the clerk. Our ultimate goal is shown in Figure 3.1. The main characteristics are as follows:

- It's a Word lookalike so it's familiar to the clerk. It is very likely that it will be more familiar than even a browser.
- It creates real XML documents that look similar to Listing 3.1.
- Developing it is quick (less than a day) because the editor does all the hard work.
- It mixes closed and open questions. The name, location, and contact information are fixed fields but the description is open-ended. It can even include formatting (bold, italic) like a word processor does.

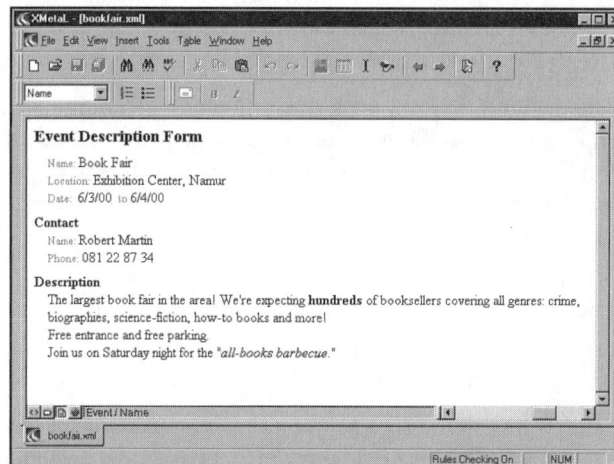

**Figure 3.1** A familiar environment to edit forms.

One of the most interesting aspects of this project is that it illustrates how XML opens up your application to tools. By choosing the XML format, you gain access to powerful tools, such as the editor, but the underlying format remains XML. So, you always can access it through other mechanisms (for example, building your own application, as you did in Chapter 1, "Lightweight Data Storage"). You also can feed it to other tools (for example, browsers, using the publishing mechanism introduced in Chapter 4, "Content Syndication").

Listing 3.1 *bookfair.xml*

```xml
<?xml version="1.0"?>
<!DOCTYPE Event SYSTEM "event.dtd">
<Event>
   <Name>Book Fair </Name>
   <Location>Exhibition Center, Namur</Location>
   <Date>
      <Start>6/3/00</Start>
      <End>6/4/00</End>
   </Date>
   <Contact>
      <Name>Robert Martin</Name>
      <Phone>081 22 87 34</Phone>
   </Contact>
   <Description>
      <Para>The largest book fair in the area! We're expecting
         <Bold>hundreds</Bold> of booksellers covering all genres:
         crime, biographies, science-fiction, how-to books and
         more!</Para>
      <Para>Free entrance and free parking.</Para>
      <Para>Join us on Saturday night for the "<Italic>all-books
         barbecue</Italic>."</Para>
   </Description>
</Event>
```

# Creating a Form with an Editor

The XML editor used in this chapter is XMetaL from SoftQuad. If you are familiar with other XML editors such as XML Spy or XML Notepad, you will find that XMetaL is significantly more powerful.

XMetaL provides tools to completely hide the markup language behind a word processor interface. This is ideal for applications targeted at non-technicians: The newspaper clerk couldn't care less about the structure document and the markup. He wants a simple form and a familiar interface.

Compare XML Notepad in Figure 3.2 with XMetaL in Figure 3.1. XML Notepad throws the markup in your face. It's great for developers—you and I love it—but it's a nightmare for average computer users.

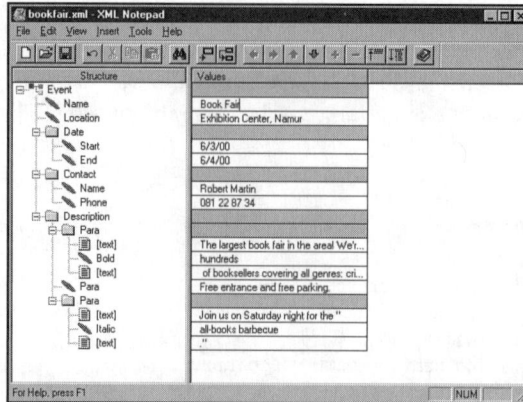

**Figure 3.2** Which looks friendlier? XMetaL or XML Notepad?

However, XMetaL is a dual-face tool. It looks like a word processor to the user, but it's a programming toolkit for the developer. In this chapter, you learn how to use this toolkit.

## Installing XMetaL

To run this project, you need a copy of XMetaL. The companion CD includes an evaluation copy of XMetaL 1.0, which you can use for testing.

For more information, visit the XMetaL Web site (www.xmetal.com) or the SoftQuad site (www.softquad.com).

### Warning

Note that XMetaL is a commercial product. Although it uses several standards, XMetaL is not a standard itself. New versions might introduce incompatibilities that I could not foresee at the time of this writing. You might want to check the Web site (www.marchal.com) for an update.

In the following sections, you will completely configure the editor so it is optimized for your XML document. The steps we will follow are

1. Define the model of the document; in other words, decide on which information to collect.
2. Create a template, which is an empty form the clerk uses to get started.
3. Style the document so it looks good onscreen.
4. Customize the behavior of the editor so it recognizes your elements.
5. Develop macros to customize toolbars and menus and to validate the document.

# Running the Project

To save yourself a lot of clicking and typing, you can turn to the files on the accompanying CD. Copy the event project on your hard disk and copy the following files in the appropriate directories. All these directories are under the XMetaL main·directory:

- `event.css` goes under `Display`.
- `event.mcr` goes under `Macros`.
- `event.dtd`, `event.ctm`, and `~event.tbr` go under `Rules`.
- For `Event Description Form.xml`, you must first create a new `Pineapplesoft` directory under `Template`. Then, copy the file in the new directory.

## Creating the Model

The first step is to model the information we want to capture. We must decide which information is relevant and how to encode it in XML (which elements). We are not concerned with the presentation but with the structure of the document.

A form to record local events is not very complicated. Essentially, it must capture the name, location, and date of the event, as well as contact information. Finally, it should provide a text area to describe the specifics of the event. You might want to propose basic formatting options (bold and italic) for the description.

Figure 3.3 shows the structure for the form. Translated into DTD format, it looks similar to Listing 3.2.

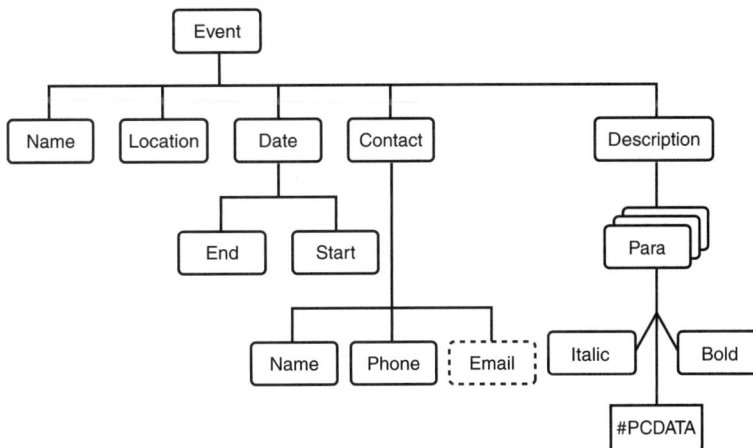

**Figure 3.3** The event form starts with closed questions and ends with a free-text description.

Listing 3.2  *event.dtd*

```
<!ELEMENT Event        (Name,Location,Date,Contact,Description)>
<!ELEMENT Name         (#PCDATA)>
<!ELEMENT Location     (#PCDATA)>
<!ELEMENT Date         (Start,End)>
<!ELEMENT Contact      (Name,Phone,Email?)>
<!ELEMENT Description  (Para+)>
<!ELEMENT Start        (#PCDATA)>
<!ELEMENT End          (#PCDATA)>
<!ELEMENT Phone        (#PCDATA)>
<!ELEMENT Email        (#PCDATA)>
<!ELEMENT Para         (#PCDATA | Bold | Italic)*>
<!ELEMENT Bold         (#PCDATA | Italic)*>
<!ELEMENT Italic       (#PCDATA | Bold)*>
```

## XML Models

In XML, markup is used to encode the structure of a document. Most XML tools manipulate the structure, making it important to have proper tools to model the structure of documents.

Therefore, XML has a modeling language, the *Document Type Definition (DTD)*. A DTD defines which elements appear in the document and what their relationships are (which element appears where). It also defines which elements can repeat and which are optional. Finally, the DTD also declares attributes and entities.

Listing 3.2 is a DTD. It lists all the elements and their content. For example,

```
<!ELEMENT Event (Name,Location,Date,Contact,Description)>
```

means that the Event element must contain a Name, Location, Date, Contact, and Description element.

XML documents fall into one of the following two categories:

- Well-formed documents follow the XML syntax. So far, our documents have been well formed.

- Valid documents follow the XML syntax and respect a model. This chapter uses valid documents.

Valid documents are helpful because XML tools will enforce their model. For example, XMetaL reports an error if you create a document in which an Event has no Location. In practice, your application benefits from a free validation routine.

For completeness, note that W3C is working on a replacement for DTD. The new modeling language, which should be called XML Schema, will be more powerful and will support object-oriented concepts.

For a comprehensive introduction to DTD and XML models, I recommend you read my other book, *XML by Example*, published by Que.

## Loading the Model in XMetaL

Copy event.dtd (refer to Listing 3.2) under the Rules directory underneath the
XMetaL main directory (on my system that is the C:\Program Files\SoftQuad\
XMetaL 1\Rules directory). XMetaL can load DTDs from any directory, but placing
them in the Rules directory ensures they are always available.

In the menu, choose File, New to open the New dialog box. Under the General tab,
select Blank XML Document and then select the event.dtd file you have just created.
XMetaL opens a dialog box to inquire about the space options; click the Apply Layout
button.

> **Note**
>
> The Preserve Space Options dialog box determines how XMetaL indents the XML code. For most docu-
> ments, you should choose Apply Layout, which produces more readable XML code.
>
> However, if you write documents in which spaces are meaningful, you should opt to Preserve Space. You
> can always change the setting later.

You now should see a blank editor window but be unable to type anything. To create
the root XML element, choose Insert, Element in the menu and double-click Event.

The editor window fills with various entry fields for name, location, and more. Click
{Name} and type Book Fair. Click {Location} and type Exhibition Center, Namur,
as illustrated in Figure 3.4.

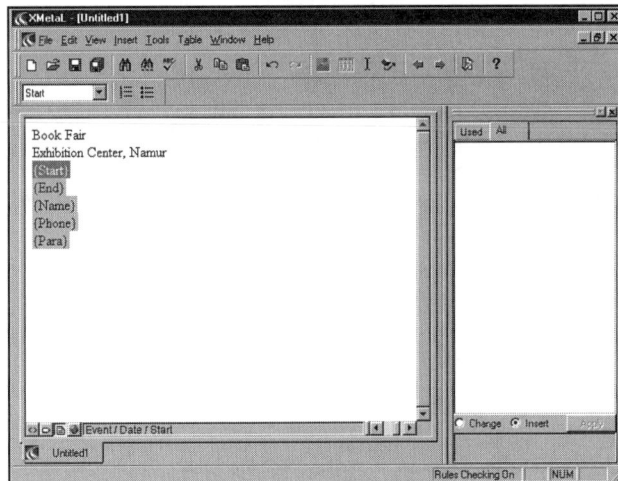

**Figure 3.4** After inserting the root element, enter some data.

> **Note**
>
> As you can see, XMetaL makes good use of the DTD. It extracts the list of elements and their relation-
> ships so that, when you insert an `Event` element, it knows which elements must appear underneath—
> `Name`, `Location`, and so on. Therefore, it creates input fields for these elements.

In the menu, choose View, Plain Text to display the XML code you have just created. The screen should look similar to Figure 3.5.

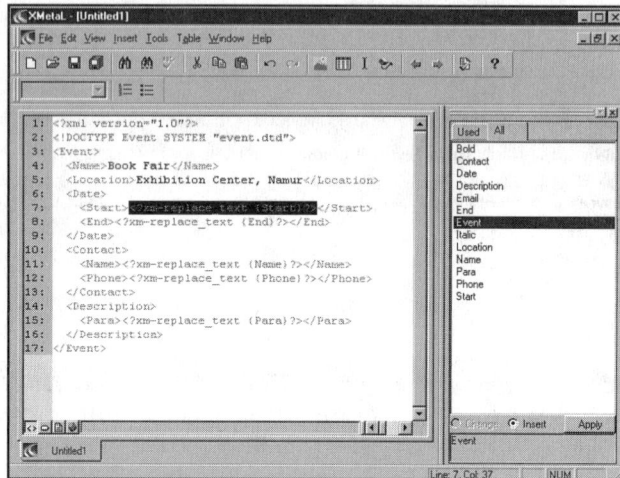

**Figure 3.5** XMetaL shows the XML code.

What happened? To find out, close the document but don't save it. Look in the XMetaL directory and you will see several new files:

- `event.rlx`—Appears under the `Rules` directory and is a so-called rules file. Essentially, it's a compiled version of the DTD.

- `event.ctm`—Appears under the `Rules` directory and is the customization file. You will learn how to edit it soon.

- `~event.tbr`—Appears in the same directory and represents the toolbars.

- `event.css`—Appears in the `Display` directory and is a cascading style sheet for this document.

These files are created with default options. They give us a starting point, but we probably want to customize them to better fit our event form.

## Creating a Template

Our second step will be to create a template or an empty form that the clerk can use to get started. Create a new empty event document as previously discussed: Choose File, New, select `event.dtd`, choose Insert, Element, and double-click Event.

Choose View, Plain Text to edit the XML code. First, though, make sure the DOCTYPE statement uses a relative path. Edit it until it looks exactly as follows (it might be correct already):

```
<!DOCTYPE Event SYSTEM "event.dtd">
```

As you can see, in this empty document, the text is replaced by processing instructions such as the following:

```
<?xm-replace_text {Name}?>
```

These processing instructions are specific to XMetaL. The editor renders them as an input area, similar to the Click Me fields in a word processor. When the user enters text, the text replaces the processing instruction.

To make the template more friendly, adopt more descriptive processing instructions, such as:

```
<?xm-replace_text {Click here to enter the event's name}?>
```

You should edit the document until it looks like Listing 3.3.

Listing 3.3 **Event Description** *Form.xml*

```
<?xml version="1.0"?>
<!DOCTYPE Event SYSTEM "event.dtd">
<Event>
  <Name><?xm-replace_text {Click here to enter the event's
➥name}?></Name>
  <Location><?xm-replace_text {Click here to enter the event's
➥location}?></Location>
  <Date>
    <Start><?xm-replace_text {Click here to enter the event's
➥start date}?></Start>
    <End><?xm-replace_text {And its end date}?></End>
  </Date>
  <Contact>
    <Name><?xm-replace_text {Click here to enter the contact
➥person's name}?></Name>
    <Phone><?xm-replace_text {Click here to enter the contact
➥person's phone number}?></Phone>
  </Contact>
  <Description>
    <Para><?xm-replace_text {Click here to enter the event's
➥description}?></Para>
  </Description>
</Event>
```

Create a new directory, called Pineapplesoft, under the Template directory below the XMetaL main directory. Save the template (Listing 3.3) under the Pineapplesoft directory and name it Event Description Form.xml.

We now have created a new template. If you close the file and choose File, New, you will see that the New dialog has a Pineapplesoft tab. The Pineapplesoft tab contains one entry: Event Description Form (see Figure 3.6).

If you double-click Event Description Form, it creates an empty document based on your template.

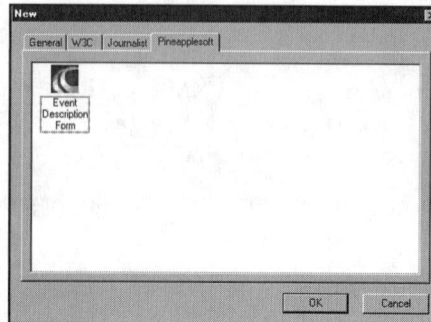

**Figure 3.6** Calling up the form is easy with custom templates.

## Styling the Form

So far, thanks to the template, we have provided the clerk with an empty form he can fill in. Also, thanks to the DTD, XMetaL makes sure the clerk provides all the required information.

However, the form is dull. At the minimum, fields should be labeled. To change the presentation of the document, you will edit the cascading style sheet.

### Cascading Style Sheet

XML markup is descriptive. Markup identifies the role of each element and its position in the structure, not how it should look. XML tools (particularly editors and browsers) need additional information to describe how to format the document for viewing.

The presentation rules are kept separated from the document itself in *style sheets*, which describe how to render the elements onscreen.

Cascading Style Sheet, or CSS, was originally created for HTML, but it was quickly extended for XML. A CSS is a list of rules, with each rule listing formatting properties associated with one or more elements.

For example, in XML, the Bold element does not automatically mean that the text must be bolded. However, you can define a CSS rule that says so:

```
Bold {
  font-weight: bold;
  display: inline;
}
```

CSS defines an extensive list of formatting properties. For the complete description, see www.w3.org/Style/CSS.

XMetaL includes a CSS editor that is convenient for getting you started. However, as you become more familiar with CSS, you will find it is faster to edit the style code directly.

First, you should format the Name element. Indent the field from the left margin and include a label.

Next, click somewhere in the Name field and choose Tools, Editor Display Style, Current Element. Make sure you are editing the Name element and then select the Box tab. Next, modify the margin-left property to 1em and click the Apply button. Notice how the two Name elements are now indented from the left margin.

**Tip**

The em unit is relative to the height of the font. Using relative units makes it easier to grow or shrink the whole document.

The Name rule you have just created applies to the element itself, so how can you insert a label before the element? The trick is to use CSS pseudo-elements. *Pseudo-elements* are not XML elements, but the style sheet treats them as such. You can think of them as virtual elements created by the style sheet.

In this case, you create a pseudo-element called Name:before. Name:before enables you to insert values before the Name element.

Still from the CSS editor, click the More button. Then, click New to open the Edit Selectors in Rule dialog box. Select Name, click Add, and click Edit to open the Edit Simple Selector dialog box. In the Pseudo/class element list (bottom-right of the box), select Before. Finally, click OK twice to return to the CSS editor.

You now have created an entry called Name:before (see Figure 3.7). Enter the following properties:

- A content property (in the Other tab) with the value Name:.
- A font-size property (in the Font tab) with the value smaller.
- A color property (in the Text tab) with the value gray.

Click OK to close the dialog box. The content property is the label. Because it is attached to the Name:before rule, it appears before the element itself. Notice that, per your selection, the label is in a smaller, gray font.

Continue adding rules for the other elements until your style sheet looks similar to Listing 3.4. Notice that the form title appears in an Event:before rule.

You probably will find it easier to edit the CSS style sheet in a text editor. To do so, from the CSS editor, click Edit Style Text.

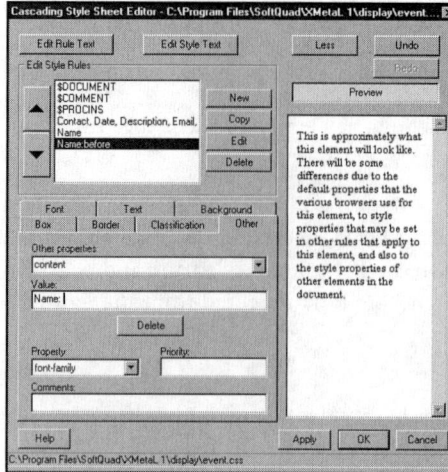

**Figure 3.7** Editing the `Name:before` rule.

▶ **Note**

$DOCUMENT, $COMMENT, and $PROCINS are not elements. They are XMetaL-specific pseudo-elements that point to the entire document, comments, and processing instructions, respectively.

Listing 3.4 *event.css*

```
/* Use Times New Roman for default font */
$DOCUMENT {
  font-family: "Times New Roman";
  font-size: 12pt;
  margin-top: 5px;
  margin-left: 5px;
}

$COMMENT {
  display: block;
  color: purple;
  white-space: pre;
}

$PROCINS {
  color: black;
  background-color: #c0c0c0;
}

Contact, Date, Description, Email, Event, Location, Name,
➥Para, Phone  {
  display: block;
}
```

Listing 3.4 **Continued**

```css
Start, End {
  display: inline;
}

Event:before {
  content: "Event Description Form";
  display: block;
  font-size: large;
  font-weight: bold;
}

Name:before, Location:before, Date:before, Phone:before,
➥Email:before, End:before {
  font-size: smaller;
  color: gray;
}

Name:before {
  content: "Name: ";
}

Location:before {
  content: "Location: ";
}

Date:before {
  content: "Date: ";
}

Phone:before {
  content: "Phone: ";
}

Email:before {
  content: "Email: ";
}

End:before {
  content: " to ";
}

Description:before, Contact:before {
  display: block;
  font-weight: bold;
}

Description:before {
  content: "Description";
}
Contact:before {
  content: "Contact";
}
```

Listing 3.4 **Continued**

```
Bold {
  font-weight: bold;
  display: inline;
}

Italic {
  font-style: italic;
  display: inline;
}

Name, Location, Date, Phone, Email, Para {
  margin-left: 1em;
}

Contact, Description {
  margin-top: 0.5em;
}

Event>Name {
  margin-top: 0.5em;
}
```

The form in the editor should now look like Figure 3.8. This is a good layout for a form: The fields are clearly labeled and the form is divided into sections separated by titles.

Remember that the labels and section titles are not part of the XML document; they appear only in the style sheet as pseudo-elements. Review the XML code in plain text view (choose View, Plain Text) to convince yourself.

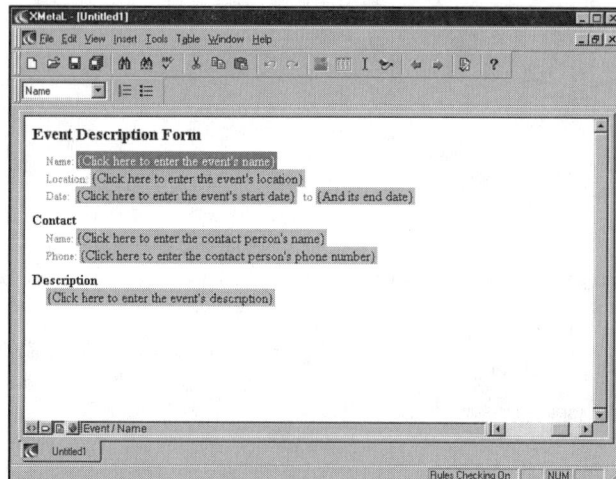

**Figure 3.8** A good-looking form in XMetaL.

# Customizing the Behavior

If we review your progress so far, it looks good. Our clerk can create an empty form, the fields are clearly labeled, and the editor still generates a valid XML document.

So far, we concentrated on the structure of the document and its presentation. In this section and the next, we customize XMetaL behavior to better fit your needs. We will

- Use the customization editor (in this section).
- Write JScript macros (in the next section) to create a specialized toolbar.

**Tip**

To save you some typing, remember you can copy event.ctm from the accompanying CD.

## Element Names

Most of the element names in the DTD, such as Name, Location, and Date, are easy to understand. Other names are not so clear, however—for example, Start, End, and Para. You should start by defining better alternatives for these names.

In the menu, choose Tools, Customization to open the customization editor. Under the General tab, enter a name for the following elements (you can leave the others empty), as follows:

- For Bold, enter Bold text.
- For Email, enter Email address.
- For End, enter End date.
- For Italic, enter Italic text.
- For Para, enter Paragraph.
- For Phone, enter Phone number.
- For Start, enter Start date.

Figure 3.9 shows the customization editor.

While we are at it, let's update the change list for the Para element. Select the Change List tab and, for Para, check both Bold and Italic. This option controls which elements appear in the list of styles in the toolbar.

Click OK to close the customization editor. Notice that the element names in the list of styles in the toolbar now reflect the changes we made. XMetaL also uses the names in the status bar.

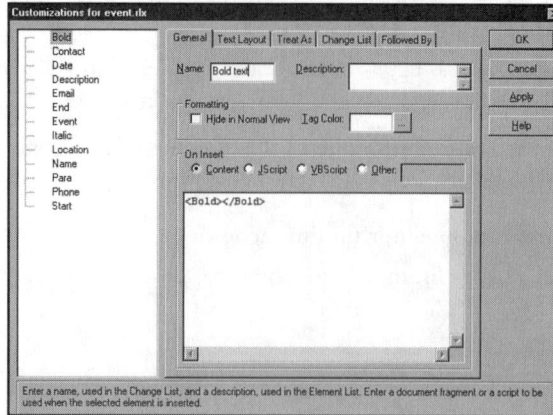

**Figure 3.9** The customization editor controls the editor's behavior.

## Creating Mini-Templates

The form editor is really taking shape now. It enables easy editing of most values, with the notable exception of the email address. In fact, because the email address is an optional element, it does not appear in the template. Therefore, to insert it, the user must position it past the Phone element and choose Insert, Element. You can do much better.

Reopen the customization editor and tab to Treat As. Set the Email element as a paragraph. This controls what the editor does when the user presses Enter. When the user presses Enter, XMetaL always tries to insert the next paragraph element. By declaring Email as a paragraph, we make it easier to insert email addresses in the document, as you will see in a moment.

> **Tip**
>
> You don't need to explicitly declare the other elements as paragraphs because your DTD is very strict. The DTD lays down strict rules on where each element should appear, and XMetaL uses these rules to insert most elements.

A further problem with email is that some people—particularly, AOL users—forget to include their domain name. Ideally, you want to remind the clerk that an email address should have the form *name@domain*.com.

The best solution is to prompt the user through a dialog box that presents the format for the email address. Return to the General tab and paste the following code in the On Insert field:

```
var email = Application.Prompt("Enter the contact person's
➥email address","name@domain.com",null,null,"Event
➥Description Form")
if(email != null && email != "")
{
   Selection.InsertElement("Email")
   Selection.TypeText(email)
}
```

Next, select `JScript` as the scripting language (see Figure 3.10). Now, whenever an `Email` element is inserted, XMetaL will run this script, which opens a dialog box.

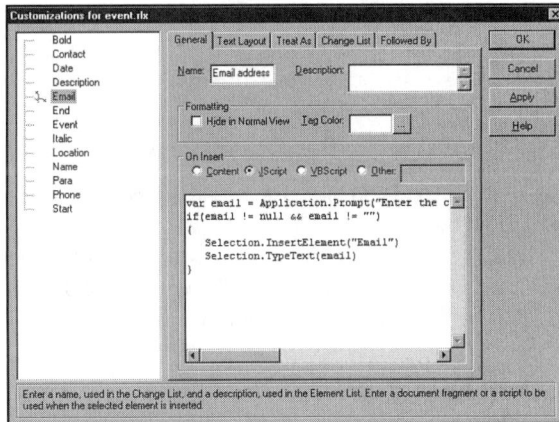

**Figure 3.10** Edit the element template.

To complete this round of customization, take a look at the On Insert field for the other elements. They always contain the XML code for the element, such as `<Location></Location>`.

By changing this code, we can control the XML code generated when creating the element. We can use it to modify the code and include the processing instructions. Edit the following elements (for these elements, leave the type as `Content`):

- For `Contact`, use
  ```
  <Contact>
      <Name><?xm-replace_text {Click here to enter the contact
  ➥person's name}?></Name>
      <Phone><?xm-replace_text {Click here to enter the contact
  ➥person's phone number}?></Phone>
  </Contact>
  ```

- For `Date`, use
  ```
  <Date>
      <Start><?xm-replace_text {Click here to enter the event's
  ➥start date}?></Start>
  ```

```
            <End><?xm-replace_text {And its end date}?></End>
         </Date>
```

- For Description, use

```
         <Description><Para><?xm-replace_text {Click here to enter the
         ↳event's description}?></Para></Description>
```

- For End, use

```
         <End><?xm-replace_text {And its end date}?></End>
```

- For Location, use

```
         <Location><?xm-replace_text {Click here to enter the event's
         ↳location}?></Location>
```

- For Phone, use

```
         <Phone><?xm-replace_text {Click here to enter the contact
         ↳person's phone number}?></Phone>
```

- For Start, use

```
         <Start><?xm-replace_text {Click here to enter the event's
         ↳start date}?></Start>
```

However, you must differentiate the event's name from the contact person's name. Right-click the Name element and select Add "In Parents" Item. Do this twice to create Name in Contact and Name in Event entries and give them different templates, respectively:

```
    <Name><?xm-replace_text {Click here to enter the contact
    ↳person's name}?></Name>
```

and

```
    <Name><?xm-replace_text {Click here to enter the event's
    ↳name}?></Name>
```

Click OK to close the customization editor. Then, position the cursor on the Phone element and press Enter. A dialog box prompts for the email address (see Figure 3.11). The following occurs internally:

- XMetaL inserts the next paragraph element, which will be Email because it is marked as a paragraph.

- XMetaL executes the script from the Email mini-template. The script opens a dialog box and inserts the element.

### Peeking at event.ctm

If you are curious, you can open event.ctm in XMetaL because it is an XML document. Listing 3.5 shows event.ctm if you applied all the customization described in this section.

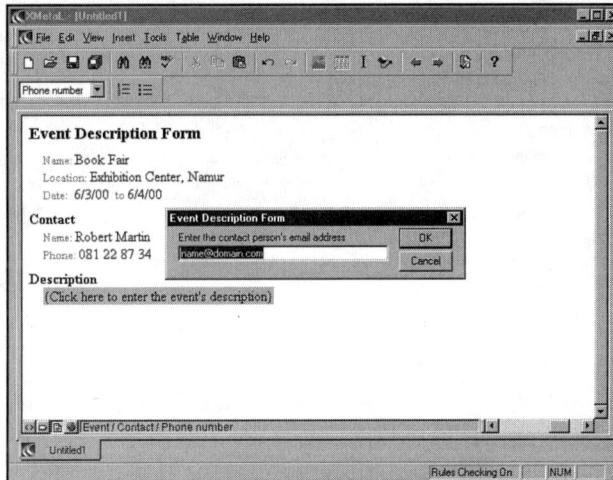

**Figure 3.11** Prompting for email information.

**Caution**

You should not modify event.ctm directly. It is both easier and safer to edit it through the customization editor.

Listing 3.5 *event.ctm*

```
<?xml version="1.0"?>
<!DOCTYPE DTDExtensions SYSTEM "ctm.dtd">
<DTDExtensions>
  <ElementPropertiesList>
    <ElementProperties>
      <Name>Contact</Name>
      <PrettyPrintOptions>
        <NewLineBeforeStartTag/>
        <IndentContent/>
        <NewLineBeforeEndTag/>
      </PrettyPrintOptions>
    </ElementProperties>
    <ElementProperties>
      <Name>Date</Name>
      <PrettyPrintOptions>
        <NewLineBeforeStartTag/>
        <NewLineBeforeEndTag/>
        <IndentContent/>
      </PrettyPrintOptions>
    </ElementProperties>
```

Listing 3.5 **Continued**

```
<ElementProperties>
  <Name>Description</Name>
  <PrettyPrintOptions>
    <NewLineBeforeStartTag/>
    <NewLineBeforeEndTag/>
    <IndentContent/>
  </PrettyPrintOptions>
</ElementProperties>
<ElementProperties>
  <Name>Email</Name>
  <ShortDescription>Email address</ShortDescription>
  <PrettyPrintOptions>
    <NewLineBeforeStartTag/>
    <IndentContent/>
  </PrettyPrintOptions>
</ElementProperties>
<ElementProperties>
  <Name>End</Name>
  <ShortDescription>End date</ShortDescription>
  <PrettyPrintOptions>
    <NewLineBeforeStartTag/>
    <IndentContent/>
  </PrettyPrintOptions>
</ElementProperties>
<ElementProperties>
  <Name>Event</Name>
  <PrettyPrintOptions>
    <NewLineBeforeStartTag/>
    <NewLineBeforeEndTag/>
    <IndentContent/>
  </PrettyPrintOptions>
</ElementProperties>
<ElementProperties>
  <Name>Location</Name>
  <PrettyPrintOptions>
    <NewLineBeforeStartTag/>
    <IndentContent/>
  </PrettyPrintOptions>
</ElementProperties>
<ElementProperties>
  <Name>Name</Name>
  <PrettyPrintOptions>
    <NewLineBeforeStartTag/>
    <IndentContent/>
  </PrettyPrintOptions>
</ElementProperties>
<ElementProperties>
  <Name>Para</Name>
  <ShortDescription>Paragraph</ShortDescription>
  <PrettyPrintOptions>
```

Listing 3.5 **Continued**

```xml
            <NewLineBeforeStartTag/>
            <IndentContent/>
          </PrettyPrintOptions>
        </ElementProperties>
        <ElementProperties>
          <Name>Phone</Name>
          <ShortDescription>Phone number</ShortDescription>
          <PrettyPrintOptions>
            <NewLineBeforeStartTag/>
            <IndentContent/>
          </PrettyPrintOptions>
        </ElementProperties>
        <ElementProperties>
          <Name>Start</Name>
          <ShortDescription>Start date</ShortDescription>
          <PrettyPrintOptions>
            <NewLineBeforeStartTag/>
            <IndentContent/>
          </PrettyPrintOptions>
        </ElementProperties>
        <ElementProperties>
          <Name>Bold</Name>
          <ShortDescription>Bold text</ShortDescription>
        </ElementProperties>
        <ElementProperties>
          <Name>Italic</Name>
          <ShortDescription>Italic text</ShortDescription>
        </ElementProperties>
      </ElementPropertiesList>
      <Paragraphs>
        <Paragraph>
          <Name>Email</Name>
        </Paragraph>
      </Paragraphs>
      <ChangeLists>
        <ChangeList>
          <Selectors>
            <Selector>
              <Name>#DEFAULT</Name>
              <Parent>Para</Parent>
            </Selector>
          </Selectors>
          <ChangeListElements>
            <ChangeListElement>Bold</ChangeListElement>
            <ChangeListElement>Italic</ChangeListElement>
          </ChangeListElements>
        </ChangeList>
      </ChangeLists>
      <Templates>
        <Template>
```

Listing 3.5 **Continued**

```
      <Name>Name</Name>
      <Parent>Contact</Parent>
      <MiniTemplate><![CDATA[<Name><?xm-replace_text
➥{Click here to enter the contact person's name}?></Name>]]>
➥</MiniTemplate>
    </Template>
    <Template>
      <Name>Name</Name>
      <Parent>Event</Parent>
      <MiniTemplate><![CDATA[<Name><?xm-replace_text
➥{Click here to enter the event's name}?></Name>]]>
➥</MiniTemplate>
    </Template>
    <Template>
      <Name>Description</Name>
      <MiniTemplate><![CDATA[<Description><Para><?xm-replace
➥text {Click here to enter the event's description}?></Para>
➥</Description>]]></MiniTemplate>
    </Template>
    <Template>
      <Name>Contact</Name>
      <MiniTemplate><![CDATA[<Contact>
  <Name><?xm-replace_text {Click here to enter the contact
➥person's name}?></Name>
  <Phone><?xm-replace_text {Click here to enter the contact
➥person's phone number}?></Phone>
</Contact>]]></MiniTemplate>
    </Template>
    <Template>
      <Name>Date</Name>
      <MiniTemplate><![CDATA[<Date>
  <Start><?xm-replace_text {Click here to enter the event's
➥start date}?></Start>
  <End><?xm-replace_text {And its end date}?></End>
</Date>]]></MiniTemplate>
    </Template>
    <Template>
      <Name>Location</Name>
      <MiniTemplate><![CDATA[<Location><?xm-replace_text
➥{Click here to enter the event's location}?></Location>]]>
➥</MiniTemplate>
    </Template>
    <Template>
      <Name>Phone</Name>
      <MiniTemplate><![CDATA[<Phone><?xm-replace_text {Click
➥here to enter the contact person's phone number}?></Phone>]]>
➥</MiniTemplate>
    </Template>
    <Template>
      <Name>Start</Name>
      <MiniTemplate><![CDATA[<Start><?xm-replace_text {Click
```

Listing 3.5 **Continued**

```
↪here to enter the event's start date}?></Start>]]>
↪</MiniTemplate>
    </Template>
    <Template>
      <Name>End</Name>
      <MiniTemplate><![CDATA[<End><?xm-replace_text {And
↪its end date}?></End> ]]></MiniTemplate>
    </Template>
  </Templates>
  <OnInsertElementList>
    <OnInsertElement>
      <Name>Email</Name>
      <Lang>JScript</Lang>
      <InsertElemScript><![CDATA[var email =
↪Application.Prompt("Enter the contact person's email address",
↪"name@domain.com",null,null,"Event Description Form")
if(email != null && email != "")
{
  Selection.InsertElement("Email")
  Selection.TypeText(email)
}]]></InsertElemScript>
    </OnInsertElement>
  </OnInsertElementList>
</DTDExtensions>
```

# Writing Macros

The next and last level of customization is performed by using macros. Macros can, amongst other things

- Add new menu items or new toolbar buttons
- Control what happens at critical moments, such as when the document is saved

You can associate one macro file with each DTD. The macros file, event.mcr, is shown in Listing 3.6. We will examine it, one macro at a time, in the following sections.

Note that the macro file is an XML document, so you can use XMetaL to edit it. To create an empty macro file, choose File, New, Blank XML Document and then select macros.dtd.

This causes a script error. You should immediately save the file as event.mcr under the Macros directory below the XMetaL directory to avoid the script errors.

**Tip**

If a macro file exists for the current DTD, you can edit it by choosing Tools, Macros, selecting Open Document Macros, and clicking Run.

Listing 3.6 *event.mcr*

```
<?xml version="1.0"?>
<!DOCTYPE MACROS SYSTEM "macros.dtd">

<MACROS>

<MACRO lang="JScript" name="Insert Email">
<![CDATA[if(ActiveDocument.documentElement)
{
   var emails = ActiveDocument.getElementsByTagName("Email")
   if(0 == emails.length)
   {
      var contacts =
ActiveDocument.getElementsByTagName("Contact")
      if(0 != contacts.length)
      {
         var phones = contacts(0).getElementsByTagName("Phone")
         if(0 != phones.length)
         {
            Selection.SelectAfterNode(phones(phones.length - 1))
            Selection.InsertWithTemplate("Email")
         }
         else
         {
            var names = contacts(0).getElementsByTagName("Name")
            if(0 != names.length)
            {
               Selection.SelectAfterNode(
names(names.length - 1))
               Selection.InsertWithTemplate("Phone")
               Selection.SelectAfterNode(contacts(0).lastChild)
               Selection.InsertWithTemplate("Email")
            }
            else
            {
               Selection.SelectNodeContents(contacts(0))
               Selection.InsertWithTemplate("Name")
               Selection.SelectAfterNode(contacts(0).lastChild)
               Selection.InsertWithTemplate("Phone")
               Selection.SelectAfterNode(contacts(0).lastChild)
               Selection.InsertWithTemplate("Email")
            }
         }
      }
   }
}]]></MACRO>

<MACRO lang="JScript" name="Italic">
<![CDATA[if(ActiveDocument.documentElement)
{
   if(Selection.ContainerName == "Italic")
```

Listing 3.6 **Continued**

```
      Selection.RemoveContainerTags()
   else if(Selection.CanSurround("Italic"))
      Selection.Surround("Italic")
}]]></MACRO>

<MACRO lang="JScript" name="Bold">
↩<![CDATA[if(ActiveDocument.documentElement)
{
   if(Selection.ContainerName == "Bold")
      Selection.RemoveContainerTags()
   else if(Selection.CanSurround("Bold"))
      Selection.Surround("Bold")
}]]></MACRO>

<MACRO lang="JScript" name="On_Document_Save">
↩<![CDATA[if(ActiveDocument.documentElement)
{
   var isStart = true,
       isEnd = true
   var invalidFields = null
   var starts = ActiveDocument.getElementsByTagName("Start")
   if(0 != starts.length)
   {
      starts(0).normalize()
      var startText = starts(0).firstChild
      if(null != startText &&
         3 == startText.nodeType)    // 3 == DOMText
         isStart = !isNaN(Date.parse(startText.data))
   }
   var ends = ActiveDocument.getElementsByTagName("End")
   if(0 != ends.length)
   {
      ends(0).normalize()
      var endText = ends(0).firstChild
      if(null != endText &&
         3 == endText.nodeType)    // 3 == DOMText
         isEnd = !isNaN(Date.parse(endText.data))
   }
   var msg = null
   if(!isStart && !isEnd)
      msg = "Both event dates are invalid.\n
↩You should fix them and save again."
   else if(!isStart)
      msg = "Event start date is invalid.\n
↩You should fix it and save again."
   else if(!isEnd)
      msg = "Event end date is invalid.\n
↩You should fix it and save again."
   if(msg != null)
      Application.Alert(msg,"Event Description Form")
}]]></MACRO>
```

Listing 3.6 **Continued**

```
<MACRO lang="JScript" name="On_Document_SaveAs">
➥<![CDATA[Application.Run("On_Document_Save")]]></MACRO>

<MACRO name="On_Update_UI" lang="JScript">
➥<![CDATA[if(!ActiveDocument.documentElement ||
   3 == ActiveDocument.ViewType)
{
   Application.DisableMacro("Insert Email")
   Application.DisableMacro("Italic")
   Application.DisableMacro("Bold")
}
else
{
   var emails = ActiveDocument.getElementsByTagName("Email")
   if(0 != emails.length)
      Application.DisableMacro("Insert Email")

   var contacts = ActiveDocument.getElementsByTagName("Contact")
   if(0 == contacts.length)
      Application.DisableMacro("Insert Email")

   if(!Selection.IsParentElement("Para"))
   {
      Application.DisableMacro("Italic")
      Application.DisableMacro("Bold")
   }
}]]></MACRO>

</MACROS>
```

## Creating a Toolbar Button

First, you should review the Italic macro (the Bold macro is almost identical):

```
<MACRO lang="JScript" name="Italic">
➥<![CDATA[if(ActiveDocument.documentElement)
{
   if(Selection.ContainerName == "Italic")
      Selection.RemoveContainerTags()
   else if(Selection.CanSurround("Italic"))
      Selection.Surround("Italic")
}]]></MACRO>
```

This macro inserts or removes the Italic element. Before running macros that will modify the document, it is good practice to test whether a document object is available. ActiveDocument is a special object that always points to the document in the active window.

The core of the macro is simple: It tests whether the cursor is within an `Italic` element, in which case the macro removes it. Otherwise, it attempts to insert an `Italic` element around the current selection.

The `RemoveContainerTags()` and `Surround()` methods modify the document. The `CanSurround()` method tests against the DTD. Our macro uses both to test against the DTD before inserting the element. For your DTD, `CanSurround()` returns true if the selection is within a `Para` element.

This macro implements the `Italic` command from word processors. You should add it to the toolbar. Make sure you have opened an empty `event.dtd` document and then select Tools, Macros to open the Macros dialog box. In the list, select the Italic macro and assign it a shortcut of Ctrl+I. XMetaL warns you that Ctrl+I conflicts with another macro, but ignore it.

> **Tip**
>
> When you edit macros in XMetaL, you can reload the macros with the Save and Refresh button on the macros toolbar.

Click Choose Image to open the Choose Toolbar Button Image dialog box. In the Formatting images, select the slanted I. Then close the macro box.

Choose View, Toolbars to open the Toolbars dialog box and click the New button. Enter `event` as the toolbar name. Immediately, an empty toolbar appears onscreen. Tab to the Buttons panel and select `event Macros`. In the list of macros, choose Italic. Finally, drag the button to the toolbar (see Figure 3.12). Repeat these steps for the Bold macro.

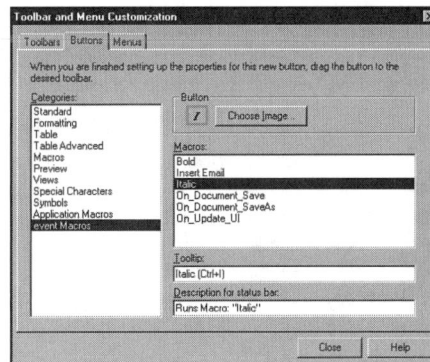

**Figure 3.12** Editing the toolbar.

## Creating an XML Element

Although you have already improved things, inserting the Email element is still difficult. Specifically, the user must be in the Phone field and press Enter. It's great if you
know it, but almost impossible to find if you don't.

Add a button to the toolbar to insert the Email element. Because the button will be
visible on the toolbar, it will be easier for the user.

This is implemented in the Insert Email macro:

```JScript
<MACRO lang="JScript" name="Insert Email">
<![CDATA[if(ActiveDocument.documentElement)
{
    var emails = ActiveDocument.getElementsByTagName("Email")
    if(0 == emails.length)
    {
        var contacts =
ActiveDocument.getElementsByTagName("Contact")
        if(0 != contacts.length)
        {
            var phones = contacts(0).getElementsByTagName("Phone")
            if(0 != phones.length)
            {
                Selection.SelectAfterNode(phones(phones.length - 1))
                Selection.InsertWithTemplate("Email")
            }
            else
            {
                var names = contacts(0).getElementsByTagName("Name")
                if(0 != names.length)
                {
                    Selection.SelectAfterNode(
names(names.length - 1))
                    Selection.InsertWithTemplate("Phone")
                    Selection.SelectAfterNode(contacts(0).lastChild)
                    Selection.InsertWithTemplate("Email")
                }
                else
                {
                    Selection.SelectNodeContents(contacts(0))
                    Selection.InsertWithTemplate("Name")
                    Selection.SelectAfterNode(contacts(0).lastChild)
                    Selection.InsertWithTemplate("Phone")
                    Selection.SelectAfterNode(contacts(0).lastChild)
                    Selection.InsertWithTemplate("Email")
                }
            }
        }
    }
}]]></MACRO>
```

Similar to Italic, this macro creates a new XML element. However, it is more complex because the Email element must appear within the Contact element and more than one Email element can't exist.

The Insert Email macro starts by testing whether an Email element already exists. If none does, it tries to locate the Contact element. If no Contact elements exist, it stops. However, if it finds Contact, it tries to locate a Phone or Name element. If Phone or Name are missing, it inserts them before inserting Email.

Insert Email is more complex than the Italic macro because it must enforce the document structure. For example, it might have to create other elements (Phone and Name) before creating the Email element.

> **Note**
> The macro uses InsertWithTemplate() to create the elements. InsertWithTemplate() uses the template defined in the customization editor, so it will end up prompting the user through a dialog box.

Don't forget to create a button on the toolbar. You can use the envelope image in the Quick Tools list.

## Improving the User Interface

The next macro is On_Update_UI. XMetaL executes it when it needs to update the user interface—for example, when the user moves to a new element or switches from normal to plain text view.

This macro is responsible for selectively disabling those macros that no longer work. For example, if the user moves from a Para element to Location, the Italic and Bold macros must be disabled.

On_Update_UI disables all the macros if no document object is available. It also disables Insert Email if an email already is in the document or if no Contact element exists. Finally, it disables Italic and Bold unless the cursor is within a Para:

```
<MACRO name="On_Update_UI" lang="JScript">
<![CDATA[if(!ActiveDocument.documentElement ||
   3 == ActiveDocument.ViewType)
{
   Application.DisableMacro("Insert Email")
   Application.DisableMacro("Italic")
   Application.DisableMacro("Bold")
}
else
{
   var emails = ActiveDocument.getElementsByTagName("Email")
   if(0 != emails.length)
      Application.DisableMacro("Insert Email")
```

```
   var contacts = ActiveDocument.getElementsByTagName("Contact")
   if(0 == contacts.length)
      Application.DisableMacro("Insert Email")

   if(!Selection.IsParentElement("Para"))
   {
      Application.DisableMacro("Italic")
      Application.DisableMacro("Bold")
   }
}]]></MACRO>
```

## Validating the Form

The last two macros are On_Document_Save and On_Document_SaveAs. They perform additional validation before the document is saved. Indeed, although XMetaL enforces the structure of the document, the user can always enter incorrect information in the fields. The DTD offers much built-in validation, but it is not always powerful enough. You can develop additional validations using On_Document_Save and On_Document_SaveAs.

Specifically, the macro extracts the start and end dates from the document and checks that they are indeed dates. In case of errors, it warns the user through a dialog box (see Figure 3.13):

```
<MACRO lang="JScript" name="On_Document_Save">
↪<![CDATA[if(ActiveDocument.documentElement)
{
   var isStart = true,
       isEnd = true
   var invalidFields = null
   var starts = ActiveDocument.getElementsByTagName("Start")
   if(0 != starts.length)
   {
      starts(0).normalize()
      var startText = starts(0).firstChild
      if(null != startText &&
         3 == startText.nodeType)    // 3 == DOMText
         isStart = !isNaN(Date.parse(startText.data))
   }
   var ends = ActiveDocument.getElementsByTagName("End")
   if(0 != ends.length)
   {
      ends(0).normalize()
      var endText = ends(0).firstChild
      if(null != endText &&
         3 == endText.nodeType)    // 3 == DOMText
         isEnd = !isNaN(Date.parse(endText.data))
   }
   var msg = null
   if(!isStart && !isEnd)
      msg = "Both event dates are invalid.\n
```

```
▸You should fix them and save again."
   else if(!isStart)
      msg = "Event start date is invalid.\n
▸You should fix it and save again."
   else if(!isEnd)
      msg = "Event end date is invalid.\n
▸You should fix it and save again."
   if(msg != null)
      Application.Alert(msg,"Event Description Form")
}]]></MACRO>
```

**Tip**

On_Document_Save does not prevent the user from saving an incorrect document; it only warns her. In practice, this is a good compromise: Good reasons might exist for the user to temporarily enter an invalid date.

If you need to prevent the user from saving incorrect documents, use the File_Save and File_SaveAs macros.

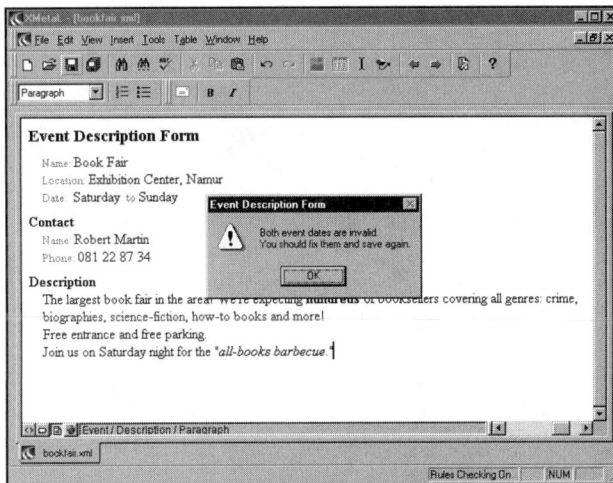

**Figure 3.13**  Oops! The dates are not acceptable.

# Advantages

This chapter demonstrated how to use an XML editor to build a customized editing environment. The main advantages of this solutions are as follows:

- It's fast and easy. The editor does most of the job already, so you only need to customize it for your DTD.

- The user interface is simple and intuitive. It looks like a word processor, which is very familiar to clerical personal.

- The result is an XML document that you can pass to other XML tools such as parsers and XSL processors (see Chapter 4).

In short, the editor is a great tool to create XML documents. Thanks to customization, you can be sure it creates the correct documents.

## Additional Resources

Current generation browsers do not recognize XML forms. The W3C is working on a standard for XML forms (XForms), but it is still a work in progress and it probably will take several years before it is widely available in browsers. For more information, visit the W3C site at www.w3.org/MarkUp/Forms.

If you need to edit forms in a browser, you can turn to special plug-ins developed by other vendors. Popular products include the following:

- PureEdge, available from www.pureedge.com
- Jetform, available from www.xfa.org

# 4

# Content Syndication

THE WEB IS MANY THINGS TO MANY people but, for publishers and authors, it is another media comparable to print, radio, and TV. Don't get me wrong, I recognize that the Internet has unique characteristics, but its reach is comparable to other popular media.

As proof, look at initiatives by existing publishers to offer their content online (visit `www.informit.com`), the emergence of new publishers (such as `www.earthweb.com`), and, of course, the growing involvement of authors (such as my own `www.marchal.com`).

Furthermore, a growing number of companies, who are not necessarily publishers, use their Web sites to distribute information, articles, and reports (such as `developer.iplanet.com`).

However, the media is still young and changing. At the peak of the rivalry between Microsoft and Netscape, the so-called "browser war," Web fashion was changing every six months. We are now enjoying more stability, but, mark my words, the browser war is about to start again with new actors. And this time, it will be more painful for the under-prepared.

According to the W3C, non-desktop browsers might account for as much as 75% of all surfers by 2002. Non-desktop browsers include mobile phones, PDAs (such as the PalmPilot), and WebTV.

Most of these devices simply won't use HTML. During the browser war, designers could at least rely on some level of commonality between the two major browsers. This won't be the case anymore because mobile phones use a special language, Wireless Markup Language (WML), which is incompatible with HTML.

What to do? Should content providers (publishers, authors, and companies) limit themselves to either HTML or WAP? Should they support both formats? Should they prepare for even more formats?

Developing original content (articles, books, reports, and so on) is expensive. To offset the cost, content owners want to distribute their content as widely as possible. Ideally, it should not matter whether the reader uses a PC, a mobile phone, or another device.

In this chapter, we will see how XML helps address this challenge. As you know, XML's roots are in the publishing industry, and that heritage guarantees that there is no lack of quality tools for publishing problems.

# Architecture

Webmasters typically edit their Web sites with an HTML editor. The major disadvantage of this approach is that it freezes the site. Indeed, to change the presentation, you must manually re-edit every page. It's possible to do, but it's a lot of work.

The XML solution is to separate authoring from publishing. The author of the pages writes the document in XML. While doing so, she ignores presentation. She instead adopts an XML vocabulary that focuses on the organization of the document: sections, titles, abstracts, and more.

Publishing the document then simply requires converting the document into HTML, WML, or another popular format. Fortunately, this can be automated because the original XML document is structure rich. The operative word here is *automated*.

For medium to large sites, it is more cost effective to automate publishing. Rewriting a couple of pages by hand is feasible; however, for a hundred pages, it is too expensive.

Figure 4.1 illustrates how we'll apply these principles in this chapter. The tree main elements are as follows:

- Documents in structure-rich XML
- XSLT style sheets that implement the conversion to HTML, WML, and RSS (more on RSS in the next section)
- A servlet that is responsible for applying the style sheets

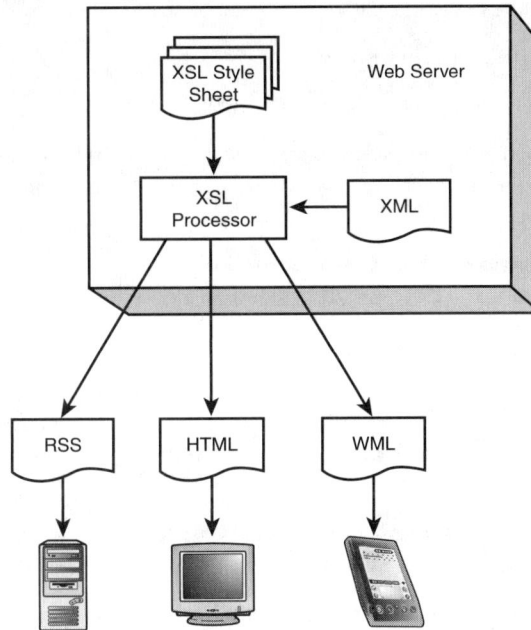

**Figure 4.1** XML separates authoring and publishing.

## XML Stylesheet Language

To publish XML documents we will use XSL, the XML Stylesheet Language. More specifically, we will use XSLT, XSL Transformation.

XSLT is a scripting language optimized for conversion between XML documents. In that respect it differs from early style sheet languages, such as CSS (Cascading Style Sheet), or word processor style sheets.

CSS describes how each element should be presented onscreen: which font, which color, which size, and more.

XSLT transforms the XML document into another XML document. It goes much further than simple presentation instructions. In fact, XSLT can completely reorganize a document and, for example, add a table of contents or delete a section.

How does that help? The trick is to transform from a structure-rich XML document into a format that contains display instructions, such as HTML or WML.

A browser (or another viewer) can render the second document onscreen or on paper. What display format should you use? The following are some popular options:

- HTML—Strictly speaking, HTML is not an XML vocabulary. This is not an XML-to-XML transformation. However, HTML is so popular, and so close to XML, that the W3C decided to support it.

- XHTML—The XML version of HTML.

- WML—The markup language for WAP devices.

- **Open eBook**—The format for eBooks, based on HTML.

- XSLFO—A new display language that is optimized for printed documents. At the time of writing, two XSLFO viewers exist: a browser (`www.indelv.com`) and a PDF converter (`xml.apache.org`).

The XSLT standard is available online at `www.w3.org/TR/xslt`.

## XML Vocabulary

As we saw in the previous chapters, XML does not define any vocabulary. It is up to developers to create vocabularies for their applications.

For this application, we have two realistic options. The first option is to use DocBook (`www.docbook.org`) or another standard SGML/XML vocabulary for documents. DocBook is particularly attractive because it is widely used and well supported.

However, DocBook is so rich that it is too complicated for such a simple project.

The second option, and the one we'll adopt in this chapter, is to create our own vocabulary—one that is simple and limited to only the tags we need.

Listing 4.1 illustrates the vocabulary we'll use in this chapter. As you can see, it is almost trivial: It's just a list of news items.

Listing 4.1  *index.xml*

```
<?xml version="1.0"?>
<News>
   <URL>http://localhost:8080/publish/index</URL>
   <Item>
      <Title>Applied XML Solutions</Title>
      <Author>Beno&#238;t Marchal</Author>
      <Abstract>A new intermediate/advanced book for XML
         developers.</Abstract>
      <Para>Learn advanced XML programming with Applied XML
         Solutions. This hands-on teaching book is filled with
         practical examples.</Para>
      <Para>Applied XML Solutions is a great complement to XML by
         Example.</Para>
   </Item>
   <Item>
      <Title>Jetty</Title>
      <Author>Greg Wilkins</Author>
            <Abstract>Open Source Java Server.</Abstract>
      <Para>Jetty is a powerful, open-source Java web server. It
```

Listing 4.1 **Continued**

```
            supports standard Java servlets making it the ideal
            development environment.</Para>
         <Para>Jetty is also highly-configurable which helps custom
            developments.</Para>
      </Item>
      <Item>
         <Title>Hypersonic SQL</Title>
         <Author>Thomas M&#252;ller</Author>
         <Abstract>Open Source SQL Database.</Abstract>
         <Para>Hypersonic SQL is an open source database that
            supports the JDBC API.</Para>
         <Para>Hypersonic SQL is efficient and can run in three
            modes: in-memory, standalone or client/server. This
            provides lots of flexibility when writing
            software.</Para>
      </Item>
   </News>
```

The list starts with a URL that points to the server where the document resides. The W3C suggests using the xml:base attribute for this purpose, but it turns out that Xalan, the XSLT processor I use, has a problem with the xml namespace, so I use a URL element as a workaround:

```
<URL>http://localhost:8080/publish/index</URL>
```

Each item has a title, author, abstract, and list of paragraphs:

```
<Item>
   <Title>Applied XML Solutions</Title>
   <Author>Beno&#238;t Marchal</Author>
   <Abstract>A new intermediate/advanced book for XML
      developers.</Abstract>
   <Para>Learn advanced XML programming with Applied XML
      Solutions. This hands-on teaching book is filled with
      practical examples.</Para>
   <Para>Applied XML Solutions is a great complement to XML by
      Example.</Para>
</Item>
```

Figure 4.2 illustrates the structure.

How can you develop such a format? When should you use existing formats (such as DocBook) rather than develop your own? Unfortunately, there are no hard rules that you can follow to guarantee success.

As you develop your XML vocabulary, remember that a good vocabulary achieves a reasonable compromise between two opposite goals: On the one hand, it must mark up as much information as possible; on the other hand, it must be simple.

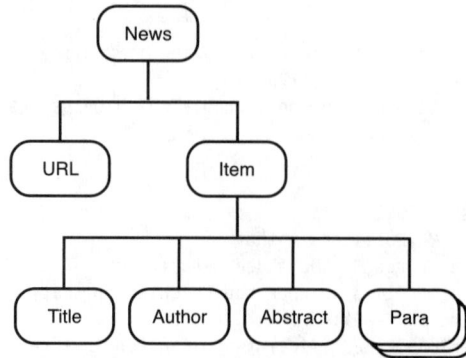

**Figure 4.2** The document structure in XML.

It is important to mark up as much data as is realistically possible because the markup drives the transformation to HTML, WML, and others. If something has not been marked up, transforming it will be difficult (or outright impossible).

Yet, as you define the vocabulary, be realistic. If you provide too many tags and too many options, you will confuse authors. This is particularly true if authors don't use the format regularly.

A format that is too complex can be dangerous because it gives the false impression that we're creating quality documents, whereas, in fact, authors usually ignore most of the markup. I am sure you have already encountered a database with a complex table organization. In most cases, developers have misused it and retrieving useful information is difficult. The same could happen with a markup vocabulary that is too complex.

▶ **Tip**

Consider using an XML editor, as introduced in the previous chapter, to guide authors.

## Publishing Formats

Ultimately, a servlet takes the XML document in Listing 4.1 and publishes it in HTML, WML, or RSS. WML is used for wireless applications, such as mobile phones, whereas RSS is used for portals.

I assume you are familiar with HTML, but I will introduce WML and RSS.

### WML

You can think of WML as an HTML for mobile users. You will recognize several HTML elements in WML, such as `<p>`, `<b>`, and `<small>`.

However, WML differs from HTML in at least one aspect: It is not organized in pages but as a deck of cards. As we will see, this is to accommodate the smaller screens of mobile phones.

In effect, the user downloads not one page but a set of related pages (called *cards*). See Figure 4.3 for an illustration of this concept.

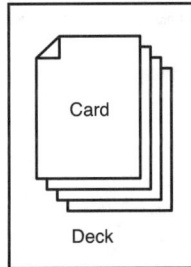

**Figure 4.3** A WML document is a set of cards.

Another difference between HTML and WML is that WML is an XML application; it respects the XML syntax. In other words, start and end tags must match. Listing 4.2 illustrates a WML document.

Listing 4.2 **WML Document**

```
<?xml version="1.0" encoding="UTF-8"?>
<!DOCTYPE wml PUBLIC "-//WAPFORUM//DTD WML 1.1//EN"
                    "http://www.wapforum.org/DTD/wml_1.1.xml">
<wml>
<card title="Pineapplesoft Daily" id="toc">
   <p align="center"><b>Today's News</b></p>
   <p><anchor>Applied XML Solutions<go href="#N8"/></anchor></p>
   <p><anchor>Jetty<go href="#N28"/></anchor></p>
   <p><anchor>Hypersonic SQL<go href="#N46"/></anchor></p>
</card>
<card title="Pineapplesoft Daily" id="N8">
   <p align="center"><b>Applied XML Solutions</b></p>
   <p><small>by Beno&#238;t Marchal</small></p>
   <p>A new intermediate/advanced book for XML developers.</p>
   <p><small><anchor>More News...<go
      href="#toc"/></anchor></small></p>
   <p>Learn advanced XML programming with Applied XML Solutions.
      This hands-on teaching book is filled with practical
      examples.</p>
   <p>Applied XML Solutions is a great complement to XML by
      Example.</p>
   <p><anchor>More News...<go href="#toc"/></anchor></p>
</card>
```

Listing 4.2 **Continued**

```
<card title="Pineapplesoft Daily" id="N28">
   <p align="center"><b>Jetty</b></p>
   <p><small>by Greg Wilkins</small></p>
   <p>Open Source Java Server.</p>
   <p><small><anchor>More News...<go
      href="#toc"/></anchor></small></p>
   <p>Jetty is a powerful, open-source Java web server.
      It supports standard Java servlets making it the ideal
      development environment.</p>
   <p>Jetty is also highly-configurable which helps custom
      developments.</p>
   <p><anchor>More News...<go href="#toc"/></anchor></p>
</card>
<card title="Pineapplesoft Daily" id="N46">
   <p align="center"><b>Hypersonic SQL</b></p>
   <p><small>by Thomas M&#252;ller</small></p>
   <p>Open Source SQL Database.</p>
   <p><small><anchor>More News...<go
      href="#toc"/></anchor></small></p>
   <p>Hypersonic SQL is an open source database that supports
      the JDBC API.</p>
   <p>Hypersonic SQL is efficient and can run in three modes:
      in-memory, standalone or client/server. This provides
      lots of flexibility when writing software.</p>
   <p><anchor>More News...<go href="#toc"/></anchor></p>
</card>
</wml>
```

Thanks to the XML declaration, there is no mistaking an XML document. The DOC-
TYPE statement is required and must point to the WAP DTD:

```
<!DOCTYPE wml PUBLIC "-//WAPFORUM//DTD WML 1.1//EN"
                     "http://www.wapforum.org/DTD/wml_1.1.xml">
```

The document itself is a deck of cards in which each card is presented independently.
Cards are used to break a large document into smaller pieces. When using a small
screen (obviously mobile phones have small screens), it is best to break information
into smaller chunks:

```
<card title="Pineapplesoft Daily" id="N8">
   <p align="center"><b>Applied XML Solutions</b></p>
   <p><small>by Beno&#238;t Marchal</small></p>
   <p>A new intermediate/advanced book for XML developers.</p>
   <p><small><anchor>More News...<go
      href="#toc"/></anchor></small></p>
   <p>Learn advanced XML programming with Applied XML Solutions.
      This hands-on teaching book is filled with practical
      examples.</p>
   <p>Applied XML Solutions is a great complement to XML by
```

```
    Example.</p>
  <p><anchor>More News...<go href="#toc"/></anchor></p>
</card>
```

As its name implies, the `title` attribute is the card title. The `id` attribute, on the other hand, is used to navigate between cards.

The `<p>`, `<b>`, and `<small>` elements correspond to paragraph, bold, and smaller font. They work similarly to their HTML counterparts.

When used together, the `<anchor>` and `<go>` elements are equivalent to HTML's `<A>`. Internal links (links that start with #) are used to navigate between cards. For example, `<go href="#toc"/>` jumps to the `toc` card.

This chapter presents only a subset of WML. You will find more information at `www.wapforum.org`.

To view a WAP site, you must have a WAP browser. It won't work with Internet Explorer or Netscape. The main browsers available are as follows:

- **A WAP-enabled telephone**—For example, the Ericsson R320 (`www.ericsson.com`) or the Nokia 7710 (`www.nokia.com`)

- **A PalmPilot browser**—For example, WAPman (`www.wap.com.sg`) or 4thpass Kbrowser (`www.4thpass.com/kbrowser`)

- **A PC browser**—For example, WinWAP (`www.winwap.org`) or, again, WAPman (`www.wap.com.sg`)

- **A mobile phone emulator**—For example, the Nokia WAP Toolkit (`www.forum.nokia.com`)

The Nokia WAP Toolkit is particularly attractive for development. Figure 4.4 shows Listing 4.2 in the Nokia emulator.

**Figure 4.4** Using the Nokia emulator.

**Note**

The WAP documentation mentions a WAP gateway sitting between the browser and the Web server.

Because mobile phones are slow, typically running at 9,600bps, the WAP *gateway* is used. This gateway is a specialized proxy that retrieves WML documents from regular Web servers and compresses them before passing them to the phone. It also communicates with the phone over a special protocol that is more efficient than HTTP.

WAP gateways are operated by phone companies and are required mainly for mobile phones. However, other browsers, such as WinWAP, can read the raw WML.

**Tip**

WML is a new markup language. Expect some surprises as you develop for this young medium. For example, I have found that the Ericsson R320 has difficulties with accentuated characters.

# RSS

*RSS (Rich Site Summary)* is a markup language for portals. Imagine your company is writing a quality daily review of developer products. Wouldn't it be great if you could list these reviews on the main portals such as Yahoo! and Netcenter? You bet it would.

So far Yahoo! does not support RSS, but Netcenter does as part of My Netscape. Figure 4.5 shows My Netscape. The various boxes are in fact RSS documents.

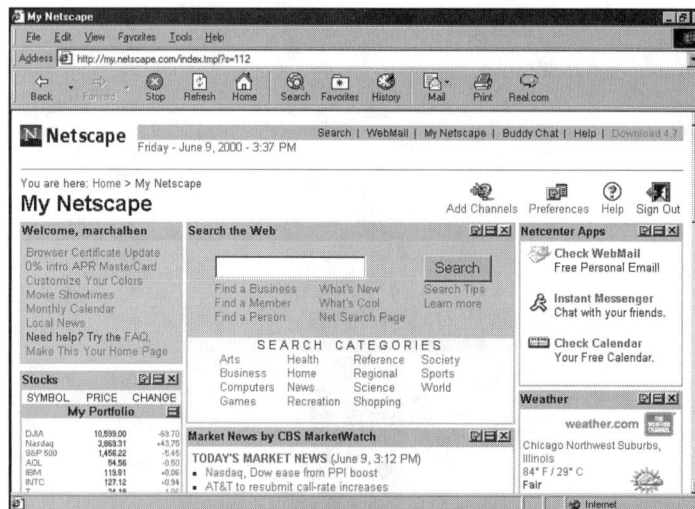

**Figure 4.5** RSS on the My Netscape portal.

How does it work? The content provider publishes an RSS file on his Web site (see Figure 4.6). Periodically, the portal fetches the file and presents it to visitors. This is called *content syndication*: The content owner syndicates his content to the portal.

This takes the separation between authoring and publishing one step further. With RSS, the content provider performs the authoring and the portal performs the publishing. As we will see, RSS does not include formatting elements—formatting is the responsibility of the portal.

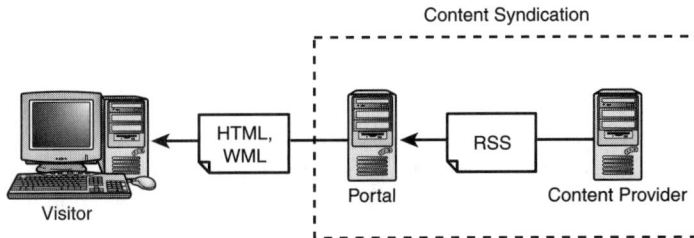

**Figure 4.6** RSS enables content syndication.

Listing 4.3 is a simple RSS document.

Listing 4.3 **RSS Document**

```
<?xml version="1.0" encoding="UTF-8"?><!DOCTYPE rss PUBLIC
    "-//Netscape Communications//DTD RSS 0.91//EN"
    "http://my.netscape.com/publish/formats/rss-0.91.dtd">
<rss version="0.91"><channel>
    <title>Pineapplesoft Daily</title>
    <description>Your source for technology news, trends and
        facts of interest to web developers.</description>
    <link>http://www.pineapplesoft.com</link>
    <language>en</language>
    <item>
        <title>Applied XML Solutions</title>
        <link>http://localhost:8080/publish/index#N8</link>
        <description>A new intermediate/advanced book for XML
            developers.</description>
    </item>
    <item>
        <title>Jetty</title>
        <link>http://localhost:8080/publish/index#N28</link>
        <description>Open Source Java Server.</description>
    </item>
    <item>
        <title>Hypersonic SQL</title>
        <link>http://localhost:8080/publish/index#N46</link>
        <description>Open Source SQL Database.</description>
    </item>
</channel></rss>
```

Again, this is unmistakably an XML document, and the DOCTYPE statement is required:

```
<!DOCTYPE rss PUBLIC
    "-//Netscape Communications//DTD RSS 0.91//EN"
    "http://my.netscape.com/publish/formats/rss-0.91.dtd">
```

An RSS document contains one (and only one) channel. The channel must have at least the following elements:

- title—The channel title
- description—A short introduction to the channel
- link—The Web page associated with the channel
- language—The channel's language

The channel also contains zero, one, or more <item> elements, where each <item> has a title, link, and description. As you can see, RSS is optimized for portals and search engines; it offers summaries and links to the complete articles on the content provider's Web site.

For more information on RSS, you can go to my.netscape.com/publish/help/ mnn20/quickstart.html. Other sites that have adopted RSS include My Userland (my.userland.com) and XMLTree (www.xmltree.com). The latter deserves a special mention: XMLTree is a catalog of all the XML content on the Internet. You will find it useful when looking for documents to include on your own site.

## Styling on Demand

Listing 4.4 is a servlet that takes XML documents and style sheets and returns HTML, WML, or RSS documents.

Listing 4.4 *Publish.java*

```
package com.psol.publish;

import java.io.*;
import java.util.*;
import org.xml.sax.*;
import javax.servlet.*;
import javax.servlet.http.*;
import org.apache.xalan.xslt.*;

public class Publish
    extends HttpServlet
{
    protected final static String
        HTML_STYLESHEET = "stylesheet/html.xsl",
        WML_STYLESHEET = "stylesheet/wml.xsl",
```

Listing 4.4 **Continued**

```
        RSS_STYLESHEET = "stylesheet/rss.xsl";
    protected Dictionary cache = new Hashtable();

    protected String getDocPath(String path)
    {
        if(null == path || path.trim().equals("/"))
            path = "index";
        File file = new File("doc",path);
        path = file.getAbsolutePath();
        if(-1 != file.getName().lastIndexOf('.'))
            // there's a dot in the filename
path = path.substring(0,path.lastIndexOf('.'));
        return path + ".xml";
    }

    protected void style(String document,
                         String stylesheet,
                         OutputStream output)
        throws IOException, SAXException
    {
        // periodically cleans the cache
        if(cache.size() > 10)
            cache = new Hashtable();
        File file = new File(document);
        String key = document +
                     stylesheet +
                     Long.toString(file.lastModified());
        ByteArrayOutputStream cached =
          (ByteArrayOutputStream)cache.get(key);
        if(null == cached)
        {
            cached = new ByteArrayOutputStream();
            XSLTProcessor processor =
               XSLTProcessorFactory.getProcessor();
            XSLTInputSource source =
               new XSLTInputSource(document);
            XSLTInputSource styleSheet =
              new XSLTInputSource(new FileInputStream(stylesheet));
            XSLTResultTarget target = new XSLTResultTarget(cached);
            processor.process(source,styleSheet,target);
            cache.put(key,cached);
        }
        cached.writeTo(output);
    }

    protected long getLastModified(HttpServletRequest request)
    {
        File file = new File(getDocPath(request.getPathInfo()));
        // read the warning in File.lastModified() but it's
        // the best thing we have :-(
```

Listing 4.4  **Continued**

```
      return file.lastModified();
   }

   public void doGet(HttpServletRequest request,
                     HttpServletResponse response)
      throws ServletException, IOException
   {
      String document = request.getPathInfo();
      String styleSheet = null;
      if(null != document &&
         document.endsWith(".rss"))
      {
         response.setContentType("text/xml");
         styleSheet = RSS_STYLESHEET;
      }
      String accept = request.getHeader("Accept");
      if(null != accept &&
         null == styleSheet)
      {
         StringTokenizer acceptTok =
            new StringTokenizer(accept,",",false);
         while(acceptTok.hasMoreTokens())
         {
            String mimeType = acceptTok.nextToken().trim();
            if(mimeType.equals("text/html"))
            {
               response.setContentType("text/html");
               styleSheet = HTML_STYLESHEET;
               break;
            }
            else if(mimeType.equals("text/vnd.wap.wml"))
            {
               response.setContentType("text/vnd.wap.wml");
               styleSheet = WML_STYLESHEET;
               break;
            }
         }
      }
      if(null == styleSheet)
      {
         if(null !=document &&
            document.endsWith(".wml"))
         {
            response.setContentType("text/vnd.wap.wml");
            styleSheet = WML_STYLESHEET;
         }
         else
         {
            response.setContentType("text/html");
            styleSheet = HTML_STYLESHEET;
```

Listing 4.4 **Continued**

```
            }
        }
        try
        {
            style(getDocPath(document),
                    styleSheet,
                    response.getOutputStream());
        }
        catch(SAXException e)
        {
            Exception ex = e.getException() != null ?
                        e.getException() : e;
            response.sendError(
                HttpServletResponse.SC_INTERNAL_SERVER_ERROR,
                ex.getMessage());
        }
    }
}
```

## Selecting the Right Style Sheet

The servlet has three style sheets from which to choose: one for HTML, one for WML, and one for RSS. It analyzes the request from the browser to decide which style sheet to apply and to which document.

Requests can take the following forms:

```
http://localhost:8080/publish
http://localhost:8080/publish/index
http://localhost:8080/publish/index.wml
http://localhost:8080/publish/index.rss
```

The servlet analyzes the request to select the XML document. The first request is a generic request to the servlet so it returns the default document. The other requests point to a specific document, index, which is really the index.xml document.

As we will see, to select an XML document, the servlet essentially discards the extension and replaces it with .xml.

To decide which style sheet to apply, the servlet studies the request headers, in which the browser passes a lot of information. A typical request looks similar to the following:

```
GET /publish/index.html HTTP/1.1
User-Agent: Mozilla/4.5 [en] (Win98; U)
Host: localhost:8080
Accept: image/gif, image/x-xbitmap, image/jpeg, image/pjpeg, image/png, */*
Accept-Encoding: gzip
```

```
Accept-Language: fr-BE,fr,en
Accept-Charset: iso-8859-1,*,utf-8
Extension: Security/Remote-Passphrase
```

This code contains a lot of useful information, and the servlet is particularly interested in the `Accept` field. `Accept` lists the MIME types that the browser recognizes.

The servlet iterates over the MIME types looking for a known type: `text/html` for HTML or `text/vnd.wap.wml` for WML. This is enough for most requests. However, if it fails, the servlet looks at the extension—`.html` selects HTML, and `.wml` selects WML.

### Warning

If you are used to file extensions, this algorithm might be confusing. Why bother with MIME types? Why not look at the extension the user requested? It is important to recognize that, on the Internet, file extensions are not very important.

Browsers and servers rely on MIME type to decide what a file is. This algorithm reflects their bias. In fact, many URLs have no extension, such as the following:

```
http://www.marchal.com/
```

For another example, point your browser to www.w3.org/Icons/WWW/w3c_home. This URL returns the W3C logo in the best format for your browser: text, HTML, or graphics.

Notice that the servlet first analyzes the `Accept` header. I have found that it is more reliable than the extension. For example, a mobile phone user might accidentally type an address of the form `http://localhost:8080/publish/index.html`, even though he should actually be requesting the WML document.

Even if visitors can make mistakes, the browser is always right. The `Accept` header field is the most reliable source of information available:

```
public void doGet(HttpServletRequest request,
                  HttpServletResponse response)
   throws ServletException, IOException
{
   String document = request.getPathInfo();
   String styleSheet = null;
   if(null != document &&
      document.endsWith(".rss"))
   {
      response.setContentType("text/xml");
      styleSheet = RSS_STYLESHEET;
   }
   String accept = request.getHeader("Accept");
   if(null != accept &&
      null == styleSheet)
   {
```

```
        StringTokenizer acceptTok =
            new StringTokenizer(accept,",",false);
        while(acceptTok.hasMoreTokens())
        {
            String mimeType = acceptTok.nextToken().trim();
            if(mimeType.equals("text/html"))
            {
                response.setContentType("text/html");
                styleSheet = HTML_STYLESHEET;
                break;
            }
            else if(mimeType.equals("text/vnd.wap.wml"))
            {
                response.setContentType("text/vnd.wap.wml");
                styleSheet = WML_STYLESHEET;
                break;
            }
        }
    }
    if(null == styleSheet)
    {
        if(null !=document &&
            document.endsWith(".wml"))
        {
            response.setContentType("text/vnd.wap.wml");
            styleSheet = WML_STYLESHEET;
        }
        else
        {
            response.setContentType("text/html");
            styleSheet = HTML_STYLESHEET;
        }
    }
}
```

Unfortunately, RSS requires a special procedure. It appears that portals don't set the Accept header properly. To work around this, the servlet gives higher priority to the .rss extension.

**Tip**

This servlet supports only one style sheet per format—one HTML style sheet, one WML style sheet, and one RSS style sheet.

However, for some applications, having different style sheets might be beneficial. For example, you might use a different "My Netscape"-branded style sheet when the visitor is coming from My Netscape. This style sheet would display a Netscape logo.

You will learn how to add this option through skins in Chapter 8, "Organize Teamwork Between Developers and Designers."

Given the flexible approach we have chosen, the `getDoc()` method must do a lot of work to convert the URLinto the proper XML file. The URL can be pointing to a file with or without an extension, and `getDoc()` will turn it into a path to an .xml file:

```
protected String getDocPath(String path)
{
    if(null == path || path.trim().equals("/"))
        path = "index";
    File file = new File("doc",path);
    path = file.getAbsolutePath();
    if(-1 != file.getName().lastIndexOf('.'))
        // there's a dot in the filename
path = path.substring(0,path.lastIndexOf('.'));
    return path + ".xml";
}
```

## Applying the Style Sheet

Applying the style sheet is the responsibility of the `style()` method, which uses Xalan, the Apache XSL processor:

```
protected void style(String document,
                     String stylesheet,
                     OutputStream output)
    throws IOException, SAXException
{
    // periodically cleans the cache
    if(cache.size() > 10)
        cache = new Hashtable();
    File file = new File(document);
    String key = document +
                    stylesheet +
                    Long.toString(file.lastModified());
    ByteArrayOutputStream cached =
      (ByteArrayOutputStream)cache.get(key);
    if(null == cached)
    {
        cached = new ByteArrayOutputStream();
        XSLTProcessor processor =
            XSLTProcessorFactory.getProcessor();
        XSLTInputSource source =
            new XSLTInputSource(document);
        XSLTInputSource styleSheet =
            new XSLTInputSource(new FileInputStream(stylesheet));
        XSLTResultTarget target = new XSLTResultTarget(cached);
        processor.process(source,styleSheet,target);
        cache.put(key,cached);
    }
    cached.writeTo(output);
}
```

> **Warning**
> No standard API, which is similar to SAX or DOM, exists for XSL processors. Currently, the API is specific to each processor. Therefore, this method works only with Xalan.

The `style()` method manages a small cache. Most documents will be called again and again, so it is more cost-effective to apply the style sheet once and store the result until the next request.

The cache is very simple and effective. After styling, `style()` stores the result in a hash table; the key to which is a combination of the filename, the style sheet, and a time-stamp for the XML document.

Although this method is simple, it can be very costly. It runs the risk of the cache growing indefinitely, consuming all the memory. Therefore, when the cache contains 10 documents, `style()` empties it.

The cache is emptied every 10 documents, not every 10 requests. If visitors make a thousand requests to a single document, that document is styled only once and served for the cache for the next 999 requests.

# The Style Sheets

This section presents the three style sheets.

## HTML Style Sheet

The style sheet for HTML documents is in Listing 4.5. It builds a short table of contents before listing the various news items.

Listing 4.5 *html.xsl*

```
<?xml version="1.0"?>

<xsl:stylesheet
    xmlns:xsl="http://www.w3.org/1999/XSL/Transform"
    xmlns="http://www.w3.org/TR/REC-html40"
    version="1.0">

<xsl:output method="html"/>

<xsl:template match="/">
<HTML><HEAD><TITLE>Pineapplesoft Daily</TITLE></HEAD>
<BODY><H1>Pineapplesoft Daily</H1>
    <H2><A NAME="toc">Today's News</A></H2>
    <xsl:for-each select="News/Item">
        <P><A HREF="#{generate-id(.)}">
```

Listing 4.5  **Continued**

```
            <xsl:value-of select="Title"/></A><BR/>
            <SMALL>by <xsl:value-of select="Author"/></SMALL><BR/>
            <xsl:value-of select="Abstract"/></P>
      </xsl:for-each>
      <H2>News Items</H2>
      <xsl:for-each select="News/Item">
         <H3><A NAME="{generate-id(.)}"><xsl:value-of
            select="Title"/></A></H3>
         <P><I>by <xsl:value-of select="Author"/></I></P>
         <xsl:for-each select="Para">
            <P><xsl:value-of select="."/></P>
         </xsl:for-each>
         <A HREF="#toc"><SMALL>More News</SMALL></A><BR/>
      </xsl:for-each>
   </BODY></HTML>
   </xsl:template>

</xsl:stylesheet>
```

Figure 4.7 presents the result in a browser.

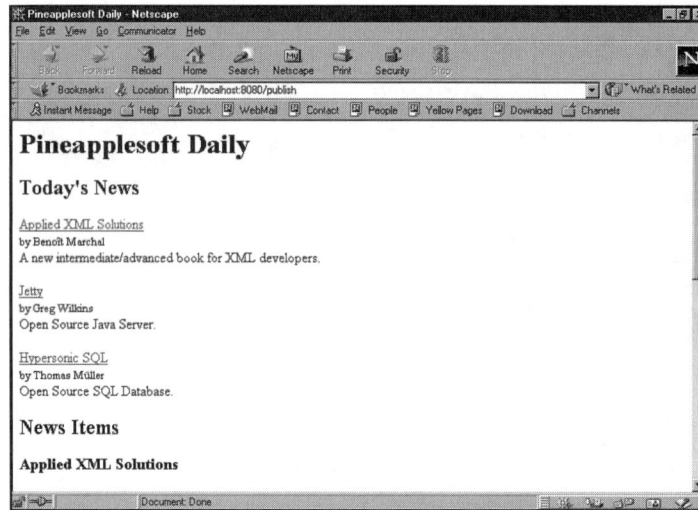

**Figure 4.7**  The HTML document in a browser.

### Crash Course in XSL

The basics of XSL are easy to learn. An XSL style sheet is a list with one or more templates. Each template describes how to transform one element (and its descendants) from the original XML document into the output format.

Let's look at a very simple template:

```
<xsl:template match="/">
      <HTML>
      <HEAD><TITLE>Today's News</TITLE></HEAD>
         <BODY><H1> Today's News </H1>
            <xsl:for-each select="News/Item/Para">
               <P><xsl:value-of select="."/></P>
            </xsl:for-each>
         </BODY>
      </HTML>
   </xsl:template>
```

As you can see, most of the template is a regular HTML document peppered with XSL statements (xsl:for-each and xsl:value-of) to extract information from the original XML document.

The match attribute points to the element to which the template applies: / is the root of the document.

It is not possible, in this book, to include a more comprehensive introduction to XSL. If you need more information, you can turn to Appendix C, "XSLT Reference," or to a tutorial such as *XML by Example*.

## WML Style Sheet

Listing 4.6 is the style sheet to generate WML. Again, it starts with a table of contents. Unlike the HTML document, however, it places each news item on a different card.

Listing 4.6 *wml.xsl*

```
<?xml version="1.0"?>

<xsl:stylesheet
   xmlns:xsl="http://www.w3.org/1999/XSL/Transform"
   version="1.0">

<xsl:output
   method="xml"
   doctype-public="-//WAPFORUM//DTD WML 1.1//EN"
   doctype-system="http://www.wapforum.org/DTD/wml_1.1.xml"/>

<xsl:template match="/">
<wml>
<card id="toc" title="Pineapplesoft Daily">
   <p align="center"><b>Today's News</b></p>
   <xsl:for-each select="News/Item">
      <p><anchor><xsl:value-of select="Title"/><go
         href="#{generate-id(.)}"/></anchor></p>
   </xsl:for-each>
</card>
<xsl:for-each select="News/Item">
   <card id="{generate-id(.)}" title="Pineapplesoft Daily">
```

Listing 4.6  **Continued**

```
      <p align="center"><b><xsl:value-of select="Title"/></b></p>
      <p><small>by <xsl:value-of select="Author"/></small></p>
      <p><xsl:value-of select="Abstract"/></p>
      <p><small><anchor>More News...<go
          href="#toc"/></anchor></small></p>
      <xsl:for-each select="Para">
          <p><xsl:value-of select="."/></p>
      </xsl:for-each>
      <p><anchor>More News...<go href="#toc"/></anchor></p>
    </card>
  </xsl:for-each>
  </wml>
</xsl:template>

</xsl:stylesheet>
```

Unlike Listing 4.5, this style sheet generates an XML document. Indeed, WML follows the XML syntax. The style sheet also issues a DOCTYPE statement, as required by the WML specification.

Figure 4.8 shows the result in a WAP browser.

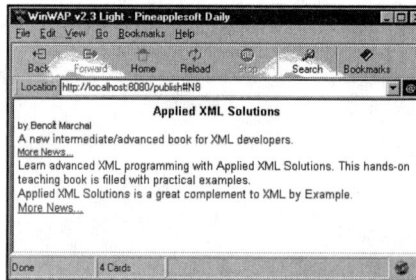

**Figure 4.8**  The WML document in a WAP browser.

## RSS Style Sheet

The last style sheet is in Listing 4.7. This style sheet generates an RSS document. Unlike the previous two style sheets, this one limits itself to a table of contents—you will recall that RSS is not designed to handle large documents. RSS is essentially a table of contents of the portal Web site.

Listing 4.7 *rss.xsl*

```xml
<?xml version="1.0"?>

<xsl:stylesheet
    xmlns:xsl="http://www.w3.org/1999/XSL/Transform"
    version="1.0">

<xsl:output
    method="xml"
    doctype-public="-//Netscape Communications//DTD RSS 0.91//EN"
    doctype-system="http://my.netscape.com/publish/formats/rss-0.91.dtd"/>

<xsl:template match="/">
<rss version="0.91"><channel>
<title>Pineapplesoft Daily</title>
<description>Your source for technology news, trends and
    facts of interest to web developers.</description>
<link>http://www.pineapplesoft.com</link>
<language>en</language>
<xsl:for-each select="News/Item">
    <item>
      <title><xsl:value-of select="Title"/></title>
      <link><xsl:value-of select="/News/URL"/>#<xsl:value-of
          select="generate-id(.)"/></link>
      <description><xsl:value-of select="Abstract"/></description>
    </item>
</xsl:for-each>
</channel></rss>
</xsl:template>

</xsl:stylesheet>
```

### Warning

The RSS style sheet is tricky—it can be used safely with Xalan, but it might not work with other XSL processors.

The problem is that the RSS document must include links to the news items. The easiest path is from RSS to the servlet. When a visitor follows a link, RSS will retrieve the news in the appropriate format: HTML or WML.

But how do you link it to a specific news item on the news page? You can simply use a reference at the end of the URL: http://localhost:8080/publish/index#N8. This is where it gets tricky.

The style sheet uses generate-id() to create the references. This works because Xalan always generates an identifier based on the original XML document. If you run the style sheet twice on the same document, you get the same identifier.

However, the XSL specification is not so strict. It guarantees only that generate-id() will generate unique identifiers for each run. Theoretically, you could run the style sheet twice on the same document and get different identifiers.

Therefore, you might find that this trick does not work with other processors. In that case, simply include identifiers in the original XML document: <Item id="N8"/>.

Figure 4.9 illustrates the result with My Userland, an RSS portal.

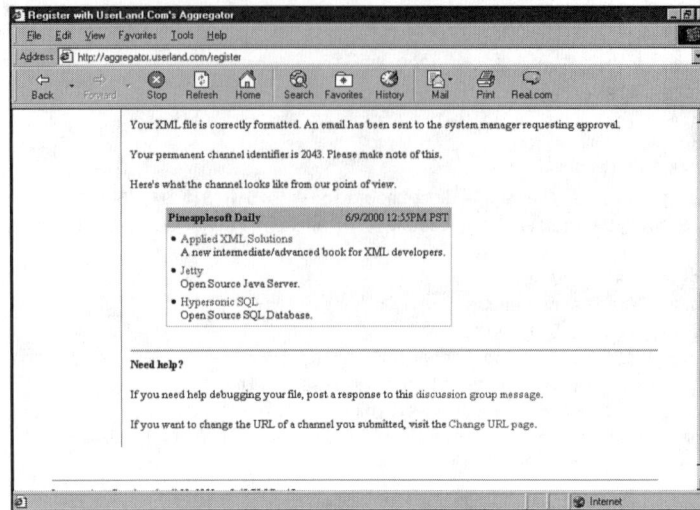

**Figure 4.9** Registering the RSS file on My Userland.

# Building and Running the Project

The publish project is available on the enclosed CD–ROM. Copy the project directory from the CD–ROM to your hard disk. Under Windows, start the server by double-clicking `publish.bat`. Next, open a browser and type the following URL (refer to Figure 4.7):

```
http://localhost:8080/publish
```

If possible, you should download at least one WAP browser and test the document again. You also might want to register the RSS channel with a portal.

**Warning**

This project uses Xalan 1.0 as the XSLT processor. If you are using another processor, you will need to adapt `style()`.

The project also uses Jetty as the Web server. However, because it is based on servlets, it should be easy to adapt to another Web server. You can add servlet support to most Web servers through JRun.

If you develop your own documents, register the corresponding RSS channels with `www.xmltree.com`, `my.netscape.com`, and `my.userland.com`.

# Additional Resources

If you find this project useful, be sure you read Chapter 8 as well. Chapter 8 presents a different twist on the same technique and many useful extensions to the servlet.

## DocBook

As has already been indicated, for more complex documents, you can turn to the DocBook DTD available from www.docbook.org. DocBook is a powerful DTD for document publishing and is available in both SGML and XML.

## XHTML

WML is the most popular markup language for mobile users, but the W3C is working on its own solution. The W3C has developed XHTML, an XML version of HTML. The recommendation is available from www.w3.org/TR/xhtml1.

The major advantage of XHTML is that it is based on HTML so it will be familiar for Web designers. The major inconvenience of XHTML is also that it is based on HTML. This results in a large and complex markup language. Therefore, XHTML currently is too complex for mobile phones.

The W3C is working to simplify XHTML. Only time will tell whether XHTML will achieve widespread acceptance.

## Open eBook

Another interesting format for mobile users is the Open eBook specification. Open eBook was designed for eBook, a different group of mobile users. An eBook can take many forms, but it is generally a palm-sized device on which readers download books.

You will find more information on Open eBook from the Open eBook Forum at www.openebook.org. A popular eBook reader is the Rocket eBook, available from www.rocketebook.com. Unfortunately, it does not support the Open eBook format yet.

## ICE

I introduced RSS as the content syndication format in this chapter because RSS is very popular. RSS is not the only choice, however.

An alternative is ICE (Information Content and Exchange protocol). ICE is a more ambitious project that aims to link content providers and publishers. You can find more information on ICE at www.w3.org/TR/NOTE-ice.

# 5

# Export to Any Format

I N THIS CHAPTER AND THE NEXT, we'll have more fun with XSLT. In the previous chapter, we were syndicating content in a variety of formats. This led us to explore transformations and the XML tool for transformation: XSLT.

Although powerful and effective, the transformations in the last chapter remained in the family because we essentially converted documents from one DTD to another DTD. Although both formats were different, they were based on XML. Yes, we also converted to HTML but, again, XML and HTML are very similar. In this chapter and the next, we'll open the door to more alien formats. Although an explosion in the number of XML-based formats has occurred, many non–XML-based formats are still out there. Some examples include the following:

- When you publish documents, you might want to convert them to RTF, which is recognized by Word, or PDF, which is Adobe Acrobat's format.
- If you are active in graphics and design, you probably don't want to throw away existing Adobe Illustrator, CorelDRAW, or CGM files.
- In electronic commerce, as we will see, legacy formats such as ANSI X12 and UN/EDIFACT need to be supported.

This chapter concentrates on transformation from XML documents to documents in non-XML format; in other words, exporting XML-based documents to other applications. The next chapter is concerned with the reverse operation and discusses how to import non-XML documents in XML applications.

These two chapters build around the same project that is related to e-commerce and, more specifically, with converting EDIFACT documents to and from XML. The two reasons I chose EDIFACT as the typical non–XML-based format are as follows:

- I'm very familiar with EDIFACT and e-commerce.
- EDIFACT gives me a chance to demonstrate both sides of the problem. It is common for an e-commerce application to convert to and from EDIFACT, which is not the case with, say, PDF.

However, the techniques introduced in these two chapters are not limited to EDI-FACT. As discussed previously, they are commonly used for PDF, RTF publishing. In e-commerce, you might also consider other legacy formats such as X12. Essentially, you need to build such a solution each time an XML application interfaces with a non-XML application.

# Meeting EDIFACT

Unfortunately, it is not possible to convert between two formats unless you are famil-iar with the input and output formats. I assume you are familiar with XML, but you might not be familiar with EDIFACT. This section is a crash course in EDIFACT. If you are in a hurry and want to jump straight into the code, I suggest you read at least the section "EDIFACT Segments."

*EDIFACT*, or UN/EDIFACT as it is formally known, is short for Electronic Data Interchange For Administration, Commerce, and Transport. It is a comprehensive e-commerce solution developed under the auspices of the United Nations (hence, the UN part of the name).

## Business-to-Business e-Commerce

*e-Commerce* is a commonly used term that has several meanings. When people think of e-commerce, though, they usually think of Amazon.com or other online shops. Other popular and older forms of e-commerce do exist, however.

Online shops cater primarily to the business-to-consumer (B2C) side of e-commerce. The other side is business-to-business (B2B) e-commerce, or the buying, selling, and other commercial transactions that take place between businesses.

Business-to-business commerce isn't as well known as the consumer-oriented side. This is mainly because it is less visible and more abstract: We shop in various stores (online and offline) every day but few of us really care from where the stores are buy-ing their goods.

This is business-to-business commerce: stores (businesses) buying goods from their suppliers (other businesses). What might surprise you is that it accounts for a very large volume because, behind the supplier is another supplier, and another, and another.

Let's look at an example. Say you have bought *Applied XML Solutions* at a bookstore. The bookstore bought the same book from a distributor, who bought it from Sams. Sams, in turn, had the book manufactured by a printer. To manufacture the book, the printer bought paper and ink. You get the idea.

So, for a single consumer-oriented transaction (you buying the book), several business-to-business transactions must occur. These transactions have a multiplying effect, which means that business-to-business commerce—and consequently, business-to-business e-commerce—is destined to outnumber consumer activities by a wide margin.

## Electronic Data Interchange

One of the oldest forms of e-commerce is Electronic Data Interchange (EDI). EDI is concerned solely with business-to-business e-commerce. The idea behind EDI is very simple: To conduct business, companies have to exchange an enormous amount of paperwork. Let's replace the paperwork with electronic files.

For example, if my company decides to buy goods from yours, we'll issue a purchase order. We also expect the goods to come with an invoice. To pay the invoice, we might cut a check.

Do we write these documents with a pen and paper? This is unlikely, because like most companies we use some sort of accounting software (by accounting software, I mean anything from QuickBooks to SAP) that tracks orders, invoices, and payments.

Go through your incoming mail and you'll find that most documents were printed by a computer (incidentally, you'll understand why Intuit makes so much money selling checkbooks). Follow the paper trail and you'll find the same documents are being routed to…your own accounting software!

So, the process is to print commercial documents, send them by postal mail, and key them in at the receiving end. The paperwork and all the manual processing it requires is just a small annoyance for small corporations such as mine, but it's a major expense for larger organizations.

More than 20 years ago, some companies realized they could simplify things by building a more direct link between the two accounting softwares. Instead of spitting out a paper purchase order, my computer produces a file. I then can email you the file and you can feed it straight into your accounting package. No paper or postal mail is required, and it's better than regular email because the commercial documents are automatically imported.

Some of the benefits of EDI include the following:

- It is faster to exchange and process electronic documents.
- Typing and retyping the same document is a major cause of errors (for example, it's easy to type 10,000 instead of 100,000). Electronic documents eliminate the retyping and associated errors.
- Processing electronic documents requires less human resources.

How big is EDI? According to Forrester Research, business-to-business e-commerce was valued at $671 billion in 1998. So, why don't we hear more about it? One of the reasons might be that most transactions take place on private networks, not the Internet. In fact, Internet transactions represented only $92 billion.

Most transactions taking place on private networks are not based on XML. Instead, they use the EDI-specific formats, such as UN/EDIFACT and ANSI X12.

However, it would be a mistake to discount XML in that space. The same study expects business-to-business e-commerce to grow to $1.3 trillion (that's trillion, not billion) within three years. And guess where most of the growth will take place? On the Internet, of course. Now guess which format will dominate on the Internet. If you chose XML, you're right again.

To summarize, business-to-business e-commerce is very important. It is several times larger than consumer-oriented activities and will remain so.

Currently, most of these transactions take place on private networks, using special formats. However, they are expected to migrate to the Internet and XML within the next three years. This is why it's important to build a bridge between the EDI formats and XML.

## The Inner Working of EDIFACT

The two dominant EDI formats are ANSI X12 and UN/EDIFACT. X12 was developed by ANSI and is used predominantly in the U.S. EDIFACT, on the other hand, enjoys a worldwide audience. Other popular formats include Odette (used in the automotive industry, including IAEG in the U.S.), Tradacoms (which is UK-based), and Swift (used in international banking).

Although they differ in details, the various EDI formats are based on the same principles.

The underlying idea is to develop electronic versions of most commercial documents. The list of documents is too long to detail here. But, some examples include an electronic purchase order, electronic invoice, and electronic catalog. An electronic custom declaration (when importing or exporting goods), electronic financial transactions (to replace checks), and electronic tax and other tax-related forms have also been developed.

Finally, some industries have even developed documents specific to their needs—for example, electronic versions of insurance contracts, reinsurance claims, statistics forms, and more.

With EDIFACT, the electronic documents are called *UNSMs*, which is short for United Nations Standard Messages.

Because the messages are developed by international (EDIFACT) or national (X12, Tradacoms, and so on) bodies, they tend to be rather large. Imagine an invoice that satisfies the legal requirements of every country, every industry, and every company in the world! Large and unmanageable? You bet.

Therefore, users must simplify these documents before using them. For example, American companies must collect the sales tax, and European companies must collect the VAT (Value-Added Tax). The worldwide invoice does both, though. So, an American company would need to simplify it to include only sales tax, whereas a European company would limit it to VAT.

Incidentally, this is one of the major criticisms of the EDI formats: Because they are all-encompassing, they are very complex. Furthermore, to bring them down to something manageable, users must spend significant effort in simplifying the messages (a process known, in EDI circles, as *creating subsets*).

A side effect is that this creates incompatibilities, which cause most of the benefits of standardized formats to be lost. In the example, one company simplified to remove VAT, and the other to remove sales tax. Now, what happens when the U.S. corporation sends a purchase order to the European one?

This problem has led a growing number of companies to look for alternatives to the EDI formats, and XML appears to be a very attractive alternative because of the following:

- XML is well supported by tools and vendors.
- It is close to object-oriented modeling such as UML.
- It offers superior conversion features.

The last point is worth reviewing. As I said, the international documents are so complex that companies must simplify them. Yet, when you study EDIFACT, you find that it has not been designed to be simplified. No support exists in the standard for simplifying orders.

On the other hand, XML has namespaces, which are a mechanism to organize large documents into smaller, more manageable subsets. Look at how XSL is divided in XSLT and XSLFO for a good example on how namespaces help simplify large standards. The standard is literally divided into two parts that can be used independently or combined at will. XML could bring that sort of benefit to EDI. For example, sales tax and VAT elements could be developed independently from the purchase order and then combined at will.

## EDIFACT Segments

What do EDI messages look like? Listing 5.1 is an EDIFACT purchase order in which the bookstore, Playfield Books, is ordering books from Que.

**Warning**

For simplicity, the purchase order in Listing 5.1 is minimalist. It has all the required information but little extra.

Listing 5.1 *orders.edi*

```
UNH+1+ORDERS:D:96A:UN'BGM+220+AGL153+9+AB'DTM+137:20000310:102'
➥DTM+61:20000410:102'NAD+BY+++PLAYFIELD BOOKS+34 FOUNTAIN
➥SQUARE PLAZA+CINCINNATI+OH+45202+US'NAD+SE+++QUE+
➥201 WEST 103RD STREET+INDIANAPOLIS+IN+46290+US'
➥LIN+1'PIA+5+0789722429:IB'QTY+21:5'PRI+AAA:24.99::SRP'
➥LIN+2'PIA+5+0789724308:IB'QTY+21:10'PRI+AAA:42.50::SRP'
➥UNS+S'CNT+3:2'UNT+17+1'
```

We will look at this purchase order in more detail in the next section. This section serves as a crash course in EDIFACT syntax. Don't worry if you don't remember everything, this is not "Applied EDIFACT Solutions." However, to convert between any format and XML, you need to know the fundamentals of the non-XML format.

The building block for the EDIFACT message is the *segment*. Segments start with a tag followed by a set of data. They end with the ' character. The tag identifies the segment. For example, the following is a price segment, recognizable by its PRI tag:

```
PRI+AAA:42.50::SRP'
```

Within a segment, the fields are delineated by the + or : character. The fields have no tags but are identified by their position. For example, in the PRI segment, the price is always the second field, which is $42.50.

The first and fourth fields are coded fields, which means their value is a code or an alphanumeric identifier for a value. For example, in the first field, the code AAA means net price. Codes are similar to enumerated parameter values in XML and are used for the same purposes.

If you are curious, SRP in the fourth field means suggested retail price. The meaning of the codes is specified by the EDIFACT standard.

You'll notice that the third field is empty, which means it has no value. However, because fields are identified by their position, the empty third field cannot be omitted. Indeed, I cannot write

```
PRI+AAA:42.50:SRP'
```

or SRP would be in the third field instead of the fourth field. The third field has a different meaning (it is reserved for the price type) from the fourth field.

▶ **Note**

When EDIFACT was originally conceived, bandwidth was more expensive than it is today. Therefore, a lot of effort was directed toward achieving the smallest file possible.

If you are curious, compare Listing 5.1 with Listing 5.2, which is the same purchase order in XML. EDIFACT is clearly the winner in terms of size.

What about the + and : characters? Fields in a segment can be either *simple* fields or *composite* fields and are separated by + characters. A composite field is a list of simple fields separated by : characters.

Therefore, the `PRI` segment

```
PRI+AAA:42.50::SRP'
```

contains one composite field, which is made up of four simple fields (`AAA`, `42.50`, empty, and `SRP`). Compare this with the `PIA` segment (product identifier):

```
PIA+5+0789722429:IB'
```

`PIA` starts with a simple data element (`5`) followed by a composite data element (`0789722429:IB`) for the ISBN number. The composite data element has two simple data elements (`0789722429` and `IB`).

Note that *ISBN* stands for International Standard Book Number. It is a worldwide identifier for books. The ISBN appears on the back of the book with the bar code, and each book has a unique one. For example, this book has been assigned ISBN 0-7897-2430-8.

Because each book has a different ISBN, using only the ISBN suffices when ordering books. In fact, less risk of confusion is involved when ordering books by ISBN than by the title or author's name. It's easy to confuse two books with the same title, but it is impossible to confuse two books' ISBNs.

> **Note**
>
> It's not always obvious why some elements become simple data elements while others end up as composite data elements. You should refer to the EDIFACT documentation to decide which is which.
>
> In theory, when two or more simple data elements are often used together, they have been grouped in a composite data element.

You are now familiar with the basics of EDIFACT. However, we should consider the following two important rules that we have not yet encountered:

- Compression
- Escape character

I explained that empty fields must be present so as not to impact the field positions. Thanks to the so-called compression mechanism, you can remove empty fields when no risk of confusion is involved. For example, in the `PIA` segment, the ISBN can repeat up to five times, so it could look similar to the following:

```
PIA+5+0789722429:IB+:+:+:+:'
```

But, because the four empty composite data elements are also the last elements in the segment, no risk of confusion exists, so you must write the following segment:

```
PIA+5+0789722429:IB'
```

The same rule applies at the end of composite data elements. The definition for the BGM (beginning of message) segment states that the first composite data element has four fields. However, if it looks like this

```
BGM+220:::+AGL153+9+AB'
```

the compression rule states that if the last three fields of the composite data elements are empty, they need not appear in the segment. Therefore, we must write

```
BGM+220+AGL153+9+AB'
```

The last syntactical rule is concerned with escape characters. Because +, :, and ' have a special role in segments, they cannot appear in data. This is similar to the < and & characters in XML, which cannot appear in data, either.

EDIFACT's solution is to escape these characters with the ? character; therefore, we would not write

```
NAD+BY+++PLAYFIELD BELGIUM+43 RUE DE L'OUVRAGE+NAMUR++5000+BE'
```

because the ' would be confused with the end of the segment. Instead, we'd write the following:

```
NAD+BY+++PLAYFIELD BELGIUM+43 RUE DE L?'OUVRAGE+NAMUR++5000+BE'
```

## The Message in Details

A *message* is a list of segments. The meaning of the segments, their positions in the message, the acceptable code for coded data elements, and more are specified in the EDIFACT standard. To decode a message, you must look up its definition in the EDIFACT standard.

The standard is conveniently available online at www.unece.org; follow the links for UN/CEFACT and then UN/EDIFACT. You can search by message and drill down to the list of segments. From the segments, you then can zoom to the data elements and code lists. See Figures 5.1 and 5.2 for examples.

To save you this rather tedious task, here are the secrets of Listing 5.1, segment by segment.

```
UNH+1+ORDERS:D:96A:UN'
```

The UNH segment marks the document as an EDIFACT document and identifies the type of document, which in this case is an order (ORDERS).

▶ **Warning**

For completeness, note that EDIFACT groups messages in interchanges. The beginning and end of interchanges are indicated through more segments. For simplicity, interchanges are not discussed in this chapter.

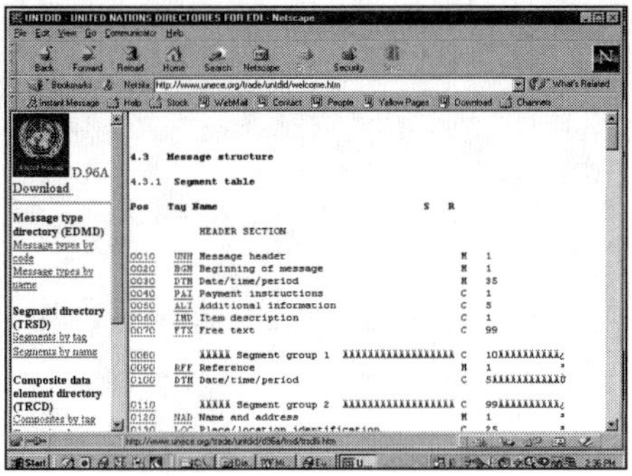

**Figure 5.1** Looking up the list of segments on the UN/ECE Web site.

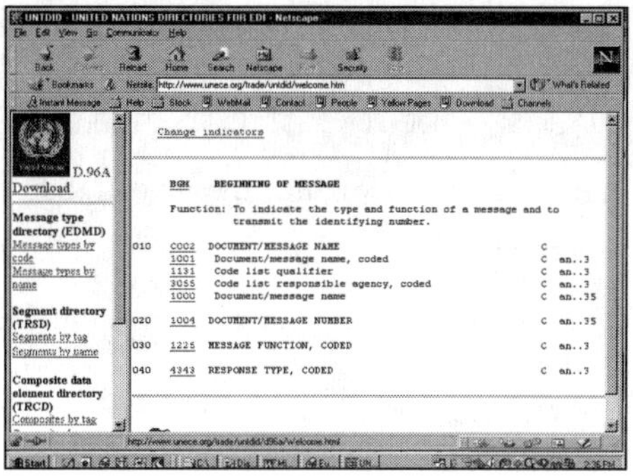

**Figure 5.2** Zooming in on one segment in the invoice shows the fields.

The 1 in the first field is a message identifier; D, 96A, and UN in the last fields identify a specific revision of the ORDERS message.

    BGM+220+AGL153+9+AB'

BGM stands for beginning of message. The code 220 confirms that the document is indeed an order. Next is the purchase order number, AGL153.

The 9 in the next field is a code that says this message is the original purchase order (other codes exist for duplicates). The last field, AB, means we want the recipient to acknowledge reception.

    DTM+137:20000310:102'

The DTM segment in the previous line is the date (actually it's the Date and Time, hence the trailing M). The code 137 says this is the purchase order date. The actual date is next. The final code, 102, means that the date is in ISO format, 10 March 2000, in this case.

When EDIFACT was originally conceived, other date formats were commonly used (including the dreadful two-digit years such as 99). Lately, it seems everybody uses the ISO date format, so 102 is becoming some sort of a constant for dates.

    DTM+61:20000410:102'

The next segment is another date. This one has the code 61 in the first field, meaning it is the last date for delivery. If the seller cannot deliver within a month (by 10 April 2000), he can forget the order.

    NAD+BY+++PLAYFIELD BOOKS+34 FOUNTAIN SQUARE PLAZA+
    ➥CINCINNATI+OH+45202+US'

The next segment is an NAD, meaning name and address. The first field is a code (BY) to indicate this is the buyer's address. After two unused fields, we find, in order of appearance, the name of the buyer (PLAYFIELD BOOKS), the street address (34 FOUNTAIN SQUARE

PLAZA), the city (CINCINNATI), the state (OH), the ZIP code or postal code (45202), and, finally, the country (US).

```
NAD+SE+++QUE+201 WEST 103RD STREET+INDIANAPOLIS+IN+46290+US'
```

A second NAD contains the seller's address (code SE).

```
LIN+1'
```

Next is the first line of the order, identified by a LIN segment and the line number (1 in this case).

```
PIA+5+0789722429:IB'
```

The PIA segment that follows contains the product identifier. The code 5, in the first field, specifies that the product identifier is related to an order line. The identifier itself follows as ISBN 0-7897-2242-9. The last code (IB) identifies the code as an ISBN.

> **Note**
>
> Why do we need a code 5 to specify that the product identifier applies to a line order? Isn't it obvious by reading the order message that this must be a line order?
>
> Yes and no. One of the issues with EDIFACT is that it uses a very flat data structure. Essentially, a message is a list of segments. With large messages, the placement of segments doesn't always indicate what's what. Code such as this 5 identify relationships between segments ("this is not any product identifier; it's the product identifier for the current product line"). These special codes are known as *qualifiers*.
>
> To be complete, note that EDIFACT has a notion of *groups of segments*, in which a *group* is a set of related segments. However, groups have no special syntax, so they are not easy to recognize in a message!

```
QTY+21:5'
```

The QTY segment indicates we are buying five books (in the last field). The 21 code (it's a qualifier again) states that the quantity applies to a line order.

```
PRI+AAA:24.99::SRP'
```

This is the product price in a PRI segment. The first field is a code (AAA) meaning net price. It is followed by the price itself (24.99), an empty field, and a code (SRP for suggested retail price).

```
LIN+2'PIA+5+0789724308:IB'QTY+21:10'PRI+AAA:42.50::SRP'
```

The second line is for the order of 10 books (ISBN 0-7897-2430-8) at a suggested retail price of $42.50.

```
UNS+S'
```

The next segment, UNS, means that the following segments are a summary of the message.

```
CNT+3:2'
```

In this case, the summary consists of only one CNT (count) segment. The code **3** in the first field indicates it counts the number of order lines, which is **2** in this case.

```
UNT+17+1'
```

The last segment is a UNT with two fields. The first field counts the total number of segments in the message (17). The second field, on the other hand, repeats the message identifier from the UNH segment (1 in this case).

## The Message Structure

To summarize, the EDIFACT message follows the classic structure of an invoice: It starts with the name and address of the parties, the date of the invoice, and a reference number. Next are order lines. Each line contains a product identifier (ISBN), the quantity, and the price.

As has already been noted, this structure is not immediately apparent in EDIFACT because it is a rather flat list of segments. In contrast, XML elements nest so the structure is immediately apparent.

# EDI Meets XML

The concept of EDI is even more relevant today than it was 20 years ago because

- Paperwork is as costly today as it was then.
- More companies have computerized their accounting functions and most are connected to a worldwide network (the Internet). They could benefit from EDI.

## EDI and the Internet

So, deploying EDI makes a lot of sense, but traditional EDI technologies, such as EDIFACT and X12, have not really taken off on the Internet. A number of reasons have been proposed to explain this lack of interest:

- EDI technologies are not familiar and do not integrate naturally in an HTML-centric Web.
- Few products, if any, ship with an EDI feature.
- No matter how effective, EDI technologies look old-fashioned and are not popular with developers.
- EDI standards have focused on building "universal" messages that are too difficult to use, as we have seen. Therefore, companies have implemented incompatible variations.
- EDI standards are complex and costly to deploy.
- Finding information on EDI on the Internet is difficult.

It is expected that XML could help alleviate some of these problems because

- XML supports complex data structures and can easily encode commercial and administrative documents as EDI does.
- An ever-growing list of products are XML-enabled (including a growing number of ERP and databases). In that respect, XML appears as the preferred format to exchange data.
- XML is popular with Web developers and interfaces neatly with the Web-centric world.
- XML supports modern, object-oriented modeling and programming.
- As we have seen before, XML has been designed to facilitate reusing vocabulary without putting unnecessary burden on the user. XML namespaces are helpful in this case.
- No shortage of resources on XML exists on the Internet.

These are all valid reasons, and I think the most important one is the integration with the Web. XML works as a natural extension of HTML for specific applications. See Figure 5.3 for an illustration.

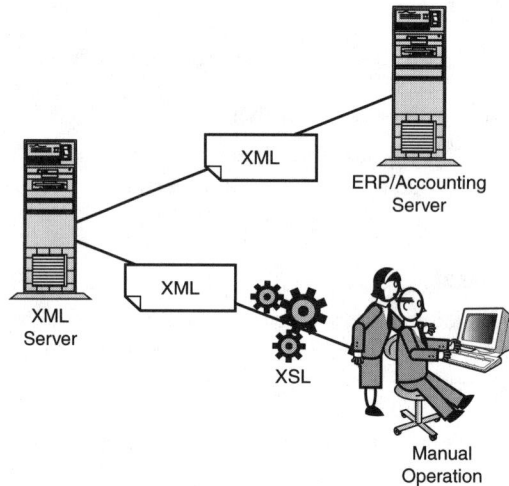

**Figure 5.3** XML supports both users on a workstation and a more automated approach.

The lower portion of Figure 5.3 is the familiar Web site, although this one is built on XML. The server of the seller uses XSL to present information to a buyer. This is similar to what we built in Chapter 4, "Content Syndication." However, instead of publishing news, it publishes commercial documents such as purchase orders, invoices, and customs declarations.

The upper portion skips the style sheet to demonstrate an EDI-like exchange of information. The same XML commercial documents are presented to the accounting system or the ERP of the buyer. What is interesting about this setup is that it uses Web technologies to integrate the two accounting systems.

The main benefit of this setup is that it enables the buyer to start with limited investments (a browser) and upgrade to the more automatic mode as the volume of transactions grows.

## XML/EDI

In 1997, the XML/EDI Group (`www.xmledi.com`) was established as a grassroots effort to promote XML in business-to-business e-commerce. Since 1997, other groups, vendors, and organizations (such as ebXML, BizTalk, CommerceOne, RosettaNet, and more) have adopted XML as their preferred syntax for business-to-business e-commerce.

Unlike EDI, no worldwide, standardized XML version of the order and other commercial document exists. In fact, it is very unlikely that there will ever be one.

Listing 5.2 is one possibility for an XML version of an order. Figure 5.4 is a graphical representation of its structure. As you can see, it is a classic order with buyer and seller information followed by order lines. The XML order is very close to the EDIFACT order for a good reason: Most orders look alike.

Listing 5.2  *orders.xml*

```
<?xml version="1.0"?>
<Order confirm="true">
    <Date>2000-03-10</Date>
    <Reference>AGL153</Reference>
    <DeliverBy>2000-04-10</DeliverBy>
    <Buyer>
        <Name>Playfield Books</Name>
        <Address>
            <Street>34 Fountain Square Plaza</Street>
            <Locality>Cincinnati</Locality>
            <PostalCode>45202</PostalCode>
            <Region>OH</Region>
            <Country>US</Country>
        </Address>
    </Buyer>
    <Seller>
        <Name>QUE</Name>
        <Address>
            <Street>201 West 103RD Street</Street>
            <Locality>Indianapolis</Locality>
            <PostalCode>46290</PostalCode>
            <Region>IN</Region>
```

Listing 5.2 **Continued**

```
            <Country>US</Country>
          </Address>
      </Seller>
      <Lines>
        <Product>
          <Code type="ISBN">0789722429</Code>
          <Description>XML by Example</Description>
          <Quantity>5</Quantity>
          <Price>24.99</Price>
        </Product>
        <Product>
          <Code type="ISBN">0789724308</Code>
          <Description>Applied XML Solutions</Description>
          <Quantity>10</Quantity>
          <Price>42.50</Price>
        </Product>
      </Lines>
  </Order>
```

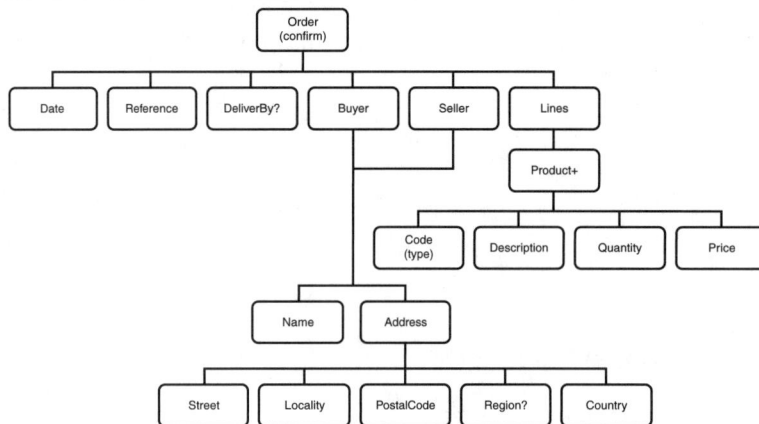

**Figure 5.4** The structure of the XML order is more readily apparent than its EDIFACT counterpart.

Although they convey the same information, the XML and EDIFACT orders are not strictly identical:

- In XML, the internal organization of the order is apparent. It is clear when looking at the document that product identifiers are included in order lines. Consequently, XML does not need qualifiers to specify the relationship between elements as EDIFACT does.

- Some codes are different. For example, the EDIFACT order relies on code `AB` to request an acknowledgement, whereas the XML order uses a `confirm` attribute with a Boolean (`true` or `false`). Likewise, the code `IB` translates into `ISBN`. Differences of this sort are very common when transforming XML to and from other formats.

- The XML document is significantly larger than the EDIFACT version. Again, EDIFACT was developed to minimize bandwidth because it was more expensive at the time.

- In the XML document, product lines include descriptions. In practice, this is very common when building transformations. The two data structures are often similar, but they are rarely identical. Our transformation must cope with these differences.

Our goal in the next sections is to convert one format into the other and vice versa.

### Warning

The XML document includes product descriptions that have no equivalent in EDIFACT. This is not a technical limitation of EDIFACT; it is more of a cultural one.

Specifically, including product descriptions using segment IMD is possible. However, EDIFACT users tend to be conservative with bandwidth, so if the ISBN is enough to identify the product, why waste resources?

### Leverage EDI Experience in XML

As explained, it is expected that business-to-business e-commerce on the Internet will be based on XML. So, if you move into that space, you will need to develop XML versions of commercial documents such as purchase orders, catalogs, packing lists, and more.

I strongly suggest that, to develop such documents, you start with an EDI basis. A lot of effort has gone into making sure the EDIFACT (or X12) documents are complete and usable. Don't reinvent the wheel.

The XML/EDI Group has been advocating precisely this approach since the early days.

Many proposals exist on how to best turn EDI into XML, but here is one that has been field-tested:

- Reverse-engineer EDI messages of interest in object-oriented models (for example, using UML). If possible, start with real implementations instead of the official standard.

- Use aggregation to express relationships between classes. This makes the structure of the original message visible.

- Simplify. The original EDI message is always too complex.

- Convert your model in XML—for example, create an XML element for every class in the model.

# Breaking Down the Conversion

In this chapter, we'll write software to convert the XML order from Listing 5.2 into the EDIFACT order in Listing 5.1. In the next chapter, we will see how to build the reverse transformation, from EDIFACT to XML.

If we analyze the conversion, we realize at least three steps are involved:

1. The converter must read the XML document.
2. The converter must convert between the two structures. Specifically, it must transform XML elements in EDI segments. This might involve splitting an XML element into several segments or grouping several elements into a single segment. It also must transform codes (such as ISBN) into their EDIFACT equivalents (IB).
3. It must write the EDIFACT document according to the rules of the EDIFACT syntax.

Which tools are available to help us? An XML parser can take care of the first step, but what about the next two? It turns out that an XSLT processor can help with the second step. Missing is the capability to write a document according to the EDIFACT rules.

Indeed, if we compare this transformation with the XML-to-HTML and XML-to-XML transformations from Chapter 4, the major difference is that our output format (EDIFACT) is not in the XML family (XML or HTML).

## Text Conversion

The simplest solution is to use `<xml:output method="text"/>` to generate the EDIFACT document. We could write rules similar to the following:

```
<xsl:template match="Price">
   <xsl:text>PRI+AAA:</xsl:text>
   <xsl:value-of select="Price"/>
   <xsl:text>::SRP</text>
</xsl:template>
```

However, in practice, this is difficult and error prone. The EDIFACT syntax is not complicated, but it would not be easy to write XSL templates that handle compression (removing empty fields where it is unambiguous) properly. Nor would it be easy to implement the escape rules (a question mark before the +, :, ', and ? characters).

## Introducing a Formatter

The trick then is to use XSLT for what it is good at, namely converting XML documents into other XML documents. In addition, we should complement it with our own software to deal with the idiosyncrasies of the EDIFACT format. Such software is called a *formatter*.

How does it work in practice? We can define an XML vocabulary that parallels the syntactic components of EDIFACT: segment, composite data element, and simple data element. For example, the segment

```
PRI+AAA:24.99::SRP'
```

would be rendered, in its XML form, as the following:

```
<Segment tag="PRI">
   <Composite>
      <Simple>AAA</Simple>
      <Simple>24.99</Simple>
      <Simple/>
      <Simple>SRP</Simple>
   </Composite>
</Segment>
```

The XSL formatter cannot produce the raw EDIFACT, but it can easily produce this XML-ized version. Furthermore, writing a formatter that takes the XML-ized code and writes it according to the EDIFACT syntax isn't that difficult. It's just a matter of putting the plus sign and quotation marks in the right place. Figure 5.5 illustrates this.

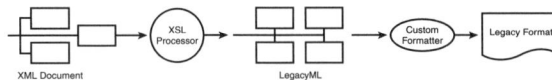

**Figure 5.5** Completing XSL with a custom formatter.

This gives us an interface into XSLT. The XSLT processor will generate the XML-ized version and our own formatter will turn it into proper EDIFACT. This technique enables us to harness the transformative power of XSLT for any file format, including EDIFACT, X12, RTF, Adobe Illustrator, and anything else (with the appropriate formatters).

At this point, you might wonder, why bother? Do we have to use XSLT? Isn't it easier to write an ad hoc Java application that parses the XML document and turns it immediately into EDIFACT? No XSLT, no need to XML-ize EDIFACT, and no problem!

In practice, using XSLT has several advantages, such as the following:

- XSLT processors are optimized for transformation and, in most cases, they are more efficient than ad hoc solutions. Furthermore, when the XSLT processor is improved, our application benefits from a free performance boost.

- It is faster to debug transformation written in XSLT than Java code because XSLT is not compiled.

- In practice, we need to convert several documents: the purchase order, corresponding invoice, order acknowledgement, and more. Using XSLT, we can build a generic transformation engine that can be adapted to any document.

- In my experience, it is easier to teach nonprogrammers style sheet coding than it is to teach them Java coding.
- In my experience, it is easier to maintain XSLT style sheets than the corresponding Java code because style sheets are declarative in nature.

Listing 5.3 is the XML-ized version of Listing 5.1. Compare it with Listing 5.1. Figure 5.6 illustrates the structure of this document. As you can see, it's flat like EDIFACT.

**Warning**

Listing 5.3 is an intermediate format for our application. Using it as an XML order would not make a lot of sense, if only because it is a flat structure like EDIFACT.

Listing 5.3 **XML-ized Version of the EDIFACT Order**

```
<?xml version="1.0"?>
<Message>
   <Segment tag="UNH">
      <Simple>1</Simple>
      <Composite>
         <Simple>ORDERS</Simple>
         <Simple>D</Simple>
         <Simple>96A</Simple>
         <Simple>UN</Simple>
      </Composite>
   </Segment>
   <Segment tag="BGM">
      <Composite>
         <Simple>220</Simple>
      </Composite>
      <Simple>AGL153</Simple>
      <Simple>9</Simple>
      <Simple>AB</Simple>
   </Segment>
   <Segment tag="DTM">
      <Composite>
         <Simple>137</Simple>
         <Simple>20000310</Simple>
         <Simple>102</Simple>
      </Composite>
   </Segment>
   <Segment tag="DTM">
      <Composite>
         <Simple>61</Simple>
         <Simple>20000410</Simple>
         <Simple>102</Simple>
      </Composite>
   </Segment>
   <Segment tag="NAD">
      <Simple>BY</Simple>
```

Listing 5.3 **Continued**

```
        <Composite><Simple/></Composite>
        <Composite><Simple/></Composite>
        <Composite>
            <Simple>PLAYFIELD BOOKS</Simple>
        </Composite>
        <Composite>
            <Simple>34 FOUNTAIN SQUARE PLAZA</Simple>
        </Composite>
        <Simple>CINCINNATI</Simple>
        <Simple>OH</Simple>
        <Simple>45202</Simple>
        <Simple>US</Simple>
    <Segment tag="NAD">
        <Simple>SE</Simple>
        <Composite><Simple/></Composite>
        <Composite><Simple/></Composite>
        <Composite>
            <Simple>QUE</Simple>
        </Composite>
        <Composite>
            <Simple>201 WEST 103RD STREET</Simple>
        </Composite>
        <Simple>INDIANAPOLIS</Simple>
        <Simple>IN</Simple>
        <Simple>46290</Simple>
        <Simple>US</Simple>
    </Segment>
    <Segment tag="LIN">
        <Simple>1</Simple>
    </Segment>
    <Segment tag="PIA">
        <Simple>5</Simple>
        <Composite>
            <Simple>0789722429</Simple>
            <Simple>IB</Simple>
        </Composite>
    </Segment>
    <Segment tag="QTY">
        <Composite>
            <Simple>21</Simple>
            <Simple>5</Simple>
        </Composite>
    </Segment>
    <Segment tag="PRI">
        <Composite>
            <Simple>AAA</Simple>
            <Simple>24.99</Simple>
            <Simple/>
            <Simple>SRP</Simple>
```

Listing 5.3 **Continued**

```xml
      </Composite>
    <Segment tag="LIN">
      <Simple>2</Simple>
    </Segment>
    <Segment tag="PIA">
      <Simple>5</Simple>
      <Composite>
        <Simple>0789724308</Simple>
        <Simple>IB</Simple>
      </Composite>
    </Segment>
    <Segment tag="QTY">
      <Composite>
        <Simple>21</Simple>
        <Simple>10</Simple>
      </Composite>
    </Segment>
    <Segment tag="PRI">
      <Composite>
        <Simple>AAA</Simple>
        <Simple>42.50</Simple>
        <Simple/>
        <Simple>SRP</Simple>
      </Composite>
    </Segment>
    <Segment tag="UNS">
      <Simple>S</Simple>
    </Segment>
    <Segment tag="CNT">
      <Composite>
        <Simple>3</Simple>
        <Simple>2</Simple>
      </Composite>
    </Segment>
    <Segment tag="UNT">
      <Simple>17</Simple>
      <Simple>1</Simple>
    </Segment>
  </Message>
```

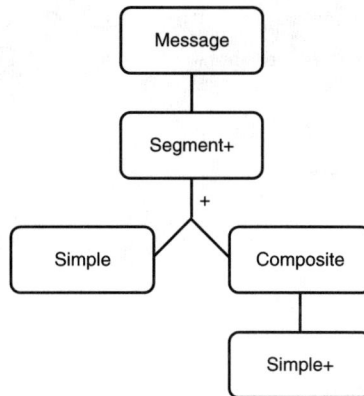

**Figure 5.6** The structure of the XML–ized message closely mimics the EDIFACT syntax.

# Building the Formatter

The only thing remaining is for us to write the EDIFACT formatter.

## Application Organization

Figure 5.7 shows the UML model for our application. The major classes are as follows:

- `EdifactFormatter`, which implements SAX's `DocumentHandler`. It interprets the XML–ized document.
- `Segment`, `CompositeDataElement`, `SimpleDataElement`, and `EdifactElement` are used by `EdifactFormatter` to take care of the EDIFACT syntax.
- `XML2Edifact` is the application's main method.

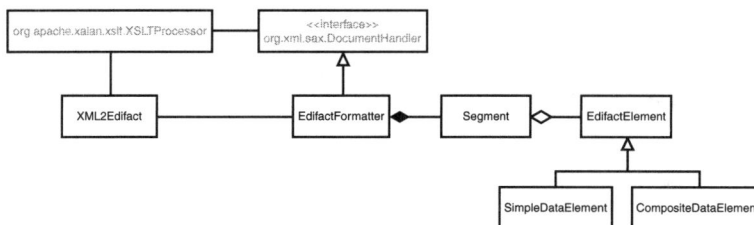

**Figure 5.7** At the heart of our application are the XSL processor and our custom formatter.

## EdifactFormatter

Listing 5.4 is the code for EdifactFormatter. It uses a SAX parser to read the XML document.

Listing 5.4  *EdifactFormatter.java*

```
package com.psol.xsledi;

import java.io.*;
import java.util.*;
import org.xml.sax.*;

public class EdifactFormatter
   implements DocumentHandler
{
   protected static final int NONE = 0,
                              MESSAGE = 1,
                              SEGMENT = 2,
                              COMPOSITE_DATA = 3,
                              SEGMENT_SIMPLE_DATA = 4,
                              COMPOSITE_SIMPLE_DATA = 5;
   protected int state = NONE;
   protected Segment segment = null;
   protected CompositeData compositeData = null;
   protected StringBuffer buffer = null;
   protected Writer writer;

   public EdifactFormatter(OutputStream out)
      throws IOException
   {
      writer = new OutputStreamWriter(out,"ISO-8859-1");
   }

   public void setDocumentLocator(Locator locator)
      {}

   public void startDocument()
      throws SAXException
      {}

   public void endDocument()
      throws SAXException
   {
      try
      {
         writer.flush();
      }
      catch(IOException e)
      {
         throw new SAXException(e);
      }
   }
```

Listing 5.4 **Continued**

```java
public void startElement(String name,AttributeList atts)
   throws SAXException
{
   if(name.equals("Message") && state == NONE)
      state = MESSAGE;
   else if(name.equals("Segment") && state == MESSAGE)
   {
      state = SEGMENT;
      String segmentTag = atts.getValue("tag");
      if(null != segmentTag)
         segment = new Segment(segmentTag);
      else
         throw new SAXException("Empty 'tag' attribute");
   }
   else if(name.equals("Composite") && state == SEGMENT)
   {
      state = COMPOSITE_DATA;
      compositeData = new CompositeData();
   }
   else if(name.equals("Simple") && state == SEGMENT)
   {
      state = SEGMENT_SIMPLE_DATA;
      buffer = new StringBuffer();
   }
   else if(name.equals("Simple") && state == COMPOSITE_DATA)
   {
      state = COMPOSITE_SIMPLE_DATA;
      buffer = new StringBuffer();
   }
}

public void endElement(String name)
   throws SAXException
{
   try
   {
      if(name.equals("Message") && state == MESSAGE)
         state = NONE;
      else if(name.equals("Segment") && state == SEGMENT)
      {
         state = MESSAGE;
         segment.toEdifact(writer);
      }
      else if(name.equals("Composite") &&
            state == COMPOSITE_DATA)
      {
         state = SEGMENT;
         segment.add(compositeData);
         compositeData = null;
      }
```

Listing 5.4 **Continued**

```
        else if(name.equals("Simple") &&
                state == SEGMENT_SIMPLE_DATA)
        {
            state = SEGMENT;
            SimpleData sd = new SimpleData(buffer.toString());
            segment.add(sd);
        }
        else if(name.equals("Simple") &&
                state == COMPOSITE_SIMPLE_DATA)
        {
            state = COMPOSITE_DATA;
            SimpleData sd = new SimpleData(buffer.toString());
            compositeData.add(sd);
        }
    }
    catch(IOException e)
    {
        throw new SAXException(e);
    }
}

public void characters(char[] ch,int start,int len)
    throws SAXException
{
    if(state == SEGMENT_SIMPLE_DATA ||
        state == COMPOSITE_SIMPLE_DATA)
        buffer.append(ch,start,len);
}

public void ignorableWhitespace(char[] ch,int start,int len)
    {}

public void processingInstruction(String target,String data)
    {}
}
```

> ► **Warning**
>
> As always, this project focuses on the XML side of things. The EdifactFormatter is limited to the most useful options in the EDIFACT syntax. It leaves out a few, seldom used, options.

Most of EdifactFormatter should be familiar, but let's review endElement() in more detail. Note that startElement() is typical and is used to track the current state in the XML document.

endElement() also tracks state and create instances of simple data elements, composite data elements, and segments. As soon as it reaches the end of a segment, endElement() calls the toEdifact() method to write the segment in EDIFACT. Then, it discards the segment:

```
public void endElement(String name)
   throws SAXException
{
   try
   {
      if(name.equals("Message") && state == MESSAGE)
         state = NONE;
      else if(name.equals("Segment") && state == SEGMENT)
      {
         state = MESSAGE;
         segment.toEdifact(writer);
      }
      else if(name.equals("Composite") &&
            state == COMPOSITE_DATA)
      {
         state = SEGMENT;
         segment.add(compositeData);
         compositeData = null;
      }
      else if(name.equals("Simple") &&
            state == SEGMENT_SIMPLE_DATA)
      {
         state = SEGMENT;
         SimpleData sd = new SimpleData(buffer.toString());
         segment.add(sd);
      }
      else if(name.equals("Simple") &&
            state == COMPOSITE_SIMPLE_DATA)
      {
         state = COMPOSITE_DATA;
         SimpleData sd = new SimpleData(buffer.toString());
         compositeData.add(sd);
      }
   }
   catch(IOException e)
   {
      throw new SAXException(e);
   }
}
```

## Segment

Listing 5.5 is Segment.java. The Segment takes a tag in its constructor. It also maintains a list of EdifactElement, which represents simple and composite data elements.

Listing 5.5  *Segment.java*

```
package com.psol.xsledi;

import java.io.*;
import java.util.*;
```

Listing 5.5  **Continued**

```java
class Segment
{
   protected String tag;
   protected Vector elements = new Vector();
   protected boolean empty = true;

   public Segment(String tag)
   {
      this.tag = tag;
   }

   public void add(EdifactElement element)
   {
      if(!element.isEmpty())
         empty = false;
      elements.addElement(element);
   }

   public EdifactElement elementAt(int i)
   {
      return (EdifactElement)elements.elementAt(i);
   }

   public int getSize()
   {
      return elements.size();
   }

   public void toEdifact(Writer writer)
      throws IOException
   {
      if(empty)
         return;
      writer.write(tag);
      int plus = 1;
      for(int i = 0;i < getSize();i++)
      {
         EdifactElement el = elementAt(i);
         if(el.isEmpty())
            plus++;
         else
         {
            for(int j = 0;j < plus;j++)
               writer.write('+');
            plus = 1;
            el.toEdifact(writer);
         }
      }
      writer.write('\'');
   }
}
```

The most interesting part of `Segment.java` is probably `toEdifact()`, the method that takes care of the EDIFACT syntax. As you can see, it loops over the `EdifactElement` and calls the `toEdifact()` method:

```java
public void toEdifact(Writer writer)
    throws IOException
{
    if(empty)
        return;
    writer.write(tag);
    int plus = 1;
    for(int i = 0;i < getSize();i++)
    {
        EdifactElement el = elementAt(i);
        if(el.isEmpty())
            plus++;
        else
        {
            for(int j = 0;j < plus;j++)
                writer.write('+');
            plus = 1;
            el.toEdifact(writer);
        }
    }
    writer.write('\'');
}
```

The tricky part is to handle compression. For example, if the following is read

```
<Segment tag="NUL"><Simple/><Simple/><Simple>1</Simple></Segment>
```

`toEdifact()` must insert three plus signs before the third field:

```
NUL+++1'
```

However, simply printing a plus sign before each field is dangerous. Consider the following:

```
<Segment tag="NUL"><Simple>1</Simple><Simple/><Simple/></Segment>
```

Because the last two fields are empty, the compression rule dictates no plus sign should exist for them. Therefore, it would read

```
NUL+1'
```

If `toEdifact()` printed a plus sign before each field, it would need to backtrack at the end of most segments and erase unnecessary trailing plus signs. Instead, `toEdifact()` delays writing the plus signs until it reaches a non-empty field.

The `plus` variable tracks how many empty fields were written, which is equal to the number of plus signs to insert before the next non-empty field.

> **Note**
>
> We are not using the visitor pattern, as we did in Chapter 1, "Lightweight Data Storage," because we don't expect to change the EDIFACT syntax any time soon. Changes in the structure of the message (such as the order of segments or fields) are being dealt with in the style sheet.

## CompositeData and SimpleData

Listing 5.6 is the `EdifactElement` interface. It defines two methods: `isEmpty()`, which is used for compression, and `toEdifact()`, which writes the field. Thanks to `EdifactElement`, `Segment` doesn't need to worry about the differences between simple and composite data elements.

Listing 5.6  *EdifactElement.java*

```
package com.psol.xsledi;

import java.io.*;

public interface EdifactElement
{
   public boolean isEmpty();
   public void toEdifact(Writer writer)
      throws IOException;
}
```

Listing 5.7 is `CompositeData`. It maintains a list of `SimpleData`. Note that its `toEdifact()` method counts colons like `Segment`'s `toEdifact()` counts plus signs.

Listing 5.7  *CompositeData.java*

```
package com.psol.xsledi;

import java.io.*;
import java.util.*;

class CompositeData
   implements EdifactElement
{
   protected Vector simples = new Vector();
   protected boolean empty = true;

   public void add(SimpleData simple)
   {
      if(!simple.isEmpty())
         empty = false;
      simples.addElement(simple);
   }
```

Listing 5.7  **Continued**

```
   public int getSize()
   {
      return simples.size();
   }

   public SimpleData simpleDataAt(int i)
   {
      return (SimpleData)simples.elementAt(i);
   }

   public boolean isEmpty()
   {
      return empty;
   }

   public void toEdifact(Writer writer)
      throws IOException
   {
      if(isEmpty())
         return;
      // the empty simple data we have encountered so far
      // in other words, the number of colons to write
      // before the next non-empty simple data
      int colons = 0;
      for(int i = 0;i < getSize();i++)
      {
         SimpleData sd = simpleDataAt(i);
         if(sd.isEmpty())
            colons++;
         else
         {
            for(int j = 0;j < colons;j++)
               writer.write(':');
            colons = 1;
            sd.toEdifact(writer);
         }
      }
   }
}
```

Listing 5.8 is the `SimpleData` class. As you can see, it's trivial: It stores a string. The most involving part is in the `toEdifact()` method, which implements a simple algorithm to escape special characters. Note that it also converts the text to uppercase; by default EDIFACT does not use lowercase characters.

Listing 5.8  *SimpleData.java*

```
package com.psol.xsledi;

import java.io.*;
```

Listing 5.8 **Continued**

```
public class SimpleData
   implements EdifactElement
{
   protected String data;

   public SimpleData(String data)
   {
      this.data = data;
   }

   public String getData()
   {
      return data;
   }

   public boolean isEmpty()
   {
      return data.length() == 0;
   }

   public void toEdifact(Writer writer)
      throws IOException
   {
      if(isEmpty())
         return;
      for(int i = 0;i < data.length();i++)
      {
         char c = data.charAt(i);
         if(c == '\'')
            writer.write("?'");
         else if(c == '+')
            writer.write("?+");
         else if(c == ':')
            writer.write("?:");
         else if(c == '?')
            writer.write("??");
         else
            writer.write(Character.toUpperCase(c));
      }
   }
}
```

## XML2Edifact

The main() method is in class XML2Edifact, which is reproduced in Listing 5.9. As you can see, it creates an EDIFACT formatter and an XSL processor and links the two together.

The Xalan XSL processor can generate its output as SAX events so that the
EDIFACT formatter plugs directly into it. With other processors, you might need
to explicitly write the XML file and parse.

Listing 5.9 **XML2Edifact.java**

```java
package com.psol.xsledi;

import java.io.*;
import java.util.*;
import org.xml.sax.*;
import org.apache.xalan.xslt.*;

public class XML2Edifact
{
   public static void main(String args[])
      throws SAXException, IOException
   {
      if(args.length < 3)
         throw new IllegalArgumentException(
            "Usage is XML2Edifact in.xml xsl.xsl out.edi");
      InputStream sin = new FileInputStream(args[0]),
                  sxsl = new FileInputStream(args[1]);
      OutputStream sout = new FileOutputStream(args[2]);
      EdifactFormatter formatter = new EdifactFormatter(sout);
      XSLTProcessor processor =
         XSLTProcessorFactory.getProcessor();
      XSLTInputSource in = new XSLTInputSource(sin),
                      xsl = new XSLTInputSource(sxsl);
      XSLTResultTarget out = new XSLTResultTarget(formatter);
      processor.process(in,xsl,out);
   }
}
```

# Writing the Style Sheet

The most interesting side of the transformation is not performed in Java, but is performed by the XSLT style sheet reproduced in Listing 5.10.

Listing 5.10 **xml2edi.xsl**

```xml
<?xml version="1.0"  encoding="ISO-8859-1"?>

<xsl:stylesheet
   xmlns:xsl="http://www.w3.org/1999/XSL/Transform"
   version="1.0">

<xsl:output method="xml"/>
```

Listing 5.10 **Continued**

```xsl
<xsl:template match="/">
   <Message>
      <xsl:apply-templates/>
   </Message>
</xsl:template>

<xsl:template name="format-date">
   <xsl:param name="date"/>
   <xsl:value-of select="substring($date,1,4)"/>
   <xsl:value-of select="substring($date,6,2)"/>
   <xsl:value-of select="substring($date,9,2)"/>
</xsl:template>

<xsl:template name="Address">
   <xsl:param name="code"/>
   <xsl:param name="value"/>
   <Segment tag="NAD">
      <Simple><xsl:value-of select="$code"/></Simple>
      <Composite><Simple/></Composite>
      <Composite><Simple/></Composite>
      <Composite>
         <Simple>
            <xsl:value-of select="$value/Name"/>
         </Simple>
      </Composite>
      <Composite>
         <Simple>
            <xsl:value-of select="$value/Address/Street"/>
         </Simple>
      </Composite>
      <Simple>
         <xsl:value-of select="$value/Address/Locality"/>
      </Simple>
      <Simple>
         <xsl:value-of select="$value/Address/Region"/>
      </Simple>
      <Simple>
         <xsl:value-of select="$value/Address/PostalCode"/>
      </Simple>
      <Simple>
         <xsl:value-of select="$value/Address/Country"/>
      </Simple>
   </Segment>
</xsl:template>

<xsl:template match="Order">
   <Segment tag="UNH">
      <Simple>1</Simple>
      <Composite>
         <Simple>ORDERS</Simple>
```

Listing 5.10  **Continued**

```
        <Simple>D</Simple>
        <Simple>96A</Simple>
        <Simple>UN</Simple>
    </Composite>
<Segment tag="BGM">
    <Composite>
        <Simple>220</Simple>
    </Composite>
    <Simple>
        <xsl:value-of select="Reference"/>
    </Simple>
    <Simple>9</Simple>
    <Simple>
        <xsl:choose>
            <xsl:when test="@confirm=true()">AB</xsl:when>
            <xsl:otherwise>NA</xsl:otherwise>
        </xsl:choose>
    </Simple>
</Segment>
<Segment tag="DTM">
    <Composite>
        <Simple>137</Simple>
        <Simple>
            <xsl:call-template name="format-date">
                <xsl:with-param name="date" select="Date"/>
            </xsl:call-template>
        </Simple>
        <Simple>102</Simple>
    </Composite>
</Segment>
<xsl:if test="DeliverBy">
    <Segment tag="DTM">
        <Composite>
            <Simple>61</Simple>
            <Simple>
                <xsl:call-template name="format-date">
                    <xsl:with-param name="date"
                                    select="DeliverBy"/>
                </xsl:call-template>
            </Simple>
            <Simple>102</Simple>
        </Composite>
    </Segment>
</xsl:if>
<xsl:call-template name="Address">
    <xsl:with-param name="code" select="'BY'"/>
    <xsl:with-param name="value" select="Buyer"/>
</xsl:call-template>
<xsl:call-template name="Address">
    <xsl:with-param name="code" select="'SE'"/>
```

Listing 5.10  **Continued**

```
            <xsl:with-param name="value" select="Seller"/>
        </xsl:call-template>
        <xsl:for-each select="Lines/Product">
            <Segment tag="LIN">
                <Simple><xsl:value-of select="position()"/></Simple>
            </Segment>
            <Segment tag="PIA">
                <Simple>5</Simple>
                <Composite>
                    <Simple>
                        <xsl:value-of select="Code"/>
                    </Simple>
                    <xsl:choose>
                        <!-- ISSN for magazines -->
                        <xsl:when test="Code/@type='ISSN'">
                            <Simple>IS</Simple>
                        </xsl:when>
                        <!-- or ISBN for books -->
                        <xsl:otherwise>
                            <Simple>IB</Simple>
                        </xsl:otherwise>
                    </xsl:choose>
                </Composite>
            </Segment>
            <Segment tag="QTY">
                <Composite>
                    <Simple>21</Simple>
                    <Simple><xsl:value-of select="Quantity"/></Simple>
                </Composite>
            </Segment>
            <Segment tag="PRI">
                <Composite>
                    <Simple>AAA</Simple>
                    <Simple><xsl:value-of select="Price"/></Simple>
                    <Simple/>
                    <Simple>SRP</Simple>
                </Composite>
            </Segment>
        </xsl:for-each>
        <Segment tag="UNS">
            <Simple>S</Simple>
        </Segment>
        <xsl:variable name="nr-lines"
                    select="count(Lines/Product)"/>
        <Segment tag="CNT">
            <Composite>
                <Simple>3</Simple>
                <Simple>
                    <xsl:value-of select="$nr-lines"/>
                </Simple>
```

Listing 5.10 **Continued**

```
            </Composite>
        <Segment tag="UNT">
            <Simple>
                <xsl:choose>
                    <xsl:when test="DeliverBy">
                        <xsl:value-of select="9 + ($nr-lines * 4)"/>
                    </xsl:when>
                    <xsl:otherwise>
                        <xsl:value-of select="8 + ($nr-lines * 4)"/>
                    </xsl:otherwise>
                </xsl:choose>
            </Simple>
            <Simple>1</Simple>
        </Segment>
    </xsl:template>

</xsl:stylesheet>
```

The bulk of the transformation is in the template matching the Order element. The template lists all the segments in the EDIFACT order. Note that this style sheet is specific to the order message, so you would need a different style sheet for other messages.

Where appropriate, the template uses xsl:choose to convert between XML and EDIFACT codes:

```
<Segment tag="BGM">
    <Composite>
        <Simple>220</Simple>
    </Composite>
    <Simple>
        <xsl:value-of select="Reference"/>
    </Simple>
    <Simple>9</Simple>
    <Simple>
        <xsl:choose>
            <xsl:when test="@confirm=true()">AB</xsl:when>
            <xsl:otherwise>NA</xsl:otherwise>
        </xsl:choose>
    </Simple>
</Segment>
```

The loop over the product lines demonstrates clearly that the EDIFACT structure is flat. In XML, the product lines are organized in a hierarchy of elements. In EDIFACT, however, it's a list of segments:

```
<xsl:for-each select="Lines/Product">
    <Segment tag="LIN">
        <!-- deleted -->
    </Segment>
```

```
    <Segment tag="PIA">
        <!-- deleted -->
    </Segment>
    <Segment tag="QTY">
        <!-- deleted -->
    </Segment>
    <Segment tag="PRI">
        <!-- deleted -->
    </Segment>
</xsl:for-each>
```

The total number of segments (which we need for the UNT segment) depends on the number of product lines and whether the optional DeliverBy element is present in the order:

```
<Segment tag="UNT">
    <Simple>
        <xsl:choose>
            <xsl:when test="DeliverBy">
                <xsl:value-of select="9 + ($nr-lines * 4)"/>
            </xsl:when>
            <xsl:otherwise>
                <xsl:value-of select="8 + ($nr-lines * 4)"/>
            </xsl:otherwise>
        </xsl:choose>
    </Simple>
    <Simple>1</Simple>
</Segment>
```

The style sheet also declares a special template to reformat the date. In XML, the date is typically written with minus characters between the year, month, and day. In contrast, EDIFACT (always obsessed with size) compresses it:

```
<xsl:template name="format-date">
    <xsl:param name="date"/>
    <xsl:value-of select="substring($date,1,4)"/>
    <xsl:value-of select="substring($date,6,2)"/>
    <xsl:value-of select="substring($date,9,2)"/>
</xsl:template>
```

This template accepts a parameter, so it can be called similar to a function:

```
<xsl:call-template name="format-date">
    <xsl:with-param name="date" select="Date"/>
</xsl:call-template>
```

# Building and Running the Project

The EDIFACT formatter project is available on the accompanying CD-ROM. Copy the project directory from the CD-ROM to your hard disk, go to the command line, and change to the root of the project. You can run the EDIFACT formatter with the xml2edi command (see Figure 5.8). The parameters are the XML file, XSL style sheet, and output file.

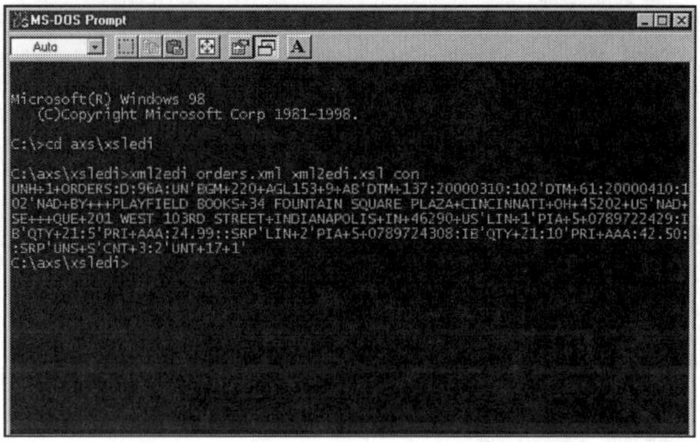

**Figure 5.8** Running with con as the output file prints the result on the console.

**Warning**

This project uses Xalan. You need Xalan and a SAX 1.0 parser to run it. The project on the enclosed CD-ROM uses Xalan and Xerces. Both are available on the CD-ROM, or you can download the latest version from xml.apache.org.

If you switch to another XSL processor, you will need to rewrite **XML2Edifact** to accommodate your processor.

**Warning**

The compiler might issue deprecation warnings if you recompile the project. At the time of this writing, Xalan uses SAX 1.0 event handlers only, but if your parser is SAX 2.0 compliant, it will warn you during recompilation.

## XSLT Benefits

One of the major advantages of using XSLT with a formatter is that modifying the input or output format is easy. Suppose you decide to include the product description in the EDIFACT order. You need to include only the following rule between the PIA and QTY segments. You don't need to modify Java code or recompile:

```
<Segment tag="IMD">
    <Simple>F</Simple>
    <Simple>81</Simple>
    <Composite>
        <Simple/>
        <Simple/>
        <Simple/>
        <Simple><xsl:value-of select="Description"/></Simple>
    </Composite>
</Segment>
```

In fact, the converter we have built is not limited to variations of purchase orders. It will work equally well with invoices, reinsurance claims, and Social Security declarations. All it takes is a different style sheet.

**Tip**

In my experience, XSL style sheets are less frightening than Java code for nonprogrammers. So, I can use the style sheet and discuss it with customers who would not understand my Java code. This alone is a major argument for using style sheets.

# Additional Resources

This technique is not limited to EDIFACT, X12, and other EDI formats! Far from it—many applications benefit from being capable of converting between XML and non-XML formats (such as other popular formats or legacy formats). You can use the same technique for the following:

- Conversion to and from RTF, the Rich Text Format recognized by most word processors.
- Conversion to proprietary formats such as the fixed-length formats used by mainframes.
- Conversion to Excel or Lotus 1-2-3 spreadsheets.
- And more. In fact, provided you can write the formatter, there is no limit to the formats your application can support.

The key to succeed is to properly analyze the output format and XML-ize it, or devise an XML vocabulary that works. The rule of thumb is to keep it simple.

For example, I could have created a more ambitious XML mapping with a different element for each EDIFACT segment, using the EDIFACT element name such as

```
<PRI>
   <C509>
      <S5125>AAA</S5125>
      <S5118>24.99</S5118>
      <S5375/>
      <S5387>SRP</S5387>
   </C509>
</PRI>
```

However, what's the point? It only makes the intermediate format and the formatter more complicated.

*Keep it simple.* The goal is to move as much intelligence as possible in the XSLT style sheet.

# 6

# Import from Any Format

IN THE PREVIOUS CHAPTER, we saw how to extend XSLT with a formatter between XML and non-XML documents. In this chapter, we'll look at the flip side—importing non-XML documents into an XML application.

Many XML applications would benefit from the capability to read non-XML documents because many formats commonly used are not based on XML. Obviously, if we can send EDIFACT orders, we need to be able to decode responses and invoices (which will be in EDIFACT) and receive EDIFACT orders from buyers.

To round off Chapter 5, "Export to Any Format," we will develop an EDIFACT-to-XML conversion. Of course, the principles demonstrated here also work for other formats, such as turning office documents (for example, RTF word processor files and Excel files) into an XML vocabulary such as DocBook. Likewise for converting Adobe Illustrator images to SVG, which is an XML-based vector graphics format currently under development at W3C.

# Parsing EDIFACT

We already know how to transform documents from one format into the other. Recall from Chapter 5 that the three steps are as follows:

1. Read the input document.
2. Convert between the two structures, which can involve grouping or splitting EDIFACT segments into one or several XML elements. It also requires transforming XML codes (such as ISBN) into their EDIFACT equivalents (IB).
3. Write the resulting document.

Again, the XSLT processor takes care of the conversion step, provided we feed it an XML document. Although the processor cannot read EDIFACT, it can write the XML document.

As the previous chapter clearly demonstrated, much can be gained from moving as much of the transformation as possible in XSLT. Some of the advantages include the following:

- Writing and maintaining style sheets is faster and easier than writing the equivalent Java code.
- Style sheets are declarative so it is easy to discuss them with non-developers.
- The XSLT processor is optimized for transformation, and as it improves, so does our application.

The only issue is that an XSLT processor chokes at EDIFACT. So, we need to roll up our sleeves and write our own parser for EDIFACT. The parser will turn the EDIFACT document into the XML-ization of EDIFACT we used in Chapter 5.

In other words, this chapter is the mirror of Chapter 5!

**Warning**

As in Chapter 5, we will limit ourselves to a reasonable subset of the EDIFACT syntax (technically a subset of the EDIFACT syntax version 3). You might need to extend the parser to recognize the most advanced (but seldom used) options of EDIFACT. The goal remains to illustrate a useful technique (importing non-XML documents into XML), not to compete with commercial products.

## Architecture of the Parser

The typical parser is composed of two modules: a *tokenizer* (also called *lexer*) and the parser itself. The tokenizer breaks the input file into its constituents. In particular, it separates special characters (+, :, ', and ?) from regular text.

The parser receives the pre-digested input, as tokens, from the tokenizer and assembles them in a higher-level construct.

Figure 6.1 illustrates how it works. The tokenizer breaks the segment into its constituents—text and special characters. Each of these becomes a different token. The parser then reads through the tokens and the higher-level constructs, such as data elements and segments.

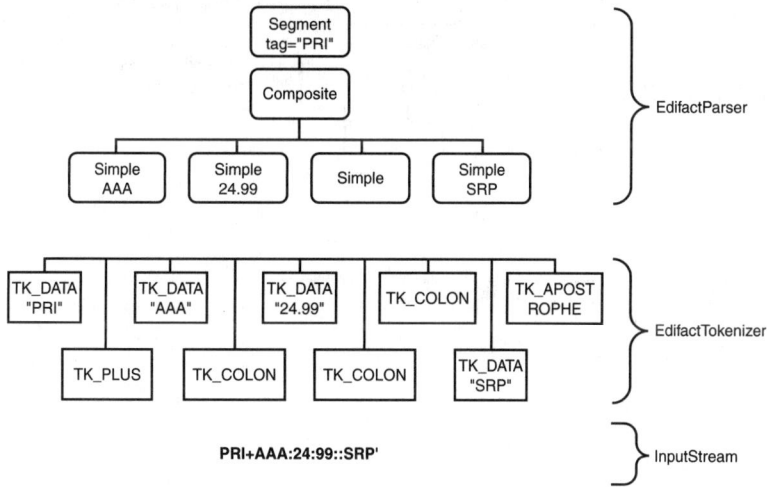

**Figure 6.1** The tokenizer interacts with the parser through tokens.

The separation between tokenizer and parser results in more manageable code. For example, one option in the EDIFACT syntax replaces the +, :, ', and ? characters with other characters. The parser introduced here does not support this option (if only because it is seldom used), but you could easily add it by changing the tokenizer. Note that such changes are limited to the tokenizer; they do not impact the parser itself.

## Classes in the Parser

Figure 6.2 illustrates a UML class diagram of the parser. The various classes are as follows:

- EdifactTokenizer—Breaks the input stream into tokens
- EdifactParser—Interacts with the tokenizer to decode the stream
- EdifactStructure—Is a helper class for the parser
- UnexpectedTokenException—Signals a parsing error
- Extensions—Implements extensions to XSL
- Edifact2XML—Is the application's main program

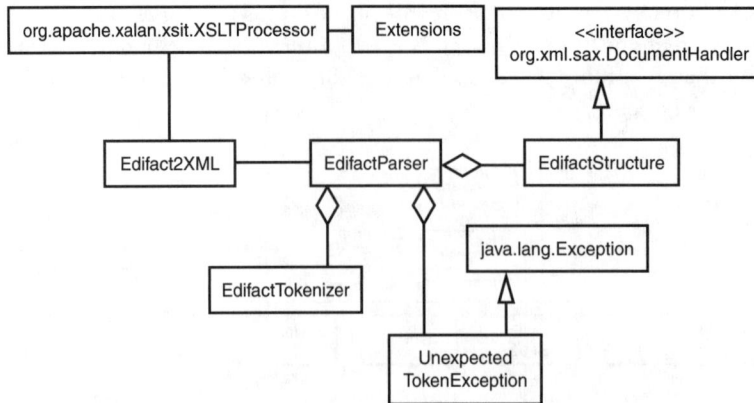

**Figure 6.2** The architecture of the application.

> **Note**
>
> For some languages, a so-called compiler-compiler can simplify the coding. We will review this option in the section "Additional Resources" at the end of this chapter.

## The EDIFACT Parser

This parser recognizes a useful subset of the EDIFACT syntax. It translates the input in the intermediate XML format introduced in Chapter 5. You will recall that segment

```
PRI+AAA:24.99::SRP'
```

becomes the following, in our XML–ized EDIFACT format:

```
<Segment tag="PRI">
   <Composite>
      <Simple>AAA</Simple>
      <Simple>24.99</Simple>
      <Simple/>
      <Simple>SRP</Simple>
   </Composite>
</Segment>
```

In this chapter, we will use the same purchase order introduced in Chapter 5. It is reproduced in Listing 6.1.

Listing 6.1 *orders.edi*

```
UNH+1+ORDERS:D:96A:UN'BGM+220+AGL153+9+AB'DTM+137:20000310:102'
➥DTM+61:20000410:102'NAD+BY+++PLAYFIELD BOOKS+34 FOUNTAIN
➥SQUARE PLAZA+CINCINNATI+OH+45202+US'NAD+SE+++QUE+
```

Listing 6.1 **Continued**

```
➡201 WEST 103RD STREET+INDIANAPOLIS+IN+46290+US'
➡LIN+1'PIA+5+0789722429:IB'QTY+21:5'PRI+AAA:24.99::SRP'
➡LIN+2'PIA+5+0789724308:IB'QTY+21:10'PRI+AAA:42.50::SRP'
➡UNS+S'CNT+3:2'UNT+17+1'
```

## Writing the Tokenizer

Let's start with the tokenizer. Fortunately, the EDIFACT syntax has only four special characters:

- +, :, and '—Separators (between fields in a segment, between fields in a composite data element, and between segments, respectively)
- ?—The escape character

The rest of the message is made up of the fields themselves. We could try to differentiate tags (three letters only), codes, and regular text, but it is easier to tokenize everything as text and sort it out in the parser itself.

Listing 6.2 is `EdifactTokenizer.java`. It recognizes the separator in the input stream, resolves escape characters, and returns text fields as strings.

Listing 6.2 *EdifactTokenizer.java*

```java
package com.psol.xsledi;

import java.io.*;

public class EdifactTokenizer
{
   public static final int TK_EOF = 0,
                           TK_APOSTROPHE = 1,
                           TK_PLUS = 2,
                           TK_COLON = 3,
                           TK_DATA = 4;
   // allocate a 10K buffer
   // for larger messages recompile with a larger buffer
   protected static final int bufferSize = 1024 * 10;
   protected char[] buffer = new char[bufferSize],
                    token = new char[bufferSize / 100];
   protected int bPos,
                 bLen,
                 tPos;

   protected void putc()
   {
      bPos--;
   }
```

Listing 6.2  **Continued**

```
protected int getc()
    {
        if(bPos < bLen)
            return buffer[bPos++];
        else
            return -1;
    }

    public int nextToken()
    {
        tPos = 0;
        int c = getc();
        switch(c)
        {
            case -1:
                return TK_EOF;
            case '+':
                return TK_PLUS;
            case '\'':
                return TK_APOSTROPHE;
            case ':':
                return TK_COLON;
            case '?':
                c = getc();
                if(c == -1)
                    return TK_EOF;
            default:
                token[tPos++] = (char)c;
        }
        for(;;)
        {
            c = getc();
            switch(c)
            {
                case -1:
                    return TK_EOF;
                case '+':
                case '\'':
                case ':':
                    putc();
                    return TK_DATA;
                case '?':
                    c = getc();
                    if(c == -1)
                        return TK_EOF;
                default:
                    token[tPos++] = (char)c;
                    break;
            }
        }
    }
```

Listing 6.2 **Continued**

```java
    }

    public String getCurrentToken()
    {
        return new String(token,0,tPos);
    }

    public static String toString(int token)
    {
        switch(token)
        {
            case TK_EOF:
                return "end of file";
            case TK_APOSTROPHE:
                return "\'";
            case TK_PLUS:
                return "+";
            case TK_COLON:
                return ":";
            case TK_DATA:
                return "data";
            default:
                throw new IllegalArgumentException();
        }
    }

    public void tokenize(InputStream in)
        throws IOException
    {
        Reader reader = new InputStreamReader(in,"ISO-8859-1");
        bLen = reader.read(buffer);
        if(bLen == buffer.length)
            throw new IOException("buffer is too small");
        if(bLen == -1)
            throw new EOFException();
        bPos = 0;
    }
}
```

Let's take a closer look at Listing 6.2. The tokenizer declares constants for the various tokens. TK_EOF stands for the end of file, whereas TK_DATA signifies a textual field. The other constants are for separators. You will notice that no constant exists for the escape character because the tokenizer resolves it transparently:

```java
public static final int TK_EOF = 0,
                        TK_APOSTROPHE = 1,
                        TK_PLUS = 2,
                        TK_COLON = 3,
                        TK_DATA = 4;
```

The tokenizer also allocates various buffers and defines two methods (`getc()` and `putc()`) to read from the buffer or replace the last read character in the buffer. We will see how useful it is when reading data fields:

```
// allocate a 10K buffer
// for larger messages recompile with a larger buffer
protected static final int bufferSize = 1024 * 10;
protected char[] buffer = new char[bufferSize],
                 token = new char[bufferSize / 100];
protected int bPos,
              bLen,
              tPos;

protected void putc()
{
    bPos--;
}

protected int getc()
{
    if(bPos < bLen)
        return buffer[bPos++];
    else
        return -1;
}
```

**Warning**

Note that the tokenizer assumes messages are smaller than 10KB. For larger messages, you need to either allocate a large buffer or rewrite `putc()` and `getc()` to support more efficient buffering.

The heart of the tokenizer is the `nextToken()` method. It reads from the buffer and recognizes data and separators. The parser will repetitively call `nextToken()` until it reaches the end of file.

`nextToken()` starts by testing whether the current character is a separator. If it is, it returns the appropriate token constant.

However, if the current character is not a separator, it must be part of a field, so `nextToken()` loops until it reaches a separator. During the loop, it fills the token array. Then, when it hits a separator, `nextToken()` replaces the separator in the input (through `putc()`) so that it will be available for the next call to `nextToken()`:

```
public int nextToken()
{
    tPos = 0;
    int c = getc();
    switch(c)
    {
        case -1:
```

```
                return TK_EOF;
        case '+':
            return TK_PLUS;
        case '\'':
            return TK_APOSTROPHE;
        case ':':
            return TK_COLON;
        case '?':
            c = getc();
            if(c == -1)
                return TK_EOF;
        default:
            token[tPos++] = (char)c;
    }
    for(;;)
    {
        c = getc();
        switch(c)
        {
            case -1:
                return TK_EOF;
            case '+':
            case '\'':
            case ':':
                putc();
                return TK_DATA;
            case '?':
                c = getc();
                if(c == -1)
                    // could return TK_DATA but a single question
                    // mark is a syntax error
                    return TK_EOF;
            default:
                token[tPos++] = (char)c;
                break;
        }
    }
}
```

Notice that nextToken() takes special care to resolve escape characters: When it hits a question mark, it immediately reads the next character and discards the question mark.

## Writing the Parser

The parser is not complicated either. It assembles the various tokens into higher-level elements: simple data elements, composite data elements, and segments.

➤ The various elements in the EDIFACT syntax were introduced in Chapter 5, in the section "Meet EDIFACT."

The only potential pitfall stems from composite and simple data elements. Consider the following segment:

```
BGM+220+AGL153+9+AC'
```

Is the first field (220) a simple data element or a composite data element? You can't tell from the segment, can you? You must turn to the EDIFACT definition of the segment. (It is a composite data element.)

However, the parser must differentiate simple and composite data elements. The correct XML-ized document for the BGM segment is as follows:

```
<Segment tag="BGM">
   <Composite>
      <Simple>220</Simple>
   </Composite>
   <Simple>AGL153</Simple>
   <Simple>AB</Simple>
</Segment>
```

The following is incorrect:

```
<Segment tag="BGM">
   <Simple>220</Simple>
   <Simple>AGL153</Simple>
   <Simple>AB</Simple>
</Segment>
```

In other words, we need to provide the parser with segment definitions. One solution is to use Listing 6.3, which is essentially an XML document listing segments used in order. For each segment, it describes its content using the following code: A simple field is represented with an S and a composite field is represented with a C.

Listing 6.3 *edifactstructure.xml*

```
<?xml version="1.0"?>
<Structure>
   <Segment tag="BGM" content="CSSSS"/>
   <Segment tag="CNT" content="C"/>
   <Segment tag="DTM" content="C"/>
   <Segment tag="LIN" content="SSCCSS"/>
   <Segment tag="NAD" content="SCCCCSSSS"/>
   <Segment tag="PIA" content="SCCCCC"/>
   <Segment tag="PRI" content="CS"/>
   <Segment tag="QTY" content="C"/>
   <Segment tag="RFF" content="C"/>
   <Segment tag="UNH" content="SCSC"/>
   <Segment tag="UNS" content="S"/>
   <Segment tag="UNT" content="SS"/>
</Structure>
```

▶ **Note**

Listing 6.3 does not break the composite data element into a simple data element. The parser does not know whether a given composite data element should be three or five simple data elements.

This is not a problem, though, because we are not too concerned about the EDIFACT message. In fact, we don't even care whether a composite has the right number of simple data elements as long as we can transform it in valid XML. Validating the order in XML using a validating parser is easier than trying to validate the original EDIFACT document.

Listing 6.4 is `EdifactStructure`, a helper class that reads Listing 6.3. The EDIFACT parser calls `setSegment()` to select a segment (for example, BGM) and repetitively calls `nextContentType()` to retrieve the type of each field in the segment. For BGM, successive calls to `nextContentType()` return C, S, S, S, and S, as specified in Listing 6.3.

Listing 6.4 *EdifactStructure.java*

```java
package com.psol.xsledi;

import java.util.*;
import org.xml.sax.*;

class EdifactStructure
    extends HandlerBase
{
    protected Dictionary dictionary = new Hashtable();
    protected String content = null;
    protected int cPos;

    public void startElement(String name,AttributeList atts)
        throws SAXException
    {
        if(name.equals("Segment"))
        {
            String tag = atts.getValue("tag"),
                   content = atts.getValue("content");
            if(null != tag && null != content)
                dictionary.put(tag,content);
            else
                throw new SAXException("Missing attribute in Segment");
        }
    }

    public void setSegment(String segment)
    {
        content = (String)dictionary.get(segment);
        cPos = 0;
        if(null == content)
            throw new NullPointerException("unknown: " + segment);
    }
```

Listing 6.4 **Continued**

```
   public char nextContentType()
   {
      if(cPos < content.length())
         return content.charAt(cPos++);
      else
         return content.charAt(content.length() - 1);
   }
}
```

The parser itself is demonstrated in Listing 6.5. It uses the `EdifactTokenizer` and `EdifactStructure` classes.

Listing 6.5 *EdifactParser.java*

```
package com.psol.xsledi;

import java.io.*;
import java.util.*;

public class EdifactParser
{
   protected EdifactStructure structure;
   protected Writer writer = null;
   protected EdifactTokenizer tokenizer =
      new EdifactTokenizer();

   public EdifactParser(EdifactStructure structure)
   {
      this.structure = structure;
   }

   public void setWriter(Writer writer)
   {
      this.writer = writer;
   }

   protected void match(int token)
      throws UnexpectedTokenException
   {
      int t = tokenizer.nextToken();
      if(t != token)
         throw new UnexpectedTokenException(token,t);
   }

   public void parse(String filename)
      throws UnexpectedTokenException, IOException
   {
      tokenizer.tokenize(new FileInputStream(filename));
      writer.write("<?xml version=\'1.0\'?>");
```

Listing 6.5  **Continued**

```
      writer.write("<Message>");
      while(nextSegment() != EdifactTokenizer.TK_EOF)
          ;
      writer.write("</Message>");
      writer.flush();
   }

   protected int nextSegment()
      throws UnexpectedTokenException, IOException
   {
      int token = tokenizer.nextToken();
      if(token == EdifactTokenizer.TK_EOF)
         return EdifactTokenizer.TK_EOF;
      else if(token != EdifactTokenizer.TK_DATA)
         throw new UnexpectedTokenException(token,
                                  EdifactTokenizer.TK_DATA);
      String tag = tokenizer.getCurrentToken();
      writer.write("<Segment tag=\'");
      writeEscape(tag);
      writer.write("\'>");
      match(EdifactTokenizer.TK_PLUS);
      structure.setSegment(tag);
      while(token != EdifactTokenizer.TK_EOF &&
            token != EdifactTokenizer.TK_APOSTROPHE)
      {
         switch(structure.nextContentType())
         {
            case 'C':
               token = nextComposite();
               break;
            case 'S':
               token = nextSimple();
               break;
            default:
               throw new IllegalStateException();
         }
      }
      writer.write("</Segment>");
      return token;
   }

   protected int nextComposite()
      throws UnexpectedTokenException, IOException
   {
      writer.write("<Composite>");
      int token = nextSimple();
      while(token == EdifactTokenizer.TK_COLON)
          token = nextSimple();
      writer.write("</Composite>");
      return token;
   }
```

Listing 6.5  **Continued**

```
protected int nextSimple()
  throws UnexpectedTokenException, IOException
{
  int token = tokenizer.nextToken();
  switch(token)
  {
    case EdifactTokenizer.TK_DATA:
      writer.write("<Simple>");
      writeEscape(tokenizer.getCurrentToken());
      writer.write("</Simple>");
      int t = tokenizer.nextToken();
      return t;
    case EdifactTokenizer.TK_PLUS:
    case EdifactTokenizer.TK_COLON:
    case EdifactTokenizer.TK_APOSTROPHE:
      writer.write("<Simple/>");
      return token;
    default:
      throw new UnexpectedTokenException(token);
  }
}

protected void writeEscape(String data)
  throws IOException
{
  // assumes a Unicode encoding since
  // it does not escape non-ASCII characters
for(int i = 0;i < data.length();i++)
  {
    char c = data.charAt(i);
    switch(c)
    {
      case '<':
        writer.write("&lt;");
        break;
      case '&':
        writer.write("&amp;");
        break;
      case '\'':
        writer.write("&apos;");
        break;
      default:
        writer.write(c);
    }
  }
}
}
```

The `parse()` method is the starting point. It uses the tokenizer to read the file. Next, it creates the root of the XML document (`Message`) and iterates over all the segment, by repetitively calling `nextSegment()`, until it finds the `TK_EOF` token:

```
public void parse(String filename)
    throws UnexpectedTokenException, IOException
{
    tokenizer.tokenize(new FileInputStream(filename));
    writer.write("<?xml version=\'1.0\'?>");
    writer.write("<Message>");
    while(nextSegment() != EdifactTokenizer.TK_EOF)
        ;
    writer.write("</Message>");
    writer.flush();
}
```

After reading the tag and writing the segment element, `nextSegment()` iterates over the various fields in the segment, calling `nextComposite()` or `nextSimple()` according to the segment structure made available by `EdifactStructure`:

```
protected int nextSegment()
    throws UnexpectedTokenException, IOException
{
    int token = tokenizer.nextToken();
    if(token == EdifactTokenizer.TK_EOF)
        return EdifactTokenizer.TK_EOF;
    else if(token != EdifactTokenizer.TK_DATA)
        throw new UnexpectedTokenException(token,
                              EdifactTokenizer.TK_DATA);
    String tag = tokenizer.getCurrentToken();
    writer.write("<Segment tag=\'");
    writeEscape(tag);
    writer.write("\'>");
    match(EdifactTokenizer.TK_PLUS);
    structure.setSegment(tag);
    while(token != EdifactTokenizer.TK_EOF &&
          token != EdifactTokenizer.TK_APOSTROPHE)
    {
        switch(structure.nextContentType())
        {
            case 'C':
                token = nextComposite();
                break;
            case 'S':
                token = nextSimple();
                break;
            default:
                throw new IllegalStateException();
        }
    }
    writer.write("</Segment>");
    return token;
}
```

`nextComposite()` and `nextSimple()` are even simpler. They read as much data as possible until they reach a separator:

```
protected int nextComposite()
   throws UnexpectedTokenException, IOException
{
   writer.write("<Composite>");
   int token = nextSimple();
   while(token == EdifactTokenizer.TK_COLON)
      token = nextSimple();
   writer.write("</Composite>");
   return token;
}
```

Listing 6.6 is `UnexpectedTokenException`, which the parser uses to report errors.

Listing 6.6 *UnexpectedTokenException.java*

```
package com.psol.xsledi;

public class UnexpectedTokenException
   extends Exception
{
   public UnexpectedTokenException(int foundToken)
   {
      super("unexpected " +
            EdifactTokenizer.toString(foundToken) +
            " token found");
   }

   public UnexpectedTokenException(int expectedToken,
                                   int foundToken)
   {
      super("unexpected " +
            EdifactTokenizer.toString(foundToken) +
            " token found, was expecting " +
            EdifactTokenizer.toString(expectedToken));
   }
}
```

# The Conversion

The parser generates only the intermediate XML–ized format. This format is just that, a temporary step in the conversion. It would not be sensible to use it as the real XML order. Therefore, the next step is to transform the intermediate format into the real XML order (see Listing 6.7).

Listing 6.7 *orders.xml*

```xml
<?xml version="1.0"?>
<Order confirm="true">
    <Date>2000-03-10</Date>
    <Reference>AGL153</Reference>
    <DeliverBy>2000-04-10</DeliverBy>
    <Buyer>
        <Name>PLAYFIELD BOOKS</Name>
        <Address>
            <Street>34 FOUNTAIN SQUARE PLAZA</Street>
            <Locality>CINCINNATI</Locality>
            <PostalCode>45202</PostalCode>
            <Region>OH</Region>
            <Country>US</Country>
        </Address>
    </Buyer>
    <Seller>
        <Name>QUE</Name>
        <Address>
            <Street>201 WEST 103RD STREET</Street>
            <Locality>INDIANAPOLIS</Locality>
            <PostalCode>46290</PostalCode>
            <Region>IN</Region>
            <Country>US</Country>
        </Address>
    </Seller>
    <Lines>
        <Product>
            <Code type="ISBN">0789722429</Code>
            <Description>XML by Example</Description>
            <Quantity>5</Quantity>
            <Price>24.99</Price>
        </Product>
        <Product>
            <Code type="ISBN">0789724308</Code>
            <Description>Applied XML Solutions</Description>
            <Quantity>10</Quantity>
            <Price>42.50</Price>
        </Product>
    </Lines>
</Order>
```

## The Style Sheet

The main transformation is the responsibility of the XSLT style sheet in Listing 6.8.

Listing 6.8 *edi2xml.xsl*

---

```xml
<?xml version="1.0"  encoding="ISO-8859-1"?>

<xsl:stylesheet
    xmlns:xsl="http://www.w3.org/1999/XSL/Transform"
    xmlns:axslt="http://xml.apache.org/xslt"
    xmlns:psol="http://www.psol.com/xsledi/extensions"
    extension-element-prefixes="psol"
    version="1.0">

<axslt:component prefix="psol"
                 functions="lookupDescription"
                 elements="register">
   <axslt:script lang="javaclass"
                 src="com.psol.xsledi.Extensions"/>
</axslt:component>

<xsl:output method="xml"/>

<xsl:template match="/Message">
   <psol:register isbn="0789722429"
                  title="XML by Example"/>
   <psol:register isbn="0789724308"
                  title="Applied XML Solutions"/>   <Order>
      <xsl:attribute name="confirm">
        <xsl:variable name="ack"
                      select="Segment[@tag='BGM']/Simple[2]"/>
        <xsl:value-of select="$ack != 'NA'"/>
      </xsl:attribute>
      <xsl:call-template name="Date"/>
      <xsl:call-template name="Reference"/>
      <xsl:call-template name="DeliverBy"/>
      <xsl:call-template name="Buyer"/>
      <xsl:call-template name="Seller"/>
      <xsl:call-template name="Lines"/>
   </Order>
</xsl:template>

<xsl:template name="format-date">
   <xsl:param name="date"/>
   <xsl:value-of select="substring($date,1,4)"/>
   <xsl:text>-</xsl:text>
   <xsl:value-of select="substring($date,5,2)"/>
   <xsl:text>-</xsl:text>
   <xsl:value-of select="substring($date,7,2)"/>
</xsl:template>

<xsl:template name="Date">
   <xsl:variable name="date"
                 select="Segment[@tag='DTM' and
                         child::Composite[Simple[1]='137']]"/>
```

Listing 6.8 **Continued**

```xsl
      <Date>
        <xsl:call-template name="format-date">
          <xsl:with-param name="date"
                          select="$date/Composite[1]/Simple[2]"/>
        </xsl:call-template>
      </Date>
</xsl:template>

<xsl:template name="Reference">
    <Reference>
        <xsl:value-of select="Segment[@tag='BGM']/Simple[1]"/>
    </Reference>
</xsl:template>

<xsl:template name="DeliverBy">
    <xsl:variable name="date"
                  select="Segment[@tag='DTM' and
                          child::Composite[Simple[1]='61']]"/>
    <xsl:if test="$date">
      <DeliverBy>
        <xsl:call-template name="format-date">
          <xsl:with-param
           name="date"
           select="$date/Composite[1]/Simple[2]"/>
        </xsl:call-template>
      </DeliverBy>
    </xsl:if>
</xsl:template>

<xsl:template name="Address">
    <xsl:param name="address"/>
    <Name>
      <xsl:for-each select="$address/Composite[3]/Simple">
        <xsl:value-of select="."/>
        <xsl:if test="not(position()=last())">
           <xsl:text> </xsl:text>
        </xsl:if>
      </xsl:for-each>
    </Name>
    <Address>
      <Street>
        <xsl:for-each select="$address/Composite[4]/Simple">
          <xsl:value-of select="."/>
          <xsl:if test="not(position()=last())">
             <xsl:text> </xsl:text>
          </xsl:if>
        </xsl:for-each>
      </Street>
      <Locality>
        <xsl:value-of select="$address/Simple[2]"/>
```

Listing 6.8 **Continued**

```xsl
            </Locality>
            <PostalCode>
              <xsl:value-of select="$address/Simple[4]"/>
            </PostalCode>
            <xsl:variable name="region"
                        select="$address/Simple[3]"/>
            <xsl:if test="string-length($region) != 0">
              <Region>
                <xsl:value-of select="$region"/>
              </Region>
            </xsl:if>
            <Country>
              <xsl:value-of select="$address/Simple[5]"/>
            </Country>
          </Address>
</xsl:template>

<xsl:template name="Buyer">
    <xsl:variable name="buyer"
                select="Segment[@tag='NAD' and
                          child::Simple[1]='BY']"/>
    <Buyer>
      <xsl:call-template name="Address">
        <xsl:with-param name="address" select="$buyer"/>
      </xsl:call-template>
    </Buyer>
</xsl:template>

<xsl:template name="Seller">
    <xsl:variable name="seller"
                select="Segment[@tag='NAD' and
                          child::Simple[1]='SE']"/>
    <Seller>
      <xsl:call-template name="Address">
        <xsl:with-param name="address" select="$seller"/>
      </xsl:call-template>
    </Seller>
</xsl:template>

<xsl:template name="Lines">
    <Lines>
      <xsl:for-each select="Segment[@tag='LIN']">
        <xsl:variable name="code"
                    select="following-sibling::Segment
➥[@tag='PIA']/Composite[1]/Simple[1]"/>
        <xsl:variable name="type"
                    select="following-sibling::Segment
➥[@tag='PIA']/Composite[1]/Simple[2]"/>
        <Product>
            <Code>
```

Listing 6.8 **Continued**

```xsl
                    <xsl:attribute name="type">
                      <xsl:choose>
                        <xsl:when test="$type = 'IS'">
                          <xsl:text>ISSN</xsl:text>
                        </xsl:when>
                        <xsl:otherwise>
                          <xsl:text>ISBN</xsl:text>
                        </xsl:otherwise>
                      </xsl:choose>
                    </xsl:attribute>
                    <xsl:value-of select="$code"/>
                </Code>
                <Description>
                    <xsl:value-of select="psol:lookupDescription(
  ⇒string($code),string($type))"/>
                </Description>
                <Quantity>
                    <xsl:value-of select="following-sibling::Segment
  ⇒[@tag='QTY']/Composite[1]/Simple[2]"/>
                </Quantity>
                <Price>
                    <xsl:value-of select="following-sibling::Segment
  ⇒[@tag='PRI']/Composite[1]/Simple[2]"/>
                </Price>
            </Product>
        </xsl:for-each>
      </Lines>
  </xsl:template>

</xsl:stylesheet>
```

The style sheet creates the XML document by extracting information from the EDIFACT document and placing it in the right order. We'll look at the register elements in a moment:

```xsl
<xsl:template match="/Message">
   <psol:register isbn="0789722429"
                  title="XML by Example"/>
   <psol:register isbn="0789724308"
                  title="Applied XML Solutions"/>
   <Order>
      <xsl:attribute name="confirm">
        <xsl:variable name="ack"
                      select="Segment[@tag='BGM']/Simple[2]"/>
        <xsl:value-of select="$ack != 'NA'"/>
      </xsl:attribute>
      <xsl:call-template name="Date"/>
      <xsl:call-template name="Reference"/>
      <xsl:call-template name="DeliverBy"/>
      <xsl:call-template name="Buyer"/>
```

```
            <xsl:call-template name="Seller"/>
            <xsl:call-template name="Lines"/>
        </Order>
    </xsl:template>
```

In these templates, the selection criteria is relatively complex. Look at the template for `Date` as an example. It extracts data with a combination of the element name (`Segment`), one of its attributes (`@tag='DTM'`), and the value of one of its children (`child::Composite[Simple[1]='137']]`).

`Date` needs this complex, multi-level selection to deal with EDIFACT qualifiers. You will recall that EDIFACT qualifiers are used to encode relationships between segments, so they must be read to re-create the structure of the document.

Fortunately, the EDIFACT parser doesn't need to deal with these; otherwise, it would have been more complicated. The parser performs a minimalist translation, and the more complex processing is relegated to the XSLT style sheet.

Incidentally, this illustrates why the XML-ized EDIFACT order should remain an intermediate format. It is more complex to manipulate than it needs to be. Simplifying it makes more sense:

```
    <xsl:template name="Date">
        <xsl:variable name="date"
                    select="Segment[@tag='DTM' and
                              child::Composite[Simple[1]='137']]"/>
        <Date>
            <xsl:call-template name="format-date">
                <xsl:with-param name="date"
                              select="$date/Composite[1]/Simple[2]"/>
            </xsl:call-template>
        </Date>
    </xsl:template>
```

The most complex template is probably the template for the `Lines` element because it groups information from several segments. Recall that, in the previous chapter, the equivalent template broke the `Product` element into segments.

Unfortunately, because an EDIFACT message is a list of segments, it is not easy to extract the information from the various segments. The least one could say is that XSLT is not optimized for relatively flat structures; it was designed for more hierarchical structures.

▶

**Note**

This illustrates a common problem when dealing with legacy formats (whether EDIFACT or another format): Modern tools are not optimized to manipulate them.

The best solution is to use the `next-sibling` axis to retrieve specific segments after the current one:

```
<xsl:template name="Lines">
   <Lines>
      <xsl:for-each select="Segment[@tag='LIN']">
         <xsl:variable name="code"
                       select="following-sibling::Segment
↪[@tag='PIA']/Composite[1]/Simple[1]"/>
         <xsl:variable name="type"
                       select="following-sibling::Segment
↪[@tag='PIA']/Composite[1]/Simple[2]"/>
         <Product>
            <Code>
               <xsl:attribute name="type">
                  <xsl:choose>
                     <xsl:when test="$type = 'IS'">
                        <xsl:text>ISSN</xsl:text>
                     </xsl:when>
                     <xsl:otherwise>
                        <xsl:text>ISBN</xsl:text>
                     </xsl:otherwise>
                  </xsl:choose>
               </xsl:attribute>
               <xsl:value-of select="$code"/>
            </Code>
            <Description>
               <xsl:value-of select="psol:lookupDescription(
↪string($code),string($type))"/>
            </Description>
            <Quantity>
               <xsl:value-of select="following-sibling::Segment
↪[@tag='QTY']/Composite[1]/Simple[2]"/>
            </Quantity>
            <Price>
               <xsl:value-of select="following-sibling::Segment
↪[@tag='PRI']/Composite[1]/Simple[2]"/>
            </Price>
         </Product>
      </xsl:for-each>
   </Lines>
</xsl:template>
```

> **Warning**
>
> For documents with more complex structures, grouping segments using the following-sibling axis is not possible. The solution is either to use XSLT extensions (see the next section) or to enhance the parser to produce a more structured intermediate format.

## Extensions

The style sheet uses an XSLT extension to deal with product descriptions. The XSL standard proposes a mechanism to recognize non-standard functions and elements.

However, the XSL standard doesn't specify how to write these extensions. This is left to the developers of the processor.

In this chapter, we use Xalan extensions, so we'll use the Xalan extension mechanism.

The XSL standard marks extensions with a specific namespace. The namespace must be registered with the `extension-element-prefixes` attribute.

In the style sheet, extensions are located in the `http://www.psol.com/xsledi/` extensions namespace:

```
<xsl:stylesheet
   xmlns:xsl="http://www.w3.org/1999/XSL/Transform"
   xmlns:axslt="http://xml.apache.org/xslt"
   xmlns:psol="http://www.psol.com/xsledi/extensions"
   extension-element-prefixes="psol"
   version="1.0">
```

Xalan declares the extensions with the `component` element, which is Xalan specific. We can declare one new element, `register`, and one new function, `lookupDescription()`. Both are implemented in the Java `com.psol.xsledi.Extensions`:

```
<axslt:component prefix="psol"
                 functions="lookupDescription"
                 elements="register">
   <axslt:script lang="javaclass"
                 src="com.psol.xsledi.Extensions"/>
</axslt:component>
```

The `lookupDescription()` retrieves a book title (product description) from its ISBN. `register`, on the other hand, initializes the list of titles (an alternative is to read them from a database):

```
<psol:register isbn="0789722429"
               title="XML by Example"/>
<psol:register isbn="0789724308"
               title="Applied XML Solutions"/>
```

The implementation of `register` and `lookupDescription()` is shown in Listing 6.9. Xalan uses the Bean Scripting Framework (BSF) to access the implementation, so the functions could have been written in any other BSF–compliant language, such as JPython (which can be downloaded from `www.jpython.org`) or JavaScript (which can be downloaded from `www.mozilla.org/rhino`).

Listing 6.9 *Extensions.java*

```
package com.psol.xsledi;

import java.util.Hashtable;
import org.apache.xalan.xslt.*;

public class Extensions
{
```

Listing 6.9 **Continued**

```
   protected Hashtable isbns = new Hashtable();

   public void register(XSLProcessorContext context,
                        ElemExtensionCall extElem)
   {
      String isbn = extElem.getAttribute("isbn"),
             title = extElem.getAttribute("title");
      isbns.put(isbn,title);
   }

   public Extensions()
      {}

   public String lookupDescription(String code,String type)
   {
      String desc = type.equals("IB") ?
                    (String)isbns.get(code) : null;
      return null != desc ? desc : "unknown";
   }
}
```

## Edifact2XML

The starting point for the application is `Edifact2XML` (see Listing 6.10). It parses the EDIFACT stream into a character array and applies the style sheet to the result.

Listing 6.10 *Edifact2XML.java*

```
package com.psol.xsledi;

import java.io.*;
import java.util.*;
import org.xml.sax.*;
import org.xml.sax.helpers.*;
import org.apache.xalan.xslt.*;

public class Edifact2XML
{
   public static final String PARSER_NAME =
      "org.apache.xerces.parsers.SAXParser";

   public static void main(String args[])
      throws UnexpectedTokenException, SAXException,
             IOException, ClassNotFoundException,
             IllegalAccessException, InstantiationException
   {
      EdifactStructure structure = new EdifactStructures);
      Parser parser = ParserFactory.makeParser(PARSER_NAME);
```

Listing 6.10 **Continued**

```
        parser.setDocumentHandler(structure);
        parser.parse("edifactstructure.xml");

        CharArrayWriter writer = new CharArrayWriter();

        EdifactParser eparser = new EdifactParser(structure);
        eparser.setWriter(writer);
        eparser.parse(args[0]);
        writer.close();

        char[] carray = writer.toCharArray();

        Reader reader = new CharArrayReader(carray);
        InputStream sxsl = new FileInputStream(args[1]);
        OutputStream sout = new FileOutputStream(args[2]);

        XSLTProcessor processor =
            XSLTProcessorFactory.getProcessor();
        XSLTInputSource in = new XSLTInputSource(reader),
                       xsl = new XSLTInputSource(sxsl);
        XSLTResultTarget out = new XSLTResultTarget(sout);
        processor.process(in,xsl,out);
    }
}
```

# Building and Running the Project

The EDIFACT parser project is available on the accompanying CD-ROM. Copy the project directory from the CD-ROM to your hard disk and then go to the command line and change to the root of the project. You can run the EDIFACT formatter with the edi2xml command (see Figure 6.3). The parameters are the EDI file, XSL style sheet, and output file.

**Warning**

This project uses Xalan. You need Xalan and a SAX 1.0 parser to run it. The project on the accompanying CD-ROM uses Xalan and Xerces. Both are available on the CD-ROM, or you can download the latest version from xml.apache.org.

If you switch to another XSL processor, you must rewrite Edifact2XML and the extensions to accommodate your processor.

**Warning**

The compiler might issue deprecation warnings if you recompile the project: Xalan works with SAX 1.0, altought SAX 2.0 is the latest version.

**Figure 6.3** Test the converted by converting back and forth between XML and EDIFACT.

# Additional Resources

Again, the technique in this chapter is not limited to EDIFACT. Any file format can be XML-ized, as was explained in Chapter 5. In fact, there is often value in designing an XML model from an existing format. However, depending on the input file format, you will have to do more or less work to parse it.

You should start by searching for existing parsers. For example, if you deal with Excel spreadsheets, you can turn to the OpenExchange DDL, (available from www.gotovbs.com) or, in Delphi only, to the TXLSRead and TXLSWrite components (available from www.axolot.com/components/xlsreadwrite.htm). If you work with RTF or PostScript, you should consider PCYACC (available from www.abxsoft.com).

If you cannot find an existing parser, you must write your own. For some formats, such as EDIFACT, I find it simpler to write the parser from scratch. In my experience, this is true for old legacy formats. Over the years, the syntax has accumulated many exceptions, so writing code around the exceptions is faster.

On the other hand, if you are lucky enough to work with a more modern format, chances are a compiler-compiler will be useful. A *compiler-compiler* is a tool used to help write parsers. The idea is that you write a high-level description of the format and the tool compiles it into an actual parser.

Two advantages to this approach exist. First, you are working at a higher level of abstraction, so it is faster. Second, the parsers are very efficient. The downside is that these tools work best with formats that were designed rigorously…which excludes many legacy formats.

Some of the most interesting tools are as follows:

- YACC is one of the oldest compiler–compilers. A PC version, PCYACC, is available commercially from Abraxas (`www.abxsoft.com`). The product ships with several pre-built parsers, including RTF, VRML, HTML, and PostScript.
- Bison is a GNU replacement for YACC. It is available from `www.gnu.org`.
- ANTLR is a powerful open–source compiler–compiler. It is available from `www.antlr.org`.
- Visual Parse++ is a commercial product from Sandstone that offers a graphical development environment. It is available from `www.sand-stone.com`.

For more information on this topic, read *Compilers Principles, Techniques and Tools* by Alfred V. Aho, Ravi Sethi, and Jeffrey D. Ullman. This book is dubbed the "Dragon book" and enjoys an almost religious following. However, at close to 800 pages in a small typeset, it is not for the faint of heart.

If you want a shorter introduction, I recommend *Compiler Construction* from Niklaus Wirth (of Pascal fame). At 180 pages, it is an easy read.

# 7

# Write an e-Commerce Server

THIS CHAPTER LOOKS AT SOLUTIONS to conduct electronic business on the Internet using XML. More specifically, it demonstrates a server for purchasing and invoicing.

I have made several simplifications in this project and I will particularly concentrate on two aspects:

- Automatically exchanging XML documents between Web servers, which is essential for high-volume transactions
- Accepting various formats through XSL style sheets for increased flexibility

If you follow the announcements of XML-based e-commerce products, you have probably heard of XML *marketplaces*. These are promising solutions that enable e-commerce for businesses. This chapter doesn't aim to compete with these products but to demonstrate a simple, low-cost solution. The concepts introduced in the chapter can serve as a basis for more sophisticated solutions as well.

## XML Marketplaces

I'd like to start this chapter by briefly looking at the impact the Internet is having on business. I will keep it short because I assume that, if you are reading *Applied XML Solutions*, you must be close to the revolution yourself.

However, at least two remarkable aspects exist when conducting business electronically. The first aspect is that location is less important.

Therefore, despite some thorny regulatory and cultural differences, a local company can act globally. My own business, Pineapplesoft, is active in Belgium, the U.S., France, the U.K., the Netherlands, and other countries from our base in Namur, Belgium. Most of our international business is conducted electronically.

Despite the physical distance, global organizations can become close to their customers by offering targeted advice, tips, or discounts. In my view, Amazon is a prime example of this.

Secondly, and most importantly, small businesses can compete effectively in that space. Internet access is so cheap no business can afford not to have it. Companies or individuals can have a Web site for a few dollars per month. And, thanks to easy-to-use editors, they don't need an HTML wizard either.

As their activities grow, small businesses can rent a shopping cart, again for a low monthly fee, from their ISP or from a large mall such as Amazon's zShop or Yahoo! Store. With credit authorization, searches, and quality ranking, these shops rank among the best offerings in e-commerce.

The openness to small businesses is fundamental because they are the foundation of our various economies, even though they seldom make it to the front page of magazines.

However, as explained in previous chapters, until recently e-commerce on the Internet was geared toward business-to-consumer (B2C) activities. Indeed, any business can open shop on Amazon, but having an Internet shop doesn't make sense when you're manufacturing windshields sold directly to automakers in Detroit!

The needs of business-to-business (B2B) e-commerce are different from those of B2C and are geared toward large-volume, more stable relationships, and a streamlined and more efficient procurement.

To put it simply, it is not effective for a car manufacturer to hire an army of Web surfers to click the online shops of its various suppliers. Instead, the manufacturer will look for a more integrated solution, ideally a product that integrates with its ERP solution. Ideally, it's the ERP package that does the clicking.

I call this "browsing on autopilot." Instead of asking a user to sit and click, the software simulates the clicking automatically. Obviously, the software must be capable of decoding the responses from the server, and the structure-centric XML is simply a better markup language for this application than presentation-centric HTML.

## A Commercial Transaction

It would not be possible to build a complete marketplace in one chapter. Indeed, such a solution needs to be very flexible and support many activities—from procurement to payment to shipping to much more.

Figure 7.1 illustrates how a company can buy goods from another electronically.

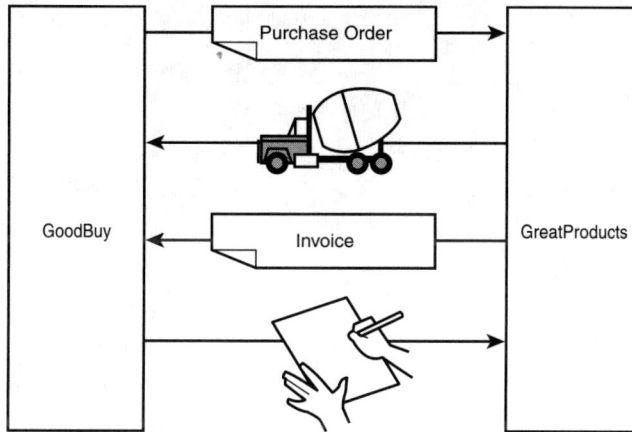

**Figure 7.1** A transaction means several interactions and just as much paperwork!

The transaction includes the following steps:

1. The buyer (GoodBuy) issues a purchase order.

2. The supplier (GreatProducts) checks the purchase order. It could approve or reject it. Not rejecting it is typically taken for approval.

3. GreatProducts manufactures the goods and delivers them through a shipper (NiceTruck).

4. GreatProducts invoices GoodBuy.

5. After receiving the goods and checking the invoice, GoodBuy pays GreatProducts.

This example has many simplifications, and many options are not covered in it. For example, it does not show how the two organizations start their relationship: typically terms and conditions must be agreed upon, including payment terms.

Furthermore, it hides the relationship between the shipper and the bank. Typically, the shipper issues bills of lading, packing lists, and its own invoices.

Also, payment can be electronic, by check, or by other means. In the U.S. checks are very popular, but other countries have different preferences. For example, in Belgium, most payments are by direct transfer between accounts.

Finally, this scenario applies to goods but doesn't cover services.

As you can see, there are probably as many variations as there are businesses, and a good e-commerce product accounts for these variations. In this chapter, we will concentrate on a few steps in the transaction, which clearly illustrate how to use XML (see Figure 7.2).

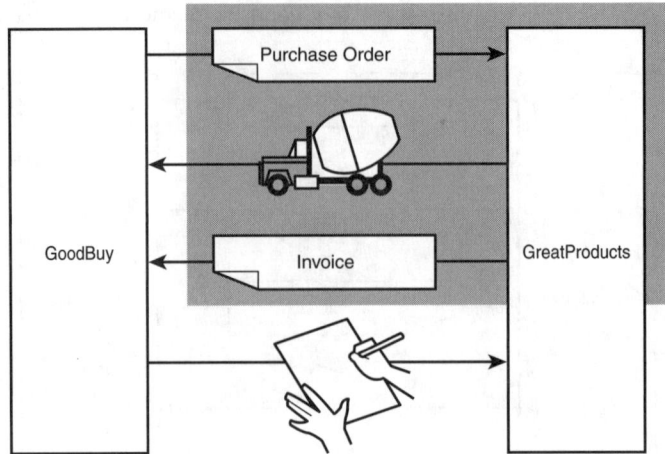

**Figure 7.2** This chapter concentrates on ordering and invoicing.

## Architecture

So far, most chapters have included a UML model of the application under development. However, in this chapter, the application consists of two servlets, several style sheets, and one HTML page, so a class diagram is not helpful. Figure 7.3 illustrates the various pieces and their relationships.

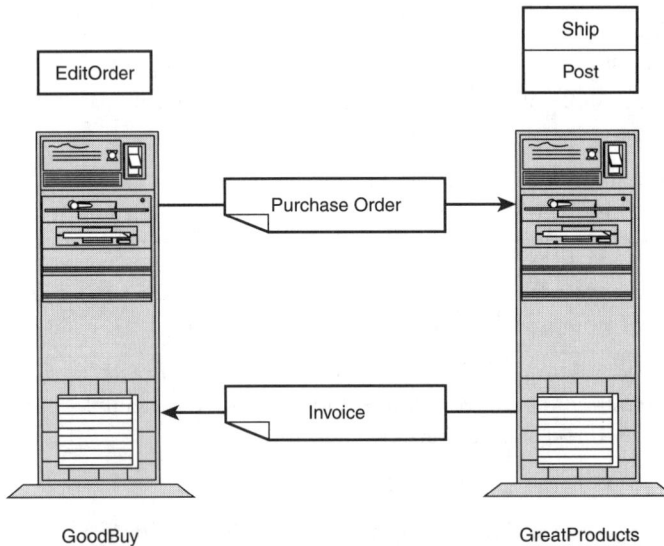

**Figure 7.3** The various components of the e-commerce application.

The tree applications are as follows:

- `Post`—A servlet to accept XML documents, such as orders and invoices. You can think of it as an XML shopping cart.
- `Ship`—A servlet to prepare invoices, after the goods have been shipped.
- `EditOrder`—An JavaScript application to create orders.

## XML Modeling

The main challenge when building an e-commerce solution with XML is not programming but the creation of good, stable, and complete data models. The programming is straightforward.

The challenge is that you're modeling documents to use within and outside your organization. This impacts modeling in the following ways:

- The model must be well thought-out to cover the needs of all the parties.
- The model must be thoroughly documented because it will be widely distributed.

Let's look at the first requirement: the need to account for third-party needs. When modeling documents for internal applications, you are concerned with only your own business. If your business needs a tag, you add it. Conversely, if you never use certain tags, you toss them.

This, however, is not true with e-commerce. The documents must account for your needs as well as the needs of your customers or suppliers.

Let's look at an example: In the textile industry, vendors use sizes (such as small, medium, and large T-shirts). Their orders, invoices, packing lists, catalogs, and other documents include size information. Therefore, they need a `<Size>` tag. However, this need is specific to the textile industry.

If yours is a pharmaceutical company, you typically wouldn't include a `<Size>` tag in your document. But what happens when you order gloves for the lab?

Likewise, requirements vary in an international context. The address is a good example—U.S. addresses include a state (or province in Canada). There's no such thing in many other countries.

When we turn to the second requirement, documentation, we hit a very costly, and often underestimated, issue. The ultimate purpose of this exercise is to communicate. When you adopt an XML model, you want your partners (customers and suppliers) to understand it.

The alternatives are either to offer expensive support in the form of corporate training and assistance to development or to develop top-notch documentation. Although developing quality documentation is expensive, it is cheaper in the long run.

To save themselves some work, many organizations turn to existing models developed by standard bodies or vendors. Oasis runs a repository of XML models, available online from xml.org. A quick search for invoices turns up a dozen hits by the likes of Commerce One, cXML.org, IBM, and Visa.

If you nevertheless decide to model your own documents, be sure your team includes experienced modelers, preferably with experience modeling open systems, and technical writers.

I also recommend working in a high-level modeling language, such as UML. UML models buy you a certain level of independence from XML. It makes it easier to design and maintain the documents.

Furthermore, UML was designed for communication. It is a universal language readily understood by all developers. It won't save you from serious technical writing, but it will reduce the effort.

In this chapter, we'll use simplified models for the order and invoice. In UML, they look similar to Figures 7.4 and 7.5. Listing 7.1 is a sample order. As you can see, there's nothing fancy here: just a list of products.

**Warning**

You will notice that this order differs from the order introduced in Chapter 6, "Import from Any Format." That order was modeled after the EDIFACT order. The order in this chapter was modeled independently and aims to be as simple as possible. In practice, as discussed in the next section, you will find that you must deal with different documents.

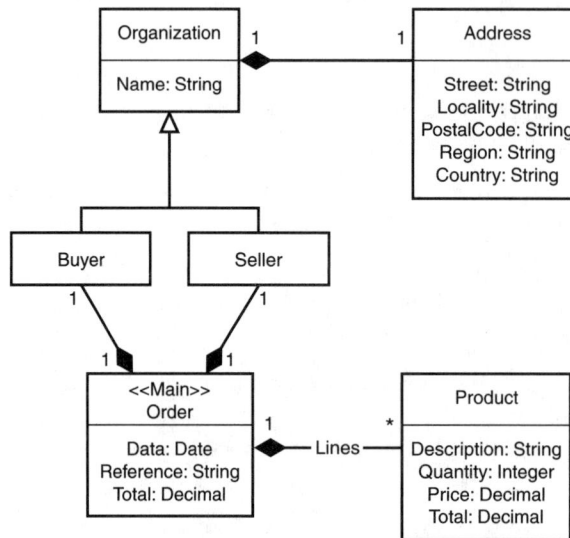

**Figure 7.4** A model for a simple purchase order.

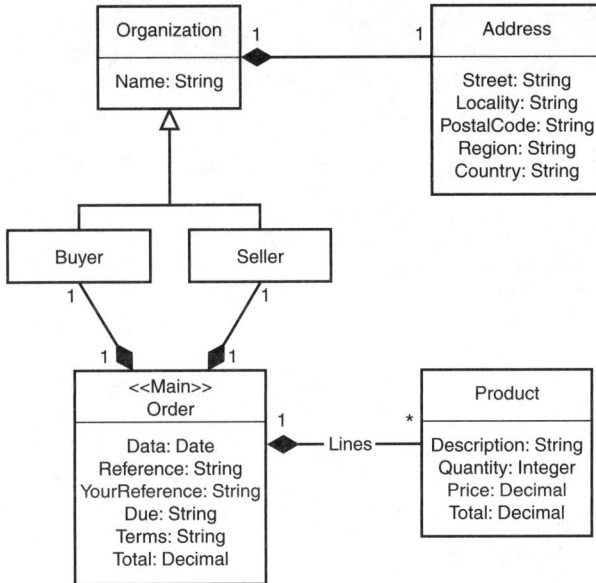

**Figure 7.5** A model for a simple invoice.

---

Listing 7.1 **A Simple Purchase Order in XML**

```xml
<?xml version="1.0"?><Order>
   <Date>2000-03-31</Date>
   <Reference>AGL153</Reference>
   <Buyer>
      <Name>Playfield Books</Name>
      <Address>
         <Street>34 Fountain Square Plaza</Street>
         <Locality>Cincinnati</Locality>
         <PostalCode>45202</PostalCode>
         <Region>OH</Region>
         <Country>US</Country>
      </Address>
   </Buyer>
   <Seller>
      <Name>QUE</Name>
      <Address>
         <Street>201 West 103RD Street</Street>
         <Locality>Indianapolis</Locality>
         <PostalCode>46290</PostalCode>
         <Region>IN</Region>
         <Country>US</Country>
      </Address>
   </Seller>
   <Lines>
```

Listing 7.1 **Continued**

```
        <Product>
            <Description>XML by Example</Description>
            <Quantity>5</Quantity>
            <Price>24.99</Price>
            <Total>124.95</Total>
        </Product>
        <Product>
            <Description>Applied XML Solutions</Description>
            <Quantity>10</Quantity>
            <Price>44.99</Price>
            <Total>449.90</Total>
        </Product>
    </Lines>
    <Total>574.85</Total>
</Order>
```

# The Post Manager

Post is the first software installed at the seller site. It consists of a servlet and a style sheet.

## Accepting Post

The servlet is presented in Listing 7.2. It waits for POST requests for XML documents and stores them in a database.

Listing 7.2 *Post.java*

```
package com.psol.xcommerce;

import java.io.*;
import java.sql.*;
import org.xml.sax.*;
import javax.servlet.*;
import javax.servlet.http.*;
import org.apache.xalan.xslt.*;

public class Post
    extends HttpServlet
{
    public void init()
        throws ServletException
    {
        try
        {
            Class.forName(getInitParameter("driver"));
        }
```

Listing 7.2 **Continued**

```
      catch(ClassNotFoundException e)
      {
          throw new ServletException(e);
      }
  }

  protected String style(String document,
                         String stylesheet)
     throws IOException, SAXException
  {

     XSLTProcessor processor =
        XSLTProcessorFactory.getProcessor();
     XSLTInputSource source =
        new XSLTInputSource(new StringReader(document));
     XSLTInputSource styleSheet =
        new XSLTInputSource(new FileInputStream(stylesheet));
     StringWriter writer = new StringWriter();
     XSLTResultTarget target = new XSLTResultTarget(writer);
     processor.process(source,styleSheet,target);
     return writer.toString();
  }

  public void doPost(HttpServletRequest request,
                     HttpServletResponse response)
     throws IOException
  {
     Writer writer = response.getWriter();
     response.setContentType("text/xml");
     try
     {
        String original = request.getParameter("document"),
               address = request.getParameter("address");
        String url = getInitParameter("url"),
               username = getInitParameter("username"),
               password = getInitParameter("password"),
               stylesheet = getInitParameter("stylesheet");
        Connection connection =
           DriverManager.getConnection(url,username,password);
        try
        {
           PreparedStatement stmt =
              connection.prepareStatement("insert into " +
                   "documents (original, document, address, new) " +
                   "values (?,?,?,true)");
           try
           {
              stmt.setString(1,original);
              if(stylesheet != null)
              {
                 String document = style(original,stylesheet);
                 stmt.setString(2,document);
              }
```

Listing 7.2 **Continued**

```
                        else
                            stmt.setNull(2,Types.VARCHAR);
                        stmt.setString(3,address);
                        stmt.executeUpdate();
                        connection.commit();
                    }
                    finally
                    {
                        stmt.close();
                    }
                    writer.write("<result error='false'>ok</result>");
                }
                finally
                {
                    connection.close();
                }
            }
        }
        catch(SQLException e)
        {
            writer.write("<result error='true'><![CDATA[");
            writer.write(e.getMessage());
            writer.write("]]></result>");
        }
        catch(SAXException e)
        {
            writer.write("<result error='true'><![CDATA[");
            writer.write(e.getMessage());
            writer.write("]]></result>");
        }
        writer.flush();
    }
}
```

The servlet expects two parameters: the XML document itself and a return address. The return address will be used to send invoices and other documents related to this order:

```
String original = request.getParameter("document"),
       address = request.getParameter("address");
```

Usually, a company has several customers. So, in practice, not all these customers will use the same XML documents. Some might use the invoice model introduced previously, while others might use completely different models. Furthermore, even if everybody uses the same format, different versions will coexist. This is illustrated in Figure 7.6.

The easiest solution to dealing with this multitude of formats is to convert them to the company's own format as soon as they are received. So only one conversion is necessary, upon receiving the message.

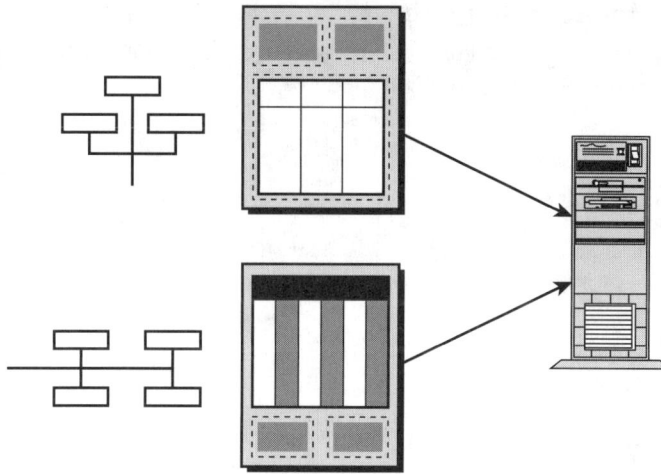

**Figure 7.6** You face a multitude of slightly different variations.

Therefore, the servlet starts by applying a style sheet. It also stores the document twice—in its original form and in the converted version. It is good practice to store the document as you received it, in case of later disputes:

```
stmt.setString(1,original);
if(stylesheet != null)
{
   String document = style(original,stylesheet);
   stmt.setString(2,document);
}
else
   stmt.setNull(2,Types.VARCHAR);
stmt.setString(3,address);
stmt.executeUpdate();
connection.commit();
```

**Note**

An alternative would be to parse the document and extract useful information, as we saw in Chapter 1, "Lightweight Data Storage." However, it is still advisable to store the original XML document, in case of later disputes.

Finally, the servlet returns an XML document to indicate success or failure:

```
writer.write("<result error='false'>ok</result>");
```

**Tip**

A simple solution to enable security is to activate HTTP username/password on the Web server.

## The Post Manager Style Sheet

The conversion style sheet is illustrated in Listing 7.3. It outputs an XML document; this is a conversion between two XML models.

Listing 7.3  *tointernal.xsl*

```
<?xml version="1.0"?>

<xsl:stylesheet xmlns:xsl="http://www.w3.org/1999/XSL/Transform"
                version="1.0">

<xsl:output method="xml"/>

<xsl:template match="/Order">
   <Order>
      <xsl:apply-templates select="@*|node()" mode="identity"/>
   </Order>
</xsl:template>

<xsl:template match="@*|node()" mode="identity">
  <xsl:copy>
     <xsl:apply-templates select="@*|node()" mode="identity"/>
  </xsl:copy>
</xsl:template>

<xsl:template match="/PurchaseOrder">
   <Order>
      <Date><xsl:value-of select="PODate"/></Date>
      <Reference><xsl:value-of select="Reference"/></Reference>
      <Buyer>
         <Name><xsl:value-of select="From/Company"/></Name>
         <Address>
            <Street><xsl:value-of
               select="From/Address"/></Street>
            <Locality><xsl:value-of
               select="From/City"/></Locality>
            <PostalCode><xsl:value-of
               select="From/ZIP"/></PostalCode>
            <Region><xsl:value-of
               select="From/StateProvince"/></Region>
            <Country>US</Country>
         </Address>
      </Buyer>
      <Seller>
         <Name><xsl:value-of select="To/Company"/></Name>
         <Address>
            <Street><xsl:value-of
               select="To/Address"/></Street>
            <Locality><xsl:value-of
               select="To/City"/></Locality>
            <PostalCode><xsl:value-of
```

Listing 7.3 **Continued**

```
                    select="To/ZIP"/></PostalCode>
                <Region><xsl:value-of
                    select="To/StateProvince"/></Region>
                <Country>US</Country>
            </Address>
        </Seller>
        <Lines>
            <xsl:for-each select="Books/Book">
                <xsl:variable name="quantity"
                            select="Unit"/>
                <xsl:variable name="price"
                            select="Price"/>
                <Product>
                    <Description><xsl:value-of
                        select="Title"/></Description>
                    <Quantity><xsl:value-of
                        select="$quantity"/></Quantity>
                    <Price><xsl:value-of
                        select="$price"/></Price>
                    <Total><xsl:value-of
        select="format-number($quantity * $price,'#0.00')"/></Total>
                </Product>
            </xsl:for-each>
        </Lines>
        <Total><xsl:value-of select="ToPay"/></Total>
    </Order>
</xsl:template>

</xsl:stylesheet>
```

The style sheet uses template matches to control the conversion. This single style sheet can convert between any number of XML documents. The following template matches the seller's own format (it simply copies the document unmodified):

```
<xsl:template match="/Order">
    <Order>
        <xsl:apply-templates select="@*|node()" mode="identity"/>
    </Order>
</xsl:template>
```

But this template matches a different structure:

```
<xsl:template match="/PurchaseOrder">
    <Order>
        <Date><xsl:value-of select="PODate"/></Date>
        <Reference><xsl:value-of select="Reference"/></Reference>
        <!-- some part deleted -->
```

**Note**

The selection procedure can be more involved. Remember that a `match` attribute can contain any XPath. For example, matching an element, its namespace, and the value of one of its attributes is as simple as

```
<xsl:template match="/xmli:PurchaseOrder[@version='1.0']">
<!-- template deleted -->

<xsl:template match="/xmli:PurchaseOrder[@version='2.0']">
<!-- template deleted -->
```

**Tip**

If writing many style sheets, you should acquire a visual XSL editor. For example, XSL Editor, from IBM (illustrated in Figure 7.7) has a drag-and-drop editor that greatly simplifies editing the style sheet. At the time of writing, XSL Editor is in pre-release and available from www.alphaworks.ibm.com. IBM will probably turn it into a commercial product, however.

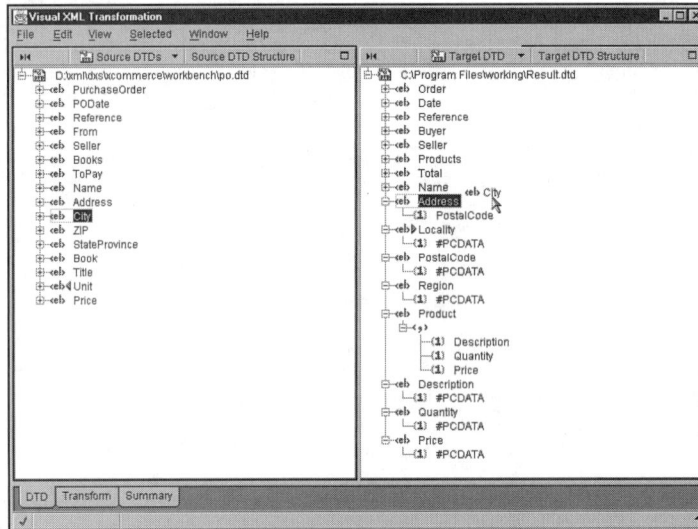

**Figure 7.7** Editing a style sheet is as simple as dragging and dropping elements.

**Tip**

To learn more about accepting non-XML documents, such as EDI orders, see Chapter 5, "Export to Any Format," and Chapter 6.

## The Customer's End

The customer will have its own application to generate orders. The application is typically integrated with the ERP solution. However, in this chapter, we won't write an ERP package for the sake of demonstrating integration. Instead, we'll use a simple JavaScript-based editor (see Listing 7.8).

> **Warning**
>
> The JavaScript editor is a simplification. In practice, the buyer probably relies on a solution that is integrated with its own ERP package. However, in this chapter, we concentrate on the merchant, not the customer.

Listing 7.8 *editorder.html*

```
<HTML>
<HEAD><TITLE>Order</TITLE>
<SCRIPT LANGUAGE="JavaScript"><!--
var products = new Array();

function addProduct(form)
{
   // collects data from the form
   var title = form.title.value,
       quantity = form.quantity.value,
       price = form.price.value;

   doAddProduct(form,title,quantity,price);
}

function doAddProduct(form,title,quantity,price)
{
   var productList = form.productlist,
       product = new Product(title,quantity,price);

   // arrays are zero-based so products.length points
   // to one past the latest product
   // JavaScript automatically allocates memory
   var pos = products.length;
   products[pos] = product;

   var option = new Option(title + " (" + price + ")",pos);

   productList.options[productList.length] = option;
}

function deleteProduct(form)
{
   var productList = form.productlist,
       pos = productList.selectedIndex;
```

Listing 7.8 **Continued**

```
    if(pos != -1)
    {
        var product = productList.options[pos].value;
        productList.options[pos] = null;
        products[product] = null;
    }
}

function exportProduct(form)
{
    var books = "";

    var i,
        total = 0;
    for(i = 0;i < products.length;i++)
        if(products[i] != null)
        {
            books += products[i].toXML();
            total += products[i].quantity * products[i].price;
        }

    books = element("Books",books);

    var from = element("Company",escapeXML(form.company.value));
    from += element("Address",escapeXML(form.street.value));
    from += element("City",escapeXML(form.city.value));
    from += element("ZIP",escapeXML(form.zip.value));
    from += element("StateProvince",escapeXML(form.state.value));
    from = element("From",from);

    var to = "<To><Company>QUE</Company>";
    to += "<Address>201 West 103RD Street</Address>";
    to += "<City>Indianapolis</City>";
    to += "<ZIP>46290</ZIP>";
    to += "<StateProvince>IN</StateProvince></To>";

    var header = element("PODate",escapeXML(form.date.value));
    header += element("Reference",
                        escapeXML(form.reference.value));

    var toPay = element("ToPay",escapeXML(String(total)));

    var doc = element("PurchaseOrder",
                        header + from + to + books + toPay);

    form.document.value = "<?xml version='1.0'?>" + doc;
}

function element(name,content)
{
```

Listing 7.8 **Continued**

```
   var result = "<" + name + ">";
   result += content;
   result += "</" + name + ">\r";
   return result;
}

function escapeXML(string)
{
   var result = "",
       i,
       c;
   for(i = 0;i < string.length;i++)
   {
      c = string.charAt(i);
      if(c == '<')
         result += "&lt;";
      else if(c == '&')
         result += "&amp;";
      else
         result += c;
   }
   return result;
}

// declares product object

function Product(title,quantity,price)
{
   this.title = title;
   this.quantity = quantity;
   this.price = price;
   this.toXML = product_toXML;
}

function product_toXML()
{
   var result = element("Title",escapeXML(this.title));
   result += element("Unit",escapeXML(this.quantity));
   result += element("Price",escapeXML(this.price));
   return element("Book",result);
}

function load(form)
{
   doAddProduct(form,"XML by Example","5","24.99");
   doAddProduct(form,"Applied XML Solutions","10","44.99");
}
// --></SCRIPT>
</HEAD>
<BODY ONLOAD="load(document.controls)">
```

Listing 7.8 **Continued**

```
<CENTER>
    <FORM NAME="controls" METHOD="POST"
            ACTION="http://localhost:8080/post">
        Title: <INPUT TYPE="TEXT" NAME="title"><BR>
        Quantity: <INPUT TYPE="TEXT" NAME="quantity"><BR>
        Price: <INPUT TYPE="TEXT" NAME="price"><BR>
        <SELECT NAME="productlist" SIZE="5"
                WIDTH="250"></SELECT><BR>
        <INPUT TYPE="BUTTON" VALUE="Add"
                ONCLICK="addProduct(controls)">
        <INPUT TYPE="BUTTON" VALUE="Delete"
                ONCLICK="deleteProduct(controls)"><BR>
        Date: <INPUT TYPE="TEXT" NAME="date"
                        VALUE="2000-03-31"><BR>
        Reference: <INPUT TYPE="TEXT" NAME="reference"
                        VALUE="AGL153"><BR>
        Company: <INPUT TYPE="TEXT" NAME="company"
                        VALUE="Books and More"><BR>
        Address: <INPUT TYPE="TEXT" NAME="street"
                        VALUE="43 Fountain Street"><BR>
        City: <INPUT TYPE="TEXT" NAME="city"
                    VALUE="Cincinnati"><BR>
        ZIP: <INPUT TYPE="TEXT" NAME="zip" VALUE="45202"><BR>
        State/Province: <INPUT TYPE="TEXT" NAME="state"
                            VALUE="OH"><BR>
        Return address: <INPUT TYPE="TEXT"
                            VALUE="http://localhost:8081"
                            NAME="address"><BR>
        <INPUT TYPE="SUBMIT" VALUE="Post"
                ONCLICK="exportProduct(controls)">
        <INPUT TYPE="HIDDEN" NAME="document">
    </FORM>
    </CENTER>
</BODY></HTML>
```

This Web page is a poor man's editor for purchase order. It is illustrated in Figure 7.8.

**Note**

This editor is written in portable JavaScript. It does not rely on the availability of an XML parser, so it should run with most browsers.

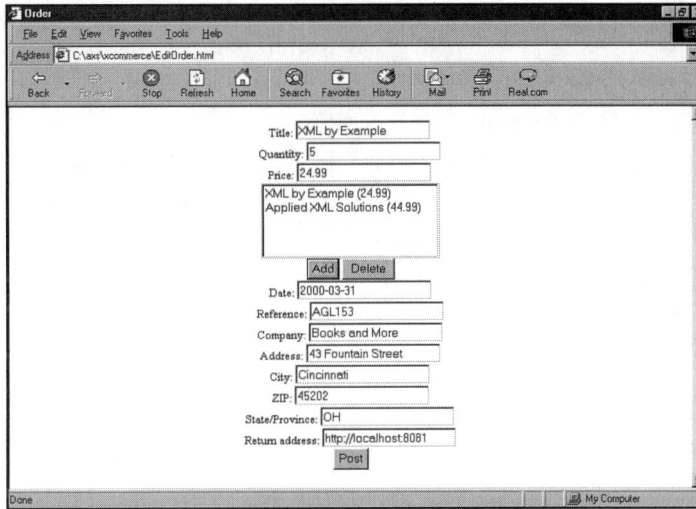

**Figure 7.8**  The editor to create and edit purchase orders.

Let's review Listing 7.8 step by step. The script maintains an array of `Product` objects, where `Products` have a title, quantity, and price:

```
function Product(title,quantity,price)
{
   this.title = title;
   this.quantity = quantity;
   this.price = price;
   this.toXML = product_toXML;
}
```

The script uses functions to add and remove products from the array. The functions take care to synchronize the display, in the HTML form, and the content of the array:

```
function doAddProduct(form,title,quantity,price)
{
   var productList = form.productlist,
      product = new Product(title,quantity,price);

   // arrays are zero-based so products.length points
   // to one past the latest product
   // JavaScript automatically allocates memory
   var pos = products.length;
   products[pos] = product;

   var option = new Option(title + " (" + price + ")",pos);

   productList.options[productList.length] = option;
}
```

To send the purchase order, the script writes the corresponding XML document in a hidden field of the form. The content of the form is posted to the server by the Web browser and, of course, includes the hidden field and XML document:

```
function exportProduct(form)
{
    var books = "";

    var i,
        total = 0;
    for(i = 0;i < products.length;i++)
        if(products[i] != null)
        {
            books += products[i].toXML();
            total += products[i].quantity * products[i].price;
        }

    books = element("Books",books);

    var from = element("Company",escapeXML(form.company.value));
    from += element("Address",escapeXML(form.street.value));
    from += element("City",escapeXML(form.city.value));
    from += element("ZIP",escapeXML(form.zip.value));
    from += element("StateProvince",escapeXML(form.state.value));
    from = element("From",from);

    var to = "<To><Company>QUE</Company>";
    to += "<Address>201 West 103RD Street</Address>";
    to += "<City>Indianapolis</City>";
    to += "<ZIP>46290</ZIP>";
    to += "<StateProvince>IN</StateProvince></To>";

    var header = element("PODate",escapeXML(form.date.value));
    header += element("Reference",
                      escapeXML(form.reference.value));

    var toPay = element("ToPay",escapeXML(String(total)));

    var doc = element("PurchaseOrder",
                      header + from + to + books + toPay);

    form.document.value = "<?xml version='1.0'?>" + doc;
}
```

## Sending the Invoice

After shipping the goods, the seller prepares an invoice for the buyer. We'll write a simple application that relies on XSLT to prepare the invoice. The main point of this section is to illustrate how to build the browser on autopilot, as I mentioned previously. Indeed, this application generates an XML document (the invoice) and sends it automatically on behalf of the user. The code for the servlet is in Listing 7.9.

Listing 7.9 *Ship.java*

```java
package com.psol.xcommerce;

import java.io.*;
import java.net.*;
import java.sql.*;
import java.text.*;
import org.xml.sax.*;
import javax.servlet.*;
import javax.servlet.http.*;
import org.xml.sax.helpers.*;
import org.apache.xalan.xslt.*;

public class Ship
   extends HttpServlet
{
   public void init()
      throws ServletException
   {
      try
      {
         Class.forName(getInitParameter("driver"));
      }
      catch(ClassNotFoundException e)
      {
         throw new ServletException(e);
      }
   }

   protected void style(String document,
                        String stylesheet,
                        Writer writer,
                        String id,
                        String servletPath)
      throws IOException, SAXException
   {
      XSLTProcessor processor =
         XSLTProcessorFactory.getProcessor();
      XSLTInputSource source =
         new XSLTInputSource(new StringReader(document));
      XSLTInputSource styleSheet =
         new XSLTInputSource(new FileInputStream(stylesheet));
      XSLTResultTarget target = new XSLTResultTarget(writer);
      processor.setStylesheetParam("id",'\'' + id + '\'');
      processor.setStylesheetParam("servletPath",
                                    '\'' + servletPath +'\'');
      processor.process(source,styleSheet,target);
   }

   protected String style(String document,
                          String stylesheet,
```

Listing 7.9 **Continued**

```java
                                String id)
        throws IOException, SAXException
    {
        XSLTProcessor processor =
            XSLTProcessorFactory.getProcessor();
        XSLTInputSource source =
            new XSLTInputSource(new StringReader(document));
        XSLTInputSource styleSheet =
            new XSLTInputSource(new FileInputStream(stylesheet));
        StringWriter writer = new StringWriter();
        XSLTResultTarget target = new XSLTResultTarget(writer);
        processor.setStylesheetParam("id",'\'' + id + '\'');
        SimpleDateFormat formatter =
            new SimpleDateFormat("yyyy-MM-dd");
        processor.setStylesheetParam("date",'\'' +
                    formatter.format(new java.util.Date()) + '\'');
        processor.process(source,styleSheet,target);
        return writer.toString();
    }

    protected void writeOrder(Connection connection,
                              String id,
                              Writer writer,
                              String servletPath)
        throws SQLException, SAXException, IOException
    {
        PreparedStatement stmt =
            connection.prepareStatement("select document from " +
                                        "documents where id=?");
        try
        {
            stmt.setString(1,id);
            ResultSet rs = stmt.executeQuery();
            try
            {
                if(rs.next())
                    style(rs.getString(1),
                            "stylesheet/toconfirm.xsl",
                            writer,
                            id,
                            servletPath);
            }
            finally
            {
                rs.close();
            }
        }
        finally
        {
            stmt.close();
        }
    }
```

Listing 7.9 **Continued**

```java
protected void writeList(Connection connection,
                         Writer writer,
                         String servletPath)
    throws IOException, SQLException
{
    Statement stmt = connection.createStatement();
    try
    {
        ResultSet rs = stmt.executeQuery("select id " +
                            "from documents where new=true");
        try
        {
            writer.write("<HTML><HEAD><TITLE>Shipping");
            writer.write("</TITLE></HEAD><BODY>");
            writer.write("<H1>Choose an order</H1><UL>");
            while(rs.next())
            {
                writer.write("<LI><A HREF=\"");
                writer.write(servletPath);
                writer.write("?id=");
                writer.write(rs.getString(1));
                writer.write("\">order #");
                writer.write(rs.getString(1));
                writer.write("</A></LI>");
            }
            writer.write("</UL></BODY></HTML>");
        }
        finally
        {
            rs.close();
        }
    }
    finally
    {
        stmt.close();
    }
}

protected void postInvoice(String document,
                           String id,
                           String post)
    throws IOException, SAXException
{
    String toPost = style(document,
                          "stylesheet/toinvoice.xsl",
                          id);
    URL url = new URL(post);
    HttpURLConnection connection =
        (HttpURLConnection)url.openConnection();
    connection.setRequestProperty("Content-type",
        "application/x-www-form-urlencoded");
```

Listing 7.9 **Continued**

```
            connection.setRequestProperty("Accept:","text/xml");
            connection.setRequestMethod("POST");
            connection.setDoOutput(true);
            connection.setDoInput(true);
            OutputStream os = connection.getOutputStream();
            os.write(new String("document=").getBytes());
            os.write(URLEncoder.encode(toPost).getBytes());
            connection.connect();
            XMLReader reader =
                XMLReaderFactory.createXMLReader(
                    "org.apache.xerces.parsers.SAXParser");
            reader.setContentHandler(new DefaultHandler()
            {
                public void startElement(String namespaceURI,
                                         String localName,
                                         String rawName,
                                         Attributes atts)
                    throws SAXException
                {
                    if(rawName.equals("result"))
                    {
                        String att = atts.getValue("error");
                        if(att == null || !att.equalsIgnoreCase("false"))
                            throw new SAXException("Error during POST");
                    }
                }
            });
            reader.parse(new InputSource(connection.getInputStream()));
        }

        public void doGet(HttpServletRequest request,
                          HttpServletResponse response)
            throws IOException
        {
            Writer writer = response.getWriter();
            try
            {
                String url = getInitParameter("url"),
                       username = getInitParameter("username"),
                       password = getInitParameter("password");
                Connection connection =
                    DriverManager.getConnection(url,username,password);
                try
                {
                    String id = request.getParameter("id");
                    if(null != id && id.length() != 0)
                        writeOrder(connection,
                                   id,
                                   writer,
                                   request.getServletPath());
                    else
```

Listing 7.9  **Continued**

```
                    writeList(connection,
                             writer,
                             request.getServletPath());
        }
        finally
        {
           connection.close();
        }
     }
     catch(SQLException e)
     {
        response.sendError(
           HttpServletResponse.SC_INTERNAL_SERVER_ERROR,
           e.getMessage());
     }
     catch(SAXException e)
     {
        response.sendError(
           HttpServletResponse.SC_INTERNAL_SERVER_ERROR,
           e.getMessage());
     }
  }

  public void doPost(HttpServletRequest request,
                     HttpServletResponse response)
     throws IOException
  {
     Writer writer = response.getWriter();
     try
     {
        String id = request.getParameter("id"),
               approved = request.getParameter("approved"),
               url = getInitParameter("url"),
               username = getInitParameter("username"),
               password = getInitParameter("password"),
               post = getInitParameter("post");
        Connection connection =
           DriverManager.getConnection(url,username,password);
        try
        {
        PreparedStatement stmt =
           connection.prepareStatement("select document, " +
              "address from documents where id=?");
        try
        {
           stmt.setString(1,id);
           ResultSet rs = stmt.executeQuery();
           try
           {
              if(rs.next())
```

Listing 7.9  **Continued**

```
                        postInvoice(rs.getString(1),
                                    id,
                                    rs.getString(2));
            }
            finally
            {
                rs.close();
            }
        }
        finally
        {
            stmt.close();
        }
        stmt = connection.prepareStatement("update " +
                "documents set new=false where id=?");
        try
        {
            stmt.setString(1,id);
            stmt.executeUpdate();
            connection.commit();
        }
        finally
        {
            stmt.close();
        }
        writer.write("<HTML><HEAD><TITLE>Payment " +
            "confirmation</TITLE></HEAD><BODY><P> " +
            "Successfully paid!<P><A HREF=\'");
        writer.write(request.getServletPath());
        writer.write("\'>Go to list</A></BODY></HTML>");
    }
    finally
    {
        connection.close();
    }
}
catch(SQLException e)
{
    response.sendError(
        HttpServletResponse.SC_INTERNAL_SERVER_ERROR,
        e.getMessage());
}
catch(SAXException e)
{
    response.sendError(
        HttpServletResponse.SC_INTERNAL_SERVER_ERROR,
        e.getMessage());
}
    }
}
```

This servlet accepts both GET and POST requests. In response to a GET request, it displays the list of invoices (see Figure 7.9) or the details of a given invoice (see Figure 7.10). The former reads data from the database, whereas the latter applies a style sheet to an invoice.

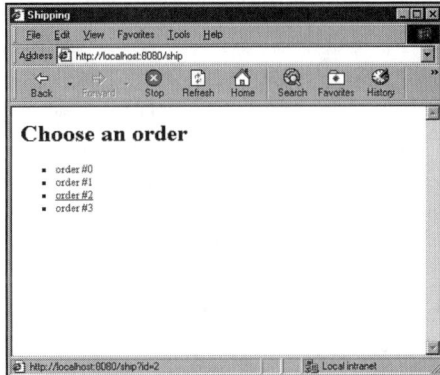

**Figure 7.9** The list of invoices.

**Figure 7.10** Details of one invoice.

The heart of this servlet is the postInvoice() method, which is called in response to the user clicking the Has been shipped button.

The method is roughly divided into three steps. First, the application uses a style sheet to convert the order into an invoice. Both are XML documents, so a style sheet is a simple and effective solution to transform one into the other:

```
String toPost = style(document,
                      "stylesheet/toinvoice.xsl",
                      id);
```

Next, it posts the result using HttpURLConnection. HttpURLConnection, part of java.net, implements the HTTP protocol:

```
URL url = new URL(post);
HttpURLConnection connection =
   (HttpURLConnection)url.openConnection();
connection.setRequestProperty("Content-type",
   "application/x-www-form-urlencoded");
connection.setRequestProperty("Accept:","text/xml");
connection.setRequestMethod("POST");
connection.setDoOutput(true);
connection.setDoInput(true);
OutputStream os = connection.getOutputStream();
os.write(new String("document=").getBytes());
os.write(URLEncoder.encode(toPost).getBytes());
connection.connect();
```

Finally, it parses the result to test whether any errors have occurred:

```
XMLReader reader =
   XMLReaderFactory.createXMLReader(
      "org.apache.xerces.parsers.SAXParser");
reader.setContentHandler(new DefaultHandler()
{
   public void startElement(String namespaceURI,
                            String localName,
                            String rawName,
                            Attributes atts)
      throws SAXException
   {
      if(rawName.equals("result"))
      {
         String att = atts.getValue("error");
         if(att == null || !att.equalsIgnoreCase("false"))
            throw new SAXException("Error during POST");
      }
   }
});
reader.parse(new InputSource(connection.getInputStream()));
```

This is a prime example of a browser on autopilot. The application creates the document and posts it on behalf of the user. It even interprets the response.

> **Tip**
>
> To test this application, you'll need a server that accepts XML calls. The easiest solution is to run another copy of the Post servlet on a different server or on the same server but on a different port.

## Transforming Orders

The style sheet in Listing 7.10 is used to transform the order into an invoice.

Listing 7.10  *toinvoice.xsl*

```
<?xml version="1.0"?>

<xsl:stylesheet
   xmlns:xsl="http://www.w3.org/1999/XSL/Transform"
   version="1.0">

<xsl:output method="xml"/>

<xsl:param name="id"/>
<xsl:param name="date"/>

<xsl:template match="/Order">
<Invoice>
```

Listing 7.10  **Continued**

```xml
    <Reference><xsl:value-of select="$id"/></Reference>
    <YourReference><xsl:value-of
        select="Reference"/></YourReference>
    <Date><xsl:value-of select="$date"/></Date>
    <Due>30 days</Due>
    <Terms>Please make your check payable to Que.</Terms>
    <Seller>
        <Name>QUE</Name>
        <Address>
            <Street>201 West 103RD Street</Street>
            <Locality>Indianapolis</Locality>
            <PostalCode>46290</PostalCode>
            <Region>IN</Region>
            <Country>US</Country>
        </Address>
    </Seller>
    <Buyer>
        <Name><xsl:value-of select="Buyer/Name"/></Name>
        <Address>
            <Street><xsl:value-of
                select="Buyer/Address/Street"/></Street>
            <Locality><xsl:value-of
                select="Buyer/Address/Locality"/></Locality>
            <PostalCode><xsl:value-of
                select="Buyer/Address/PostalCode"/></PostalCode>
            <Region><xsl:value-of
                select="Buyer/Address/Region"/></Region>
            <Country><xsl:value-of
                select="Buyer/Address/Country"/></Country>
        </Address>
    </Buyer>
    <Lines>
        <xsl:for-each select="Lines/Product">
            <Product>
                <Description><xsl:value-of
                    select="Description"/></Description>
                <Quantity><xsl:value-of
                    select="Quantity"/></Quantity>
                <Price><xsl:value-of
                    select="Price"/></Price>
                <Total><xsl:value-of
                    select="Total"/></Total>
            </Product>
        </xsl:for-each>
    </Lines>
    <Total><xsl:value-of select="Total"/></Total>
</Invoice>
</xsl:template>

</xsl:stylesheet>
```

The only remarkable aspect of this style sheet is that it takes two parameters:

```
<xsl:param name="id"/>
<xsl:param name="date"/>
```

The `style()` method in `Ship` passes the parameter values to the style sheet:

```
SimpleDateFormat formatter = new SimpleDateFormat("yyyy-MM-dd");
processor.setStylesheetParam("date",'\'' +
    formatter.format(new java.util.Date()) + '\'');
```

> **Note**
>
> To improve the conversion, you could create extensions, as we used in Chapter 6, and validate the pricing against a database of products. As it stands, if the buyer sends an order with incorrect pricing, he will be invoiced with these prices, which might not be acceptable.

## Viewing Invoices

For completeness, Listing 7.11 is the style sheet `Ship` uses to display invoices. It also takes a parameter with the invoice number.

**Listing 7.11** *toconfirm.xsl*

```
<?xml version="1.0"?>

<xsl:stylesheet
    xmlns:xsl="http://www.w3.org/1999/XSL/Transform"
    xmlns="http://www.w3.org/TR/REC-html40"
    version="1.0">

<xsl:output method="html"
            encoding="ISO-8859-1"/>

<xsl:param name="id"/>

<xsl:template match="/Order">
    <HTML>
    <HEAD><TITLE>Order</TITLE></HEAD>
    <BODY><TABLE>
      <TR><TD><FORM ACTION="/ship" METHOD="POST">
        <INPUT TYPE="HIDDEN" NAME="id" VALUE="{$id}"/>
        <INPUT TYPE="SUBMIT" VALUE="Has been shipped"/>
      </FORM></TD>
      <TD><FORM ACTION="/ship" METHOD="GET">
        <INPUT TYPE="SUBMIT" VALUE="Will ship later"/>
      </FORM></TD></TR></TABLE>
      <TABLE><TR><TD COLSPAN="2" BGCOLOR="black">
        <FONT COLOR="white">Order</FONT></TD></TR>
      <TR><TD>Date:</TD>
```

Listing 7.11 **Continued**

```
            <TD><xsl:value-of select="Date"/></TD></TR>
        <TR><TD>Reference:</TD>
            <TD><xsl:value-of select="Reference"/></TD></TR>
        <TR><TD VALIGN="TOP">Seller:</TD>
            <TD>
                <xsl:value-of select="Seller/Name"/><BR/>
                <xsl:value-of select="Seller/Address/Street"/><BR/>
                <xsl:value-of select="Seller/Address/Locality"/>
                <xsl:if test="Seller/Address/Region">
                    <xsl:text>, </xsl:text>
                    <xsl:value-of select="Seller/Address/Region"/>
                </xsl:if>
                <xsl:text> </xsl:text>
                <xsl:value-of
                    select="Seller/Address/PostalCode"/><BR/>
                <xsl:value-of select="Seller/Address/Country"/>
            </TD></TR>
        <TR><TD VALIGN="TOP">Buyer:</TD>
            <TD>
                <xsl:value-of select="Buyer/Name"/><BR/>
                <xsl:value-of select="Buyer/Address/Street"/><BR/>
                <xsl:value-of select="Buyer/Address/Locality"/>
                <xsl:if test="Buyer/Address/Region">
                    <xsl:text>, </xsl:text>
                    <xsl:value-of select="Buyer/Address/Region"/>
                </xsl:if>
                <xsl:text> </xsl:text>
                <xsl:value-of
                    select="Buyer/Address/PostalCode"/><BR/>
                <xsl:value-of select="Buyer/Address/Country"/>
            </TD></TR>
    </TABLE><TABLE>
        <TR><TD>Qty</TD><TD>Description</TD>
            <TD>Price</TD><TD>Total</TD></TR>
        <xsl:for-each select="Lines/Product">
            <TR><TD><xsl:value-of select="Quantity"/></TD>
                <TD><xsl:value-of select="Description"/></TD>
                <TD><xsl:value-of select="Price"/></TD>
                <TD><xsl:value-of select="Total"/></TD></TR>
        </xsl:for-each>
        <TR>
            <TD><xsl:text
                disable-output-escaping="yes"> </xsl:text>
            </TD><TD><xsl:text
                disable-output-escaping="yes"> </xsl:text>
            </TD><TD><xsl:text
                disable-output-escaping="yes"> </xsl:text>
            </TD><TD><xsl:value-of select="Total"/></TD></TR>
    </TABLE></BODY></HTML>
</xsl:template>

</xsl:stylesheet>
```

# Building and Running the Project

The e-commerce project is available on the enclosed CD-ROM. Copy the project directory from the CD-ROM to your hard disk. Under Windows, start the server by double-clicking `server.bat`. Next double-click `PostOrder.html` to open it in a browser. Create one or more orders and send them to the supplier.

Now, point your browser to `http://localhost:8080/ship`, which is the address for the shipping application. Review the orders you have just created and confirm shipping. This will create invoices and post them to the buyer.

▶ **Warning**

This project uses Xalan 1.0 as the XSLT processor. If you're using another processor, you will need to adapt `Post` and `Ship`.

The project also uses Jetty as the Web server. However, because it is based on servlets, it should be easy to adapt to another Web server. You can add servlet support to most Web servers through JRun.

The project on the CD includes a database, but if you need to re-create it, you can use the following statement:

```
CREATE TABLE documents (id INTEGER IDENTITY,original VARCHAR,
↪document VARCHAR,address VARCHAR,new BIT);
```

Use Hypersonic SQL DatabaseManager to execute the statement. You must create two databases. To do so, follow these steps:

1. Select Hypersonic SQL Standalone.
2. The URL is `jdbc:HypersonicSQL:db/buyer`.
3. Issue the  previously mentioned `CREATE TABLE` statement.
4. Select File, Connect.
5. Select Hypersonic SQL Standalone.
6. The second URL is `jdbc:HypersonicSQL:db/buyer`.
7. Execute the statement again to create the second database.

▶ **Warning**

The project uses Hypersonic SQL for the database. Because Hypersonic SQL is a JDBC database, adapting it to other JDBC databases (including Access, Oracle, and SQL Server) should be easy.

# Additional Resources

In this chapter, we built a simple e-commerce application to illustrate browsing on autopilot and explored the use of XSL for conversion. The three cornerstones of the project are

- Good modeling of the XML document
- The ability to accept XML documents in a variety of formats but convert them to your internal format
- The ability to post requests automatically, in effect implementing a browser on autopilot

If you are looking for ready-made models, you can turn to any of the following:

- `www.rosettanet.org`—A group developing XML-based standards for e-commerce
- `www.ebxml.org`—A group developing an XML-based framework for e-commerce
- `www.xmledi.com`—A grassroots effort to promote the use of XML in e-commerce
- `www.ariba.com`—A vendor developing XML marketplaces
- `www.bolero.net`—An e-commerce marketplace for international trade

However, if you are looking for software, you should turn to the following:

- `www.iplanet.com`—Look for the ECXpert range of products, one of the most mature range of B2B e-commerce products.
- `www.commerceone.com`—A vendor of XML marketplace software.
- `www.webmethods.com`—A vendor of XML integration products.
- `www.mercator.com`—Another vendor of integration products.
- `www.neonsoft.com`—Another vendor of integration products.

# 8

# Organize Teamwork Between Developers and Designers

Over the years, the Web development team has grown in size and in sophistication. Although many Web sites are still the work of one person (the mythical Webmaster), companies increasingly rely on a multi-talented team to build and manage their Web sites.

The best teams employ many talents: not only graphic designers, HTML coders, and programmers, but also copywriters, Flash animators, marketers, sales consultants, translators, and sometimes even an ergonomist.

In practice, coordinating such a diverse team isn't always easy. In this chapter, you explore the use of XML and XSL as tools to separate the work of engineers (programmers and the like) from artistic personalities (designers). This separation matches the organization of many teams.

## Servlets and Teams

Servlets come in two shapes: the regular servlets, which inherit from classes in `javax.servlet.http`, and the newer Java Server Pages (JSP) located in the `javax.servlet.jsp` package.

However, regardless of their form, servlets suffer from mixing HTML and Java code. The following code sample illustrates the problem:

```
protected void doGet(HttpServletRequest request,
                        HttpServletResponse response)
    throws IOException
{
    Writer w = response.getWriter();
    String string = request.getParameter("string");
    w.write("<HTML><HEAD><TITLE>Upper Case</TITLE></HEAD>");
    w.write("<BODY><P>" + string + " in uppercase is <B>");
w.write(string.toUpperCase());
    w.write("</B></BODY></HTML>");
    w.flush();
}
```

This servlet is trivial, but it illustrates the mixing of Java and HTML code. The Java code implements the application logic and is the responsibility of engineers, whereas the HTML code deals with the look and feel of the application and is the responsibility of designers.

However, because of the mixing of Java and HTML, when the designer needs to change the look and feel, he must rely on the programmer. This causes much frustration because

- Designers often complain that developers are too slow to integrate their changes.
- Programmers would rather focus their energy on improving performance or adding new functions rather than on implementing so-called frivolous changes from designers.

In fact, the fundamental problem is that servlets, like CGI scripts and ASP, force a very close collaboration between two groups (designers and developers) who have different priorities. Understandably, designers are very concerned with presentation, while programmers concentrate on coding.

### Note

JSP does not solve this problem; it merely switches it around. Instead of having HTML in the middle of Java code, JSP places Java code right in the middle of HTML. Although writing JSP is often faster than writing regular servlets, it does not solve the fundamental problem of mixing HTML and Java.

In short, it's the old rivalry between engineers and artistic persons. The situation is particularly difficult in Web design because Web teams are under enormous pressure to deliver quickly.

## Creating an Interface

If you're reading this book, you are probably more like the Java programmers than the designers. In this chapter, you build a solution to cleanly separate your work (Java development) from the design work. The main goals are to

- Separate HTML and Java coding in the servlet
- Provide the designer with tools to modify the presentation without requiring the assistance of the programmer
- Allow the programmer to concentrate on the application logic

The solution is close to what you did in Chapter 4, "Content Syndication." In that chapter, you relied on a presentation-neutral XML document and used XSLT style sheets to produce the HTML. One of the major differences between that and what you'll do in this chapter is that the XML document will be dynamically generated by the servlet in this chapter.

In other words, the programmer will generate presentation-neutral XML code, while the designer will use XSLT to render it in an aesthetically pleasing layout. This provides a clear-cut separation between the two groups that mimics the organization of the team.

## Additional Benefits

Although the primary motivation to use XML was to improve the day-to-day working of the Web team, the technique outlined in this chapter is also very valuable in the following cases:

- A Web site revamping occurs and all the pages, including the servlets, must adopt the new look. However, programmers are typically busy working on new applications.
- An application is shared among different sites; each site has its own look and feel; and the servlet must support them all.
- Multilingual sites exist. For example, I live in Belgium where many sites are multilingual. In practice, accommodating the differences is difficult—French words are often longer than their English counterparts. This might force you to redesign the page to provide more room on the button bar.

# Using XSL in Servlets

The servlets need to output XML and call an XSLT processor to turn it into HTML. If every servlet is calling the XSLT processor, it makes sense to encapsulate this behavior in a library. The library, in this chapter, is called `XslServlet`.

## Encapsulating the XSL Processor

Figure 8.1 shows the UML class model for the library. The main classes are as follows:

- XslServlet—Extends HttpServlet and redirects HTTP requests to XSL-enhanced versions of doGet() and doPost().

- XslServletLiaison—An interface for an additional parameter of the XSL-enhanced version of doGet() and doPost(). As its name implies, it establishes the liaison with the XSLT processor.

- XslServletLiaisonImpl—An implementation of XslServletLiaison specialized for Xalan. If you're using another XSLT processor, you must provide another implementation of XslServletLiaison.

- XslWriter—Derived from PrintWriter, it provides helper methods to escape XML delimiters such as <.

- BugList and BugForm—Examples of servlets built with the XslServlet library. They inherit from XslServlet instead of inheriting directly from HttpServlet.

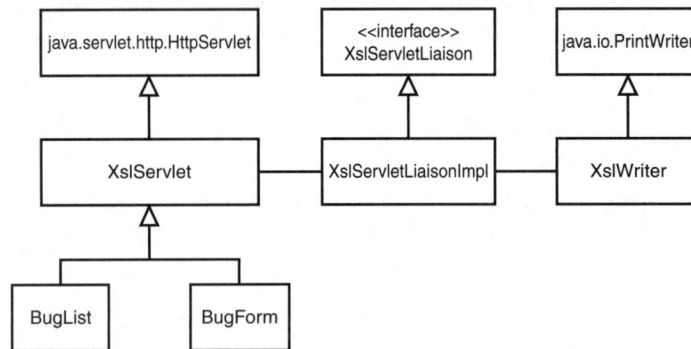

**Figure 8.1**  The XslServlet library encapsulates the XSL processor.

## Introducing Pesticide

To illustrate the use of XslServlet, you will write a Web-based bug tracker called Pesticide. Hopefully, the name will have a dissuasive effect on your code.

As always, your focus is on the application of XML, not on building an industrial-strength bug tracker. Therefore, some simplifications will be made:

- Bug descriptions are limited to the essentials—a name, description, programmer, and application name.

- No mechanism exists to add new applications or programmers, other than typing SQL commands.

- No workflow management exists to notify programmers when new bugs have appeared.

Figure 8.2 is Pesticide's main screen. As you can see, it centers on the list of bugs.

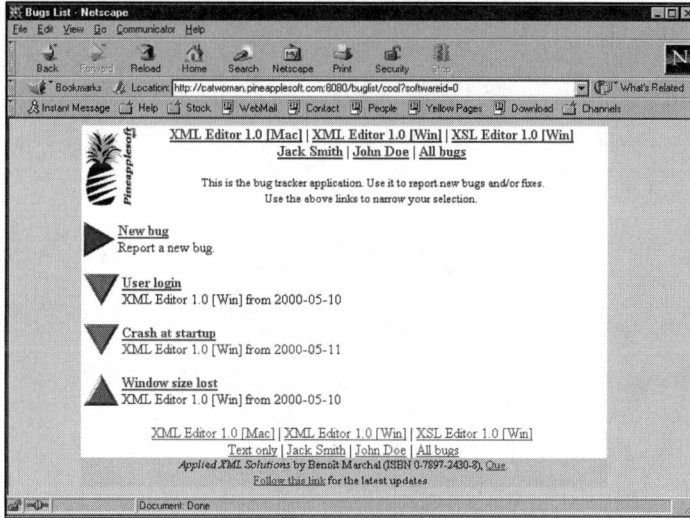

**Figure 8.2**  Pesticide is a Web–based bug tracker.

# Building `XslServlet`

`XslServlet` and `XslServletLiaisonImpl` perform all the work of calling the XSLT processor.

## `XslServlet`

Listing 8.1 is `XslServlet`, your specialized `HttpServlet`. It replaces `doGet()` and `doPost()` with its own version. The new methods have an additional parameter of type `XslServletLiaison`.

Listing 8.1  *XslServlet.java*

```
package com.psol.pesticide;

import java.io.*;
import javax.servlet.*;
import javax.servlet.http.*;
```

Listing 8.1 **Continued**

```
public class XslServlet
   extends HttpServlet
{
   public void doGet(HttpServletRequest request,
                     HttpServletResponse response)
      throws ServletException, IOException
   {
      XslServletLiaisonImpl liaison =
         new XslServletLiaisonImpl(getClass(),request);
      doGet(request,response,liaison);
      liaison.writeResponse(response);
   }

   public void doGet(HttpServletRequest request,
                     HttpServletResponse response,
                     XslServletLiaison liaison)
      throws ServletException, IOException
   {
      response.sendError(HttpServletResponse.SC_BAD_REQUEST);
   }

   public void doPost(HttpServletRequest request,
                      HttpServletResponse response)
      throws ServletException, IOException
   {
      XslServletLiaisonImpl liaison =
         new XslServletLiaisonImpl(getClass(),request);
      doPost(request,response,liaison);
      liaison.writeResponse(response);
   }

   public void doPost(HttpServletRequest request,
                      HttpServletResponse response,
                      XslServletLiaison liaison)
      throws ServletException, IOException
   {
      response.sendError(HttpServletResponse.SC_BAD_REQUEST);
   }
}
```

In answer to an HTTP request (GET or POST), the servlet creates an
XslServletLiaisonImpl, passes the request to the specialized doGet() or doPost(), and
uses the liaison to write the following response:

```
public void doGet(HttpServletRequest request,
                  HttpServletResponse response)
   throws ServletException, IOException
{
   XslServletLiaisonImpl liaison =
```

```
          new XslServletLiaisonImpl(getClass(),request);
      doGet(request,response,liaison);
      liaison.writeResponse(response);
  }
```

## XslServletLiaison

The declaration for `XslServletLiaison` is shown in Listing 8.2. It enables the servlet
to communicate with the XSL processor. The main methods are as follows:

- `getWriter()`—Returns the `Writer` for the servlet to write the XML document.
  It replaces `HttpServletResponse.getWriter()`.
- `getXSL()` and `setXSL()`—Select the XSL style sheet that will be applied.
- `getSkin()`—Returns the servlet's skin, which is described in the next section.

Listing 8.2 *XslServletLiaison.java*
```
package com.psol.pesticide;

import java.io.*;

public interface XslServletLiaison
{
    public XslWriter getWriter()
        throws IOException;
    public File getXSL();
    public void setXSL(File xsl);
    public String getSkin();
}
```

## Servlet Skins

`XslServletLiaison` must select the appropriate style before applying it. Experience
shows that the most flexible solution is to extract a reference to the style sheet from
the URL. However, it is not safe to pass it directly as a URL parameter, such as

```
http://catwoman.pineapplesoft.com/buglist?xsl=xsl/buglist.xsl
```

because hackers can forge URLs that point to their XSL files. In other words, it
enables them to run their own code (their style sheet) on your server:

```
http://catwoman.pineapplesoft.com/buglist?
➥xsl=http://www.hacker.com/malign-style-sheet.xsl
```

Instead, pass a shorter reference in the URL and turn into a safe file path on the
server. In this project, the shorter reference is called a skin. The skin is simply a generic
name for a given look and feel.

For example, the following URLs respectively apply the `cool` and `fast` skins to the `buglist` servlet:

```
http://catwoman.pineapplesoft.com/buglist/cool
http://catwoman.pineapplesoft.com/buglist/fast
```

**Tip**

The alternatives to extracting the style sheet from the URL are

- A configuration file, which is less flexible. In particular, it is more difficult to provide the user with different links, such as a graphic-heavy (cool) and text-only (fast) versions of the same page.

- Having the servlet explicitly call setXSL(), which creates a dependency between the designer and the programmer—precisely what we try to avoid.

`XslServletLiaisonImpl` maps the skin (`cool`) to a file. It builds the filename by concatenating the skin to the servlet classname:

```java
// extract the "skin" from the URL
String pathInfo = request.getPathInfo();
if(null != pathInfo)
{
   StringTokenizer tokenizer =
      new StringTokenizer(pathInfo,"/",false);
   if(tokenizer.hasMoreTokens())
      skin = tokenizer.nextToken();
}
// turn the skin in the path to the style sheet
if(null != skin)
   if(skin.equals("none"))
      return;
   else
      xsl = new File("stylesheet",skin);
else
   xsl = new File("stylesheet");
StringTokenizer tokenizer =
   new StringTokenizer(clasz.getName(),".",false);
while(tokenizer.hasMoreTokens())
   if(tokenizer.countTokens() == 1)
      xsl = new File(xsl,tokenizer.nextToken() + ".xsl");
   else
      xsl = new File(xsl,tokenizer.nextToken());
```

As you can see, the skin `none` is not converted to a filename. `none` returns the raw XML file (applying no XSL style sheet). This is useful for debugging.

The following are several advantages of skins:

- The style sheet is guaranteed to be a local file, which minimizes the chances of a hacker substituting a rogue style sheet.

- Different servlets have different style sheets, but all the style sheets are grouped by the look and feel, or skin, that they implement.
- The servlet can always use setXSL() for special cases.

### Tip

Why use a special skin name, such as none, for raw XML? Why not reserve it for the empty skin, as in the following:

```
http://catwoman.pineapplesoft.com/buglist
```

In practice, it is best to use a special name because visitors might forget the skin when typing the URL. The empty skin should be reserved to a default style sheet rather than raw XML.

## XslServletLiaisonImpl

Listing 8.3 is XslServletLiaisonImpl, the default implementation of XslServletLiaison using Xalan 1.0. If you elect another XSL processor, you must provide an implementation of XslServletLiaison for that processor.

Listing 8.3  *XslServletLiaisonImpl.java*

```java
package com.psol.pesticide;

import java.io.*;
import java.util.*;
import org.xml.sax.*;
import javax.servlet.*;
import javax.servlet.http.*;
import org.apache.xalan.xslt.*;

public class XslServletLiaisonImpl
    implements XslServletLiaison
{
    protected String skin = null;
    protected File xsl = null;
    protected ByteArrayOutputStream ostream = null;
    protected XslWriter writer = null;
    protected static Dictionary stylesheets = new Hashtable();

    public XslServletLiaisonImpl(Class clasz,
                                 HttpServletRequest request)
    {
        // extract the "skin" from the path information
        String pathInfo = request.getPathInfo();
        if(null != pathInfo)
        {
            StringTokenizer tokenizer =
                new StringTokenizer(pathInfo,"/",false);
```

Listing 8.3 **Continued**

```
            if(tokenizer.hasMoreTokens())
                skin = tokenizer.nextToken();
        }
        // turn the skin in the path to the style sheet
        if(null != skin)
            if(skin.equals("none"))
                return;
            else
                xsl = new File("stylesheet",skin);
        else
            xsl = new File("stylesheet");
        StringTokenizer tokenizer =
            new StringTokenizer(clasz.getName(),".",false);
        while(tokenizer.hasMoreTokens())
            if(tokenizer.countTokens() == 1)
                xsl = new File(xsl,tokenizer.nextToken() + ".xsl");
            else
                xsl = new File(xsl,tokenizer.nextToken());
    }

    public XslWriter getWriter()
    {
        if(null == writer)
        {
            ostream = new ByteArrayOutputStream();
            writer = new XslWriter(ostream);
        }
        return writer;
    }

    public File getXSL()
    {
        return xsl;
    }

    public void setXSL(File xsl)
    {
        this.xsl = xsl;
    }

    public String getSkin()
    {
        return skin;
    }

    protected class Struct
    {
        public long lastModified;
        public StylesheetRoot stylesheet;
```

Listing 8.3 **Continued**

```java
    public Struct(long lastModified,StylesheetRoot stylesheet)
    {
        this.lastModified = lastModified;
        this.stylesheet = stylesheet;
    }
}

protected void writeStyledXml(InputStream istream,
                              HttpServletResponse response)
    throws SAXException, ServletException, IOException
{
    XSLTProcessor processor =
        XSLTProcessorFactory.getProcessor();

    // deal with precompiled style sheets
    Struct s = (Struct)stylesheets.get(xsl);
    if(null == s ||
        s.lastModified < xsl.lastModified())
    {
        XSLTInputSource source =
            new XSLTInputSource(new FileInputStream(xsl));
        s = new Struct(xsl.lastModified(),
                       processor.processStylesheet(source));
        stylesheets.put(xsl,s);
    }
    else
        processor.setStylesheet(s.stylesheet);

    // set the content-type
    String ct = s.stylesheet.getOutputMediaType(),
           cs = s.stylesheet.getOutputEncoding();
    if(null == ct)
    {
        if(s.stylesheet.isOutputMethodSet())
        {
            String method = s.stylesheet.getOutputMethod();
            if(method.equalsIgnoreCase("xml"))
                ct = "text/xml";
            else if(method.equalsIgnoreCase("html"))
                ct = "text/html";
            else if(method.equalsIgnoreCase("text"))
                ct = "text/plain";
            else
                throw new ServletException("Unknown method");
        }
        else
            ct = "text/xml";
    }
    if(null != cs)
        ct += "; charset=\"" + cs + "\"";
    response.setContentType(ct);
```

Listing 8.3 **Continued**

```
        // transform and write the result
        XSLTInputSource source = new XSLTInputSource(istream);
        XSLTResultTarget target =
            new XSLTResultTarget(response.getOutputStream());
        processor.process(source,null,target);
    }

    protected void writeRawXml(InputStream istream,
                                 HttpServletResponse response)
        throws IOException
    {
        response.setContentType("text/xml");
        OutputStream ostream = response.getOutputStream();
        int c = istream.read();
        while(-1 != c)
        {
            ostream.write(c);
            c = istream.read();
        }
    }

    public void writeResponse(HttpServletResponse response)
        throws IOException, ServletException
    {
        if(null != writer)
            writer.flush();
        if(null == ostream || 0 == ostream.size())
            return;

        writer.flush();
        InputStream istream =
            new ByteArrayInputStream(ostream.toByteArray());

        if(null == xsl)
            writeRawXml(istream,response);
        else
            try
            {
                writeStyledXml(istream,response);
            }
            catch(SAXException e)
            {
                throw new ServletException(e.getMessage());
            }
    }
}
```

You saw how the constructor selects the style sheet in the previous section.
`writeResponse()` is called by `XslServlet` to perform the XSL transformation. It then
delegates the actual work to `writeRawXml()` and `writeStyledXml()`.

`writeStyledXml()` is the method that calls the XSL processor. It takes advantage of Xalan precompiled style sheets, and it won't reread a style sheet unless it has been modified:

```
// deal with precompiled style sheets
Struct s = (Struct)stylesheets.get(xsl);
if(null == s ||
   s.lastModified < xsl.lastModified())
{
   XSLTInputSource source =
      new XSLTInputSource(new FileInputStream(xsl));
   s = new Struct(xsl.lastModified(),
                  processor.processStylesheet(source));
   stylesheets.put(xsl,s);
}
else
   processor.setStylesheet(s.stylesheet);
```

The method also sets the content type, according to the media type and character set selected in the style sheet:

```
// set the content-type
String ct = s.stylesheet.getOutputMediaType(),
       cs = s.stylesheet.getOutputEncoding();
if(null == ct)
{
   if(s.stylesheet.isOutputMethodSet())
   {
      String method = s.stylesheet.getOutputMethod();
      if(method.equalsIgnoreCase("xml"))
         ct = "text/xml";
      else if(method.equalsIgnoreCase("html"))
         ct = "text/html";
      else if(method.equalsIgnoreCase("text"))
         ct = "text/plain";
      else
         throw new ServletException("Unknown method");
   }
   else
      ct = "text/xml";
}
if(null != cs)
   ct += "; charset=\"" + cs + "\"";
response.setContentType(ct);
```

Finally, the method calls Xalan to perform the transformation:

```
// transform and write the result
XSLTInputSource source = new XSLTInputSource(istream);
XSLTResultTarget target =
   new XSLTResultTarget(response.getOutputStream());
processor.process(source,null,target);
```

# Writing Pesticide Using `XslServlet`

Pesticide, the bug tracker application, demonstrates `XslServlet` in its two servlets, `BugList` and `BugForm`.

## Writing `BugList`

The first `XslServlet` is `BugList`, which prints the list of bugs (see Listing 8.4).

Listing 8.4  *BugList.java*

```java
package com.psol.pesticide;

import java.io.*;
import java.sql.*;
import javax.servlet.*;
import javax.servlet.http.*;

public class BugList
    extends XslServlet
{
    public void init()
        throws ServletException
    {
        try
        {
            Class.forName(getInitParameter("driver"));
        }
        catch(ClassNotFoundException e)
        {
            throw new ServletException(e);
        }
    }

    protected void writeBugList(Connection conn,
                                String pid,
                                String sid,
                                XslWriter writer)
        throws SQLException, IOException
    {
        StringBuffer query = new StringBuffer("select " +
            "bug.id, bug.name, solved, created, software.name " +
            " from bug inner join software on " +
            "bug.softwareid=software.id");
        boolean isPid = null != pid && 0 != pid.length(),
                isSid = null != sid && 0 != sid.length();
        if(isPid)
            query.append(" where bug.programmerid=?");
        if(isSid)
            if(isPid)
```

Listing 8.4 **Continued**

```java
            query.append(" and bug.softwareid=?");
         else
            query.append(" where bug.softwareid=?");
      query.append(" order by solved, created");
      PreparedStatement stmt =
         conn.prepareStatement(query.toString());
      try
      {
         if(isPid)
            stmt.setString(1,pid);
         if(isSid)
            if(isPid)
               stmt.setString(2,sid);
            else
               stmt.setString(1,sid);
         ResultSet rs = stmt.executeQuery();
         try
         {
            writer.write("<bug-list>");
            String[] fields =
            {
               "id", "name", "solved",
               "created", "software-name"
            };
            while(rs.next())
               SQLUtil.writeRow("bug",fields,rs,writer);
            writer.write("</bug-list>");
         }
         finally
         {
            rs.close();
         }
      }
      finally
      {
         stmt.close();
      }
   }

   public void doGet(HttpServletRequest request,
                     HttpServletResponse response,
                     XslServletLiaison liaison)
      throws IOException, ServletException
   {
      try
      {
         String url = getInitParameter("url"),
                username = getInitParameter("username"),
                password = getInitParameter("password");
         Connection conn =
```

Listing 8.4 **Continued**

```
            DriverManager.getConnection(url,username,password);
        XslWriter writer = liaison.getWriter();
        writer.write("<page>");
        try
        {
            String pid = request.getParameter("programmerid"),
                    sid = request.getParameter("softwareid");
            if(null != pid)
                pid = pid.trim();
            if(null != sid)
                sid = sid.trim();
            writeBugList(conn,pid,sid,writer);
            SQLUtil.writeProgrammerList(conn,pid,writer);
            SQLUtil.writeSoftwareList(conn,sid,writer);
        }
        finally
        {
            conn.close();
        }
        writer.write("</page>");
    }
    catch(SQLException e)
    {
        throw new ServletException(e);
    }
    catch(Exception e)
    {
        throw new ServletException(e);
    }
  }
}
```

**Warning**

For simplicity, the servlet does not maintain a pool of database connections. Although this is not a problem with Hypersonic SQL (see the section "Building and Running the Project" later in this chapter), it
might negatively impact performances with other databases.

BugList is very similar to a regular servlet. It connects to the database, extracts information, and writes the result. The only remarkable aspect is that it overrides your version of doGet() and writes the result in presentation-neutral XML. Some of the
database code is shared between BugList and BugForm. It has been moved to SQLUtil
(see Listing 8.5).

> **Tip**
>
> You might wonder why the servlet uses a PreparedStatement, even though it runs the statement only once. Briefly, it simplifies parameter processing because it is possible to use the setString() methods.

Listing 8.5  *SQLUtil.java*

```java
package com.psol.pesticide;

import java.io.*;
import java.sql.*;

public class SQLUtil
{
    public static void writeFields(String[] fields,
                                   ResultSet rs,
                                   XslWriter writer)
        throws SQLException, IOException
    {
        for(int i = 0;i < fields.length;i++)
        {
            String value = rs.getString(i + 1);
            writer.write('<');
            writer.write(fields[i]);
            writer.write('>');
            if(!rs.wasNull())
                writer.escape(value);
            writer.write("</");
            writer.write(fields[i]);
            writer.write('>');
        }
    }

    public static void writeRow(String name,
                                String[] fields,
                                ResultSet rs,
                                XslWriter writer)
        throws SQLException, IOException
    {
        writeRow(name,null,null,fields,rs,writer);
    }

    public static void writeRow(String name,
                                String id,
                                String attribute,
                                String[] fields,
                                ResultSet rs,
                                XslWriter writer)
        throws SQLException, IOException
    {
```

Listing 8.5 **Continued**

```java
        writer.write('<');
        writer.write(name);
        if(null != attribute)
        {
            String value = rs.getString(1);
            if(id != null && id.equals(value))
            {
                writer.write(' ');
                writer.write(attribute);
            }
        }
        writer.write('>');
        writeFields(fields,rs,writer);
        writer.write("</");
        writer.write(name);
        writer.write('>');
    }

    public static void writeSoftwareList(Connection conn,
                                         String id,
                                         XslWriter writer)
        throws SQLException, IOException
    {
        Statement stmt = conn.createStatement();
        try
        {
            ResultSet rs = stmt.executeQuery("select id, " +
                "name from software order by name");
            try
            {
                String[] fields =
                {
                    "id", "name"
                };
                writer.write("<software-list>");
                while(rs.next())
                    writeRow("software",id,"selected='yes'",
                             fields,rs,writer);
                writer.write("</software-list>");
            }
            finally
            {
                rs.close();
            }
        }
        finally
        {
            stmt.close();
        }
    }
```

Listing 8.5 **Continued**

```java
public static void writeProgrammerList(Connection conn,
                                       String id,
                                       XslWriter writer)
    throws SQLException, IOException
{
    Statement stmt = conn.createStatement();
    try
    {
        ResultSet rs = stmt.executeQuery("select id, " +
            "name from programmer order by name");
        try
        {
            String[] fields =
            {
                "id", "name"
            };
            writer.write("<programmer-list>");
            while(rs.next())
                writeRow("programmer",id,"selected='yes'",
                         fields,rs,writer);
            writer.write("</programmer-list>");
        }
        finally
        {
            rs.close();
        }
    }
    finally
    {
        stmt.close();
    }
}
```

## The **BugList** Style Sheet

Obviously, BugList needs a style sheet, such as that shown in Listing 8.6. Note that the complete filename for this file is fast/com/psol/pesticide/BugList.xsl for the fast skin.

The style sheet should be familiar; it turns a list of bugs into a nicely formatted HTML page. In a browser, it looks similar to Figure 8.3.

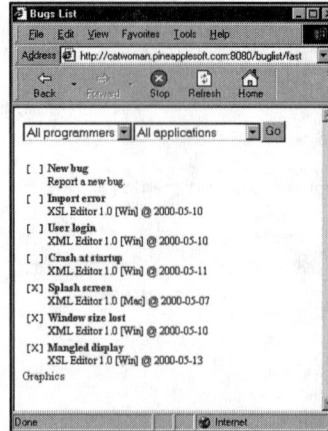

**Figure 8.3** The servlet with the fast skin.

Listing 8.6 *BugList.xsl* (cool version)

```xml
<?xml version="1.0"?>

<xsl:stylesheet
   xmlns:xsl="http://www.w3.org/1999/XSL/Transform"
   xmlns="http://www.w3.org/TR/REC-html40"
   version="1.0">

<xsl:output method="html"
            encoding="ISO-8859-1"/>

<xsl:template match="/">
   <HTML>
      <HEAD><TITLE>Bugs List</TITLE></HEAD>
      <BODY>
         <xsl:apply-templates/>
         <A HREF="/buglist/cool">Graphics</A>
         </BODY>
      </HTML>
</xsl:template>

<xsl:template match="page">
   <FORM METHOD="GET" ACTION="/buglist/fast">
      <SELECT NAME="programmerid">
         <OPTION VALUE="">All programmers</OPTION>
         <xsl:apply-templates select="programmer-list"/>
      </SELECT>
      <SELECT NAME="softwareid">
         <OPTION VALUE="">All applications</OPTION>
         <xsl:apply-templates select="software-list"/>
      </SELECT>
```

Listing 8.6 **Continued**

```
         <INPUT TYPE="SUBMIT" VALUE="Go"/>
   </FORM>
   <xsl:apply-templates select="bug-list"/>
</xsl:template>

<xsl:template match="software | programmer">
   <OPTION>
      <xsl:attribute name="VALUE">
         <xsl:apply-templates select="id"/>
      </xsl:attribute>
      <xsl:apply-templates select="name"/>
   </OPTION>
</xsl:template>

<xsl:template match="software[@selected='yes'] |
                     programmer[@selected='yes']">
   <OPTION SELECTED="SELECTED">
      <xsl:attribute name="VALUE">
         <xsl:apply-templates select="id"/>
      </xsl:attribute>
      <xsl:apply-templates select="name"/>
   </OPTION>
</xsl:template>

<xsl:template match="bug-list">
   <TABLE>
      <TR>
         <TD VALIGN="TOP"><TT>[ ]</TT></TD>
         <TD><SMALL>
            <B><A HREF="/bugform/fast">New bug</A></B><BR/>
            Report a new bug.</SMALL></TD>
         <TD></TD>
      </TR>
      <xsl:apply-templates/>
   </TABLE>
</xsl:template>

<xsl:template match="bug">
   <TR>
      <TD VALIGN="TOP"><xsl:choose>
         <xsl:when test="solved='true'"><TT>[X]</TT></xsl:when>
         <xsl:otherwise><TT>[ ]</TT></xsl:otherwise>
      </xsl:choose></TD>
      <TD><SMALL>
         <B><A>
            <xsl:attribute name="HREF">
            <xsl:text>/bugform/fast?id=</xsl:text>
            <xsl:value-of select="id"/>
            </xsl:attribute>
            <xsl:apply-templates select="name"/></A>
         </B><BR/>
```

Listing 8.6 **Continued**

```
        <xsl:apply-templates select="software-name"/>
        <xsl:text> @ </xsl:text>
        <xsl:apply-templates select="created"/></SMALL>
      </TD>
    </TR>
</xsl:template>

</xsl:stylesheet>
```

## Writing BugForm

Listing 8.7 illustrates BugForm, the servlet used to edit a bug. Again, the servlet is not remarkable but for its use of XML.

Listing 8.7 *BugForm.java*

```
package com.psol.pesticide;

import java.io.*;
import java.sql.*;
import javax.servlet.*;
import javax.servlet.http.*;

public class BugForm
    extends XslServlet
{
    public void init()
       throws ServletException
    {
      try
      {
         Class.forName(getInitParameter("driver"));
      }
      catch(ClassNotFoundException e)
      {
         throw new ServletException(e);
      }
    }

    protected void writeEmptyForm(Connection conn,
                                 XslWriter writer)
       throws SQLException, IOException
    {
      writer.write("<bug><id/><name/><created/>");
      writer.write("<description/><solution/><solved/>");
      SQLUtil.writeProgrammerList(conn,null,writer);
      SQLUtil.writeSoftwareList(conn,null,writer);
      writer.write("</bug>");
    }
```

Listing 8.7 **Continued**

```
protected void writeNonEmptyForm(Connection conn,
                                 String id,
                                 XslWriter writer)
    throws SQLException, IOException
{
    PreparedStatement stmt = conn.prepareStatement("select " +
        "id, name, created, description, solution, solved, " +
        "programmerid, softwareid from bug where id=?");
    try
    {
        stmt.setString(1,id);
        ResultSet rs = stmt.executeQuery();
        try
        {
            writer.write("<bug>");
            if(rs.next())
            {
                String[] fields =
                {
                    "id", "name", "created", "description",
                    "solution", "solved"
                };
                SQLUtil.writeFields(fields,rs,writer);
                SQLUtil.writeProgrammerList(conn,
                                            rs.getString(7),
                                            writer);
                SQLUtil.writeSoftwareList(conn,
                                          rs.getString(8),
                                          writer);
            }
            writer.write("</bug>");
        }
        finally
        {
            rs.close();
        }
    }
    finally
    {
        stmt.close();
    }
}

protected void setValue(PreparedStatement stmt,
                        int pos,
                        String value,
                        int type)
    throws SQLException
{
    if(null == value)
        stmt.setNull(pos,type);
```

Listing 8.7 **Continued**

```java
    else
      stmt.setString(pos,value);
  }

  protected void writePage(Connection conn,
                           String id,
                           HttpServletRequest request,
                           HttpServletResponse response,
                           XslServletLiaison liaison)
    throws IOException, SQLException
  {
    XslWriter writer = liaison.getWriter();
    writer.write("<page>");
    if(null != id && 0 != id.length())
      writeNonEmptyForm(conn,id,writer);
    else
      writeEmptyForm(conn,writer);
    writer.write("</page>");
  }

  protected String updateBug(Connection conn,
                             String id,
                             HttpServletRequest request)
    throws SQLException
  {
    PreparedStatement stmt = null;
    if(null != id && 0 != id.length())
      stmt = conn.prepareStatement("update bug set name=?," +
          " created=?, description=?, solution=?, solved=?," +
          " programmerid=?, softwareid=? where id=?");
    else
      stmt = conn.prepareStatement("insert into bug (name, " +
          "created, description, solution, solved, " +
          "programmerid, softwareid) values (?,?,?,?,?,?,?)");
    try
    {
      setValue(stmt,1,request.getParameter("name"),
               Types.VARCHAR);
      setValue(stmt,2,request.getParameter("created"),
               Types.DATE);
      setValue(stmt,3,request.getParameter("description"),
               Types.VARCHAR);
      setValue(stmt,4,request.getParameter("solution"),
               Types.VARCHAR);
      setValue(stmt,5,request.getParameter("solved"),
               Types.BIT);
      setValue(stmt,6,request.getParameter("programmerid"),
               Types.INTEGER);
      setValue(stmt,7,request.getParameter("softwareid"),
               Types.INTEGER);
```

Listing 8.7 **Continued**

```java
      if(null != id && 0 != id.length())
         stmt.setString(8,id);
      stmt.executeUpdate();
      if(null == id || 0 == id.length())
      {
         Statement s = conn.createStatement();
         try
         {
            ResultSet rs = s.executeQuery(
               "select max(id) from bug");
            try
            {
               if(rs.next())
                  id = rs.getString(1);
            }
            finally
            {
               rs.close();
            }
         }
         finally
         {
            s.close();
         }
      }
   }
   finally
   {
      stmt.close();
   }
   return id;
}

public void doGet(HttpServletRequest request,
               HttpServletResponse response,
               XslServletLiaison liaison)
   throws IOException, ServletException
{
   try
   {
      String url = getInitParameter("url"),
            username = getInitParameter("username"),
            password = getInitParameter("password");
      Connection conn =
         DriverManager.getConnection(url,username,password);
      try
      {
         String id = request.getParameter("id");
         if(null != id)
            id = id.trim();
```

Listing 8.7 **Continued**

```
            writePage(conn,id,request,response,liaison);
        }
        finally
        {
            conn.close();
        }
    }
    catch(SQLException e)
    {
        throw new ServletException(e);
    }
}

public void doPost(HttpServletRequest request,
                   HttpServletResponse response,
                   XslServletLiaison liaison)
    throws IOException, ServletException
{
    try
    {
        String url = getInitParameter("url"),
               username = getInitParameter("username"),
               password = getInitParameter("password");
        Connection conn =
            DriverManager.getConnection(url,username,password);
        try
        {
            String id = request.getParameter("id");
            if(null != id)
                id = id.trim();
            id = updateBug(conn,id,request);
            writePage(conn,id,request,response,liaison);
        }
        finally
        {
            conn.close();
        }
    }
    catch(SQLException e)
    {
        throw new ServletException(e);
    }
}
```

You should notice writeEmptyForm(), which writes an empty XML document. The style sheet needs an empty XML document to produce an empty HTML form:

```
protected void writeEmptyForm(Connection conn,
                              XslWriter writer)
    throws SQLException, IOException
{
```

```
    writer.write("<bug><id/><name/><created/>");
    writer.write("<description/><solution/><solved/>");
    SQLUtil.writeProgrammerList(conn,null,writer);
    SQLUtil.writeSoftwareList(conn,null,writer);
    writer.write("</bug>");
}
```

## The `BugForm` Style Sheet

Listing 8.8 is the style sheet for `BugForm`, using the `fast` skin.

Listing 8.8 *BugForm.xsl* **(fast version)**

```xml
<?xml version="1.0"?>

<xsl:stylesheet
   xmlns:xsl="http://www.w3.org/1999/XSL/Transform"
   xmlns="http://www.w3.org/TR/REC-html40"
   version="1.0">

<xsl:output method="html"
            encoding="ISO-8859-1"/>

<xsl:template match="/">
   <HTML>
      <HEAD><TITLE>Edit a Bug</TITLE></HEAD>
      <BODY>
         <xsl:apply-templates/>
         <A HREF="/buglist/cool">Graphics</A>
      </BODY>
   </HTML>
</xsl:template>

<xsl:template match="page">
   <FORM ACTION="/buglist/fast" METHOD="GET">
      <SELECT NAME="programmerid">
         <OPTION VALUE="">All programmers</OPTION>
         <xsl:apply-templates select="bug/programmer-list"
                              mode="menu"/>
      </SELECT>
      <SELECT NAME="softwareid">
         <OPTION VALUE="">All applications</OPTION>
         <xsl:apply-templates select="bug/software-list"
                              mode="menu"/>
      </SELECT>
      <INPUT TYPE="SUBMIT" VALUE="Go"/>
   </FORM>
   <xsl:apply-templates select="bug"/>
</xsl:template>
```

Listing 8.8 **Continued**

```
<xsl:template match="software | programmer" mode="menu">
   <OPTION>
      <xsl:attribute name="VALUE">
         <xsl:value-of select="id"/>
      </xsl:attribute>
      <xsl:apply-templates select="name"/>
   </OPTION>
</xsl:template>

<xsl:template match="software[@selected='yes'] |
                     programmer[@selected='yes']"
            mode="menu">
   <OPTION SELECTED="SELECTED">
      <xsl:attribute name="VALUE">
         <xsl:value-of select="id"/>
      </xsl:attribute>
      <xsl:apply-templates select="name"/>
   </OPTION>
</xsl:template>

<xsl:template match="bug">
   <xsl:choose>
      <xsl:when test="count(child::*) = 0">
         <P><B>Empty!</B></P>
      </xsl:when>
      <xsl:otherwise>
         <FORM ACTION="/bugform/fast" METHOD="POST">
            <TABLE>
               <xsl:apply-templates/>
               <TR><TD>
                  <INPUT TYPE="SUBMIT" VALUE="Save"/>
               </TD></TR>
            </TABLE>
         </FORM>
      </xsl:otherwise>
   </xsl:choose>
</xsl:template>

<xsl:template match="bug/id">
   <INPUT TYPE="HIDDEN" NAME="id">
      <xsl:attribute name="VALUE">
         <xsl:value-of select="."/>
      </xsl:attribute>
   </INPUT>
</xsl:template>

<xsl:template match="bug/name">
   <TR>
      <TD VALIGN="TOP"><SMALL>Name:</SMALL></TD>
      <TD><INPUT NAME="name">
```

Listing 8.8 **Continued**

```
                <xsl:attribute name="VALUE">
                    <xsl:value-of select="."/>
                </xsl:attribute>
            </INPUT></TD>
        </TR>
</xsl:template>

<xsl:template match="created">
    <TR>
        <TD VALIGN="TOP"><SMALL>Created:</SMALL></TD>
        <TD><INPUT NAME="created">
            <xsl:attribute name="VALUE">
                <xsl:value-of select="."/>
            </xsl:attribute>
        </INPUT><SMALL> (yyyy-mm-dd)</SMALL></TD>
    </TR>
</xsl:template>

<xsl:template match="description">
    <TR>
        <TD VALIGN="TOP"><SMALL>Description:</SMALL></TD>
        <TD><TEXTAREA NAME="description">
            <xsl:value-of select="."/>
        </TEXTAREA></TD>
    </TR>
</xsl:template>

<xsl:template match="solved">
    <TR>
        <TD VALIGN="TOP"><SMALL>Status:</SMALL></TD>
        <TD><SELECT NAME="solved">
            <xsl:choose>
                <xsl:when test="text()='true'">
                    <OPTION VALUE="TRUE"
                        SELECTED="SELECTED">Resolved</OPTION>
                    <OPTION VALUE="FALSE">Unresolved</OPTION>
                </xsl:when>
                <xsl:otherwise>
                    <OPTION VALUE="TRUE">Resolved</OPTION>
                    <OPTION VALUE="FALSE"
                        SELECTED="SELECTED">Unresolved</OPTION>
                </xsl:otherwise>
            </xsl:choose>
        </SELECT></TD>
    </TR>
</xsl:template>

<xsl:template match="solution">
    <TR>
        <TD VALIGN="TOP"><SMALL>Solution:</SMALL></TD>
        <TD><TEXTAREA NAME="solution">
```

Listing 8.8 **Continued**

```
          <xsl:value-of select="."/>
        </TEXTAREA></TD>
      </TR>
    </xsl:template>

    <xsl:template match="programmer-list">
      <TR>
        <TD VALIGN="TOP"><SMALL>Programmer:</SMALL></TD>
        <TD><SELECT NAME="programmerid">
          <xsl:apply-templates/>
        </SELECT></TD>
      </TR>
    </xsl:template>

    <xsl:template match="software-list">
      <TR>
        <TD VALIGN="TOP"><SMALL>Application:</SMALL></TD>
        <TD><SELECT NAME="softwareid">
          <xsl:apply-templates/>
        </SELECT></TD>
      </TR>
    </xsl:template>

    <xsl:template match="software | programmer">
      <OPTION>
        <xsl:attribute name="VALUE">
          <xsl:value-of select="id"/>
        </xsl:attribute>
        <xsl:apply-templates select="name"/>
      </OPTION>
    </xsl:template>

    <xsl:template match="software[@selected='yes'] |
                         programmer[@selected='yes']">
      <OPTION SELECTED="SELECTED">
        <xsl:attribute name="VALUE">
          <xsl:value-of select="id"/>
        </xsl:attribute>
        <xsl:apply-templates select="name"/>
      </OPTION>
    </xsl:template>

  </xsl:stylesheet>
```

# Building and Running the Project

The Pesticide project is available on the enclosed CD-ROM. Copy the project
directory from the CD-ROM to your hard disk. Under Windows, start the server by

double-clicking `pesticide.bat`. Next, open a browser and type one of following URLs (see Figure 8.4):

```
http://localhost:8080/buglist/cool
http://localhost:8080/buglist/fast
http://localhost:8080/buglist/fr
```

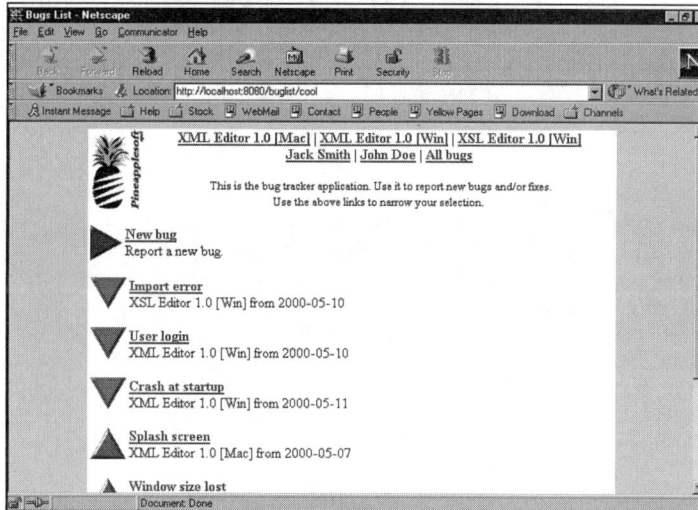

**Figure 8.4** Navigate the list of bugs.

**Warning**

This project uses Xalan 1.0 as the XSLT processor. If you are using another processor, you will need to adapt `XslServletLiaisonImpl`.

The project also uses Jetty as the Web server. However, because it is based on servlets, it should be easy to adapt to another Web server. You can add servlet support to most Web servers through JRun.

The project on the CD-ROM includes a database, but if you need to re-create it, you can use Listing 8.9. Use HypersonicSQL Database Manager to execute the script. To connect to the database, perform the following (see Figure 8.5):

- Select HypersonicSQL Standalone.
- The URL is `jdbc:HypersonicSQL:db/pesticide`.

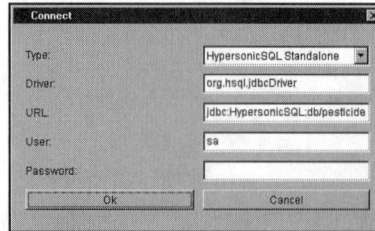

**Figure 8.5** Use the Database Manager to connect to the database.

Listing 8.9 **Creating the Initial Database**

```
CREATE TABLE software (id INTEGER IDENTITY,name VARCHAR);
CREATE TABLE programmer (id INTEGER IDENTITY,name VARCHAR);
CREATE TABLE bug (id INTEGER IDENTITY,name VARCHAR,created DATE,
➥description LONGVARCHAR,solution LONGVARCHAR,solved BIT,
➥softwareid INTEGER,programmerid INTEGER);
INSERT INTO software (name) VALUES ('XML Editor 1.0 [Win]');
INSERT INTO software (name) VALUES ('XML Editor 1.0 [Mac]');
INSERT INTO software (name) VALUES ('XSL Editor 1.0 [Win]');
INSERT INTO programmer (name) VALUES ('John Doe');
INSERT INTO programmer (name) VALUES ('Jack Smith');
INSERT INTO bug (name,created,description,solved,softwareid,
➥programmerid) SELECT 'User login', '2000-05-10', 'Creating
➥a new user throws an exception "Access Denied"', FALSE,
➥software.id, programmer.id FROM software, programmer WHERE
➥software.name='XML Editor 1.0 [Win]' AND
➥programmer.name='John Doe';
INSERT INTO bug (name,created,description,solved,solution,
➥softwareid,programmerid) SELECT 'Window size lost',
➥ '2000-05-10', 'Does not properly save the window size and
➥placement between sessions', TRUE,'Added new registry key',
➥software.id, programmer.id FROM software, programmer WHERE
➥software.name='XML Editor 1.0 [Win]' AND
➥programmer.name='John Doe';
INSERT INTO bug (name,created,description,solved,softwareid,
➥programmerid) SELECT 'Crash at startup', '2000-05-11', 'Random
➥crash at startup when low-memory', FALSE, software.id,
➥programmer.id FROM software, programmer WHERE software.
➥name='XML Editor 1.0 [Win]' AND programmer.name='John Doe';
INSERT INTO bug (name,created,description,solved,solution,
➥softwareid,programmerid) SELECT 'Splash screen', '2000-05-07',
➥ 'Splash screen does not go away until the user clicks it', TRUE,
➥ 'Added timer', software.id, programmer.id FROM software,
➥programmer WHERE software.name='XML Editor 1.0 [Mac]' AND
➥programmer.name='Jack Smith';
INSERT INTO bug (name,created,description,solved,softwareid,
➥programmerid) SELECT 'Import error', '2000-05-10', 'Cannot
➥open legacy XSL files', FALSE, software.id, programmer.id FROM
```

Listing 8.9 **Continued**

```
↪software, programmer WHERE software.name='XSL Editor 1.0 [Win]'
↪AND programmer.name='Jack Smith';
INSERT INTO bug (name,created,description,solved,solution,
↪softwareid,programmerid) SELECT 'Mangled display', '2000-05-13',
↪'For large style sheets, the display is not readable', TRUE,
↪'Added zoom', software.id, programmer.id FROM software,
↪programmer WHERE software.name='XSL Editor 1.0 [Win]' AND
↪programmer.name='Jack Smith';
```

**Warning**

The project uses Hypersonic SQL for the database. Because Hypersonic SQL is a JDBC database, it should be easy to adapt it to other JDBC databases (including Access, Oracle, and SQL Server).

However, you will need to adapt Listing 8.9 and the servlets to your database flavor of SQL. In particular, the identity column must be converted into the auto-increment columns for your database.

You might also want to take advantage of foreign keys, which Hypersonic SQL currently does not support.

# Playing with Style Sheets

Even if you are convinced of the virtue of XML and XSL as tools to organize your team's next Web project, you might still have some questions. This section deals with frequent issues that arise when deploying this solution.

## Teaching XSL

One of the hypotheses behind `XslServlet` is that designers know XSL. Clearly, at the time of this writing, this is optimistic. So is it worth all the effort?

Not necessarily. First, XSLT is not so complicated that it can't be learned in a few days. You might find it easier to start with style sheets based on `<xsl:for-each>`. Listing 8.10 illustrates this. It looks almost like an HTML document peppered with `<xsl:for-each>` and `<xsl:value-of>` to extract values from the XML document.

Listing 8.10 *BugList.xsl* **(version cool)**

```
<?xml version="1.0"?>

<xsl:stylesheet
   xmlns:xsl="http://www.w3.org/1999/XSL/Transform"
   xmlns="http://www.w3.org/TR/REC-html40"
   version="1.0">

<xsl:output method="html"
            encoding="ISO-8859-1"/>
```

Listing 8.10 **Continued**

```
<xsl:template match="/">
  <HTML>
  <HEAD><TITLE>Bugs List</TITLE></HEAD>
  <BODY BGCOLOR="#ffcc33" TEXT="#000000" LINK="#0000ff"
        VLINK="#800080" ALINK="#ffff00">
  <TABLE BORDER="0" ALIGN="CENTER" BGCOLOR="#ffffff"
         WIDTH="600" CELLSPACING="0" CELLPADDING="0">
  <TR><TD ALIGN="CENTER">
  <IMG SRC="/images/psol.gif" ALIGN="LEFT" ALT="Pineapplesoft"
       HEIGHT="93" WIDTH="60"/>
  <xsl:for-each select="page/software-list/software">
    <B><A><xsl:attribute name="HREF">
      <xsl:text>/buglist/cool?softwareid=</xsl:text>
      <xsl:value-of select="id"/></xsl:attribute>
      <xsl:value-of select="name"/></A></B>
    <xsl:if test="not(position()=last())"> | </xsl:if>
  </xsl:for-each><BR/>
  <xsl:for-each select="page/programmer-list/programmer">
    <B><A><xsl:attribute name="HREF">
      <xsl:text>/buglist/cool?programmerid=</xsl:text>
      <xsl:value-of select="id"/></xsl:attribute>
      <xsl:value-of select="name"/></A></B>
    <xsl:text> | </xsl:text>
  </xsl:for-each>
  <B><A HREF="/buglist/cool">All bugs</A></B>
  <P><SMALL>This is the bug tracker application. Use it to
  report new bugs and/or fixes.<BR/>
  Use the above links to narrow your selection.</SMALL></P>
  </TD></TR>
  </TABLE>
  <TABLE BORDER="0" ALIGN="CENTER" BGCOLOR="#ffffff"
         WIDTH="600" CELLSPACING="0" CELLPADDING="0">
  <TR><TD><BR/>
  <P><IMG ALIGN="LEFT" SRC="/images/new.gif"/>
    <B><A HREF="/bugform/cool">New bug</A></B><BR/>
    Report a new bug.
    <BR CLEAR="LEFT"/></P>
  <xsl:for-each select="page/bug-list/bug">
    <P><IMG ALIGN="LEFT"><xsl:attribute name="SRC">
      <xsl:text>/images/</xsl:text>
      <xsl:value-of select="solved"/>
      <xsl:text>.gif</xsl:text>
    </xsl:attribute></IMG>
    <B><A><xsl:attribute name="HREF">
      <xsl:text>/bugform/cool?id=</xsl:text>
      <xsl:value-of select="id"/>
    </xsl:attribute>
    <xsl:value-of select="name"/></A></B><BR/>
    <xsl:value-of select="software-name"/>
    <xsl:text> from </xsl:text>
```

Listing 8.10 **Continued**

```
            <xsl:value-of select="created"/>
            <BR CLEAR="LEFT"/></P>
      </xsl:for-each>
      </TD></TR>
      </TABLE>
      <TABLE BORDER="0" ALIGN="CENTER" BGCOLOR="#ffffff"
            WIDTH="600" CELLSPACING="0" CELLPADDING="0">
      <TR><TD ALIGN="CENTER"><BR/>
      <xsl:for-each select="page/software-list/software">
         <A><xsl:attribute name="HREF">
            <xsl:text>/buglist/cool?softwareid=</xsl:text>
            <xsl:value-of select="id"/></xsl:attribute>
            <xsl:value-of select="name"/></A>
         <xsl:if test="not(position()=last())"> | </xsl:if>
      </xsl:for-each><BR/>
      <A HREF="/buglist/fast">Text only</A> |
      <xsl:for-each select="page/programmer-list/programmer">
         <A><xsl:attribute name="HREF">
            <xsl:text>/buglist/cool?programmerid=</xsl:text>
            <xsl:value-of select="id"/></xsl:attribute>
            <xsl:value-of select="name"/></A>
         <xsl:text> | </xsl:text>
      </xsl:for-each>
      <A HREF="/buglist/cool">All bugs</A>
      </TD></TR>
      </TABLE>
      <TABLE BORDER="0" ALIGN="CENTER" BGCOLOR="#d3d3d3"
            WIDTH="600" CELLSPACING="0" CELLPADDING="0">
      <TR><TD VALIGN="MIDDLE" ALIGN="CENTER">
      <P><SMALL><I>Applied XML Solutions</I>
         by Beno&#238;t Marchal (ISBN 0-7897-2430-8),
<A HREF="http://www.mcp.com">Que</A>.<BR/>
         <A HREF="http://www.marchal.com">Follow this link</A>
         for the latest updates.</SMALL></P>
      </TD></TR>
      </TABLE>
      </BODY>
      </HTML>
   </xsl:template>

</xsl:stylesheet>
```

Second, several companies are readying XSLT editors. Although not (yet) as convivial as HTML editors, they really simplify coding. Figure 8.6 shows the XSL Editor from IBM (still in preview at the time of this writing).

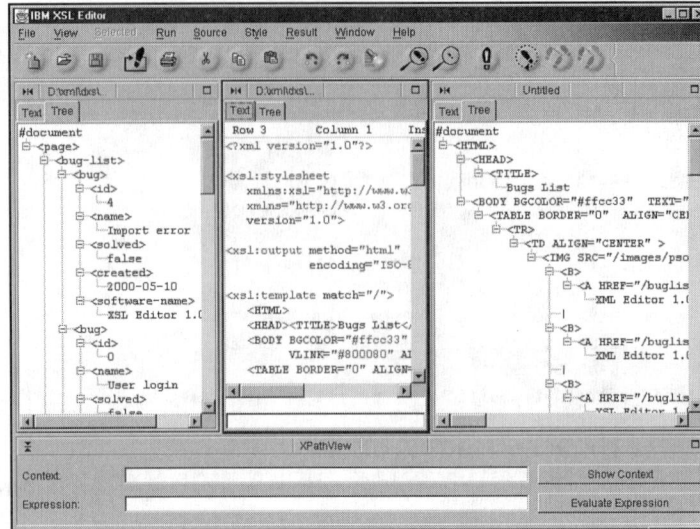

**Figure 8.6**  IBM's XSL Editor simplifies style sheet writing.

## Casting Your Servlet Skin

Incidentally, Listing 8.10 demonstrates an added benefit of this technique. By selecting another skin, the visitor enjoys a different presentation. Compare Figure 8.7 with Figure 8.2.

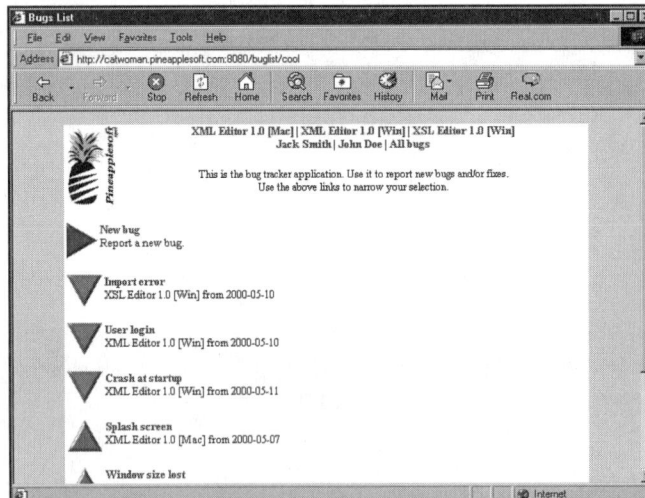

**Figure 8.7**  Change the URL for a different skin.

Furthermore, you can use the same technique to translate the Web site. Listing 8.11 is the style sheet for the French version of Pesticide. In a browser, it looks similar to Figure 8.8. Obviously, though, the data (coming from the database) is not translated.

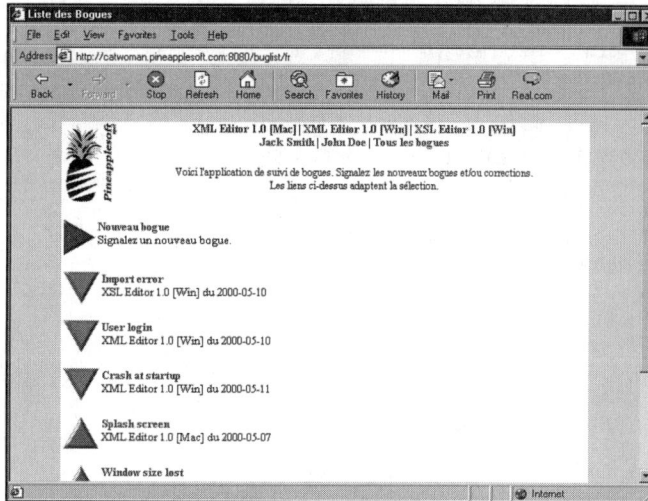

**Figure 8.8** The French version requires no programming.

Listing 8.11 *BugList.xsl* (French version)

```xml
<?xml version="1.0"?>

<xsl:stylesheet
    xmlns:xsl="http://www.w3.org/1999/XSL/Transform"
    xmlns="http://www.w3.org/TR/REC-html40"
    version="1.0">

<xsl:output method="html"
            encoding="ISO-8859-1"/>

<xsl:template match="/">
  <HTML>
  <HEAD><TITLE>Liste des Bogues</TITLE></HEAD>
  <BODY BGCOLOR="#ffcc33" TEXT="#000000" LINK="#0000ff"
        VLINK="#800080" ALINK="#ffff00">
  <TABLE BORDER="0" ALIGN="CENTER" BGCOLOR="#ffffff"
         WIDTH="600" CELLSPACING="0" CELLPADDING="0">
  <TR><TD ALIGN="CENTER">
  <IMG SRC="/images/psol.gif" ALIGN="LEFT" ALT="Pineapplesoft"
       HEIGHT="93" WIDTH="60"/>
  <xsl:for-each select="page/software-list/software">
    <B><A><xsl:attribute name="HREF">
```

Listing 8.11 **Continued**

```
        <xsl:text>/buglist/fr?softwareid=</xsl:text>
        <xsl:value-of select="id"/></xsl:attribute>
        <xsl:value-of select="name"/></A></B>
    <xsl:if test="not(position()=last())"> | </xsl:if>
</xsl:for-each><BR/>
<xsl:for-each select="page/programmer-list/programmer">
    <B><A><xsl:attribute name="HREF">
        <xsl:text>/buglist/fr?programmerid=</xsl:text>
        <xsl:value-of select="id"/></xsl:attribute>
        <xsl:value-of select="name"/></A></B>
    <xsl:text> | </xsl:text>
</xsl:for-each>
<B><A HREF="/buglist/fr">Tous les bogues</A></B>
<P><SMALL>Voici l'application de suivi de bogues. Signalez
les nouveaux bogues et/ou corrections.<BR/>
Les liens ci-dessus adaptent la s&#233;lection.</SMALL></P>
</TD></TR>
</TABLE>
<TABLE BORDER="0" ALIGN="CENTER" BGCOLOR="#ffffff"
        WIDTH="600" CELLSPACING="0" CELLPADDING="0">
<TR><TD><BR/>
<P><IMG ALIGN="LEFT" SRC="/images/new.gif"/>
    <B><A HREF="/bugform/fr">Nouveau bogue</A></B><BR/>
    Signalez un nouveau bogue.<BR CLEAR="LEFT"/></P>
<xsl:for-each select="page/bug-list/bug">
    <P><IMG ALIGN="LEFT"><xsl:attribute name="SRC">
        <xsl:text>/images/</xsl:text>
        <xsl:value-of select="solved"/>
        <xsl:text>.gif</xsl:text>
    </xsl:attribute></IMG>
    <B><A><xsl:attribute name="HREF">
        <xsl:text>/bugform/fr?id=</xsl:text>
        <xsl:value-of select="id"/>
    </xsl:attribute>
    <xsl:value-of select="name"/></A></B><BR/>
    <xsl:value-of select="software-name"/>
    <xsl:text> du </xsl:text>
    <xsl:value-of select="created"/>
    <BR CLEAR="LEFT"/></P>
</xsl:for-each>
</TD></TR>
</TABLE>
<TABLE BORDER="0" ALIGN="CENTER" BGCOLOR="#ffffff"
        WIDTH="600" CELLSPACING="0" CELLPADDING="0">
<TR><TD ALIGN="CENTER"><BR/>
<xsl:for-each select="page/software-list/software">
    <A><xsl:attribute name="HREF">
        <xsl:text>/buglist/fr?softwareid=</xsl:text>
        <xsl:value-of select="id"/></xsl:attribute>
        <xsl:value-of select="name"/></A>
```

Listing 8.11 **Continued**

```
      <xsl:if test="not(position()=last())"> | </xsl:if>
   </xsl:for-each><BR/>
   <A HREF="/buglist/fast">Version texte</A> |
<xsl:for-each select="page/programmer-list/programmer">
      <A><xsl:attribute name="HREF">
         <xsl:text>/buglist/fr?programmerid=</xsl:text>
         <xsl:value-of select="id"/></xsl:attribute>
         <xsl:value-of select="name"/></A>
      <xsl:text> | </xsl:text>
   </xsl:for-each>
   <A HREF="/buglist/fr">Tous les bogues</A>
   </TD></TR>
   </TABLE>
   <TABLE BORDER="0" ALIGN="CENTER" BGCOLOR="#d3d3d3"
         WIDTH="600" CELLSPACING="0" CELLPADDING="0">
   <TR><TD VALIGN="MIDDLE" ALIGN="CENTER">
   <P><SMALL><I>Applied XML Solutions</I>
      par Beno&#238;t Marchal (ISBN 0-7897-2430-8),
<A HREF="http://www.mcp.com">Que</A>.<BR/>Visitez
      <A HREF="http://www.marchal.com">www.marchal.com</A>
      ou abonnez-vous &#224; la lettre gratuite,
      <A HREF="http://www.pineapplesoft.com">Pineapplesoft
      Link</A>, pour les derni&#232;res nouvelles.</SMALL></P>
   </TD></TR>
   </TABLE>
   </BODY>
   </HTML>
</xsl:template>

</xsl:stylesheet>
```

You could also use different style sheets to do the following:

- Optimize your pages for a given browser. You would need to detect the browser type and select the style sheet that works best with the browser.
- Support non-PC devices. In fact, by combining the techniques introduced in Chapter 4 with the technique in this chapter, you can write servlets that support HTML and WAP devices!

## What About Speed?

How fast is the XSL processing? Does it penalize the servlet to go through all these steps? Of course, the XSL processing is one more step and it is doomed to slow down the servlet, but, in practice, it is rarely a problem.

Indeed, unless your application has very strict time constraints, the user is unlikely to notice the difference. Furthermore, one of the beauties of adopting a standard such as XSL is that you benefit from improvements to the processor.

When new and faster processors appear on the market, you can integrate them in your servlet.

## Additional Resources

In this chapter, we built a simple but effective framework to implement XSL in servlets. Although it is primarily intended to provide a clean interface between programmers and designers, the technique offers additional benefits.

If you like the approach but would prefer a more extensive framework, you can turn to the Cocoon project, part of XML Apache at `xml.apache.org`.

Finally, this approach is not limited to Java servlets. All you need is an XSL processor in the language of your choice. I can almost hear you inquiring about Perl scripts. Well, it works with XML::XSLT, which is available from `www.sci.kun.nl/sigma/ Persoonlijk/egonw/xslt`.

**9**

# Provide Up-to-the-Minute Information to Business Partners

FOR THE PURPOSE OF THIS CHAPTER, imagine that you are in the wholesale business. Your company buys goods from different suppliers, stores them in one or more warehouses, and resells them to retailers. Although you ship most products to the retailers, increasingly, you ship directly to the end buyer.

At the heart of this business is a strong commitment to managing logistics: A wholesaler is a buffer between manufacturing and retailing. Obviously, this business is highly computerized. Wholesalers typically accept orders electronically, possibly using a server similar to the one introduced in Chapter 7, "Write an e-Commerce Server."

Furthermore, imagine that your company decides to improve services to its retailers. You participate in a brainstorming session and one of the conclusions is to provide more timely information—for example, up-to-the-minute inventory information over the Internet. You are tasked with the implementation.

The availability of products in your warehouse is precious information for your retailers, particularly the online ones. It enables them to better inform their customers: "This product is available, you'll have it tomorrow morning" or "Looks like this item is very popular. I'm afraid it might take longer for delivery." In exchange for the improved service, they might have to sign an exclusive agreement with your company.

▶ **Note**

Some companies do just the opposite: They ask their suppliers (not customers) to check their stock and proactively supply goods when their warehouse is empty.

In effect, the supplier manages the stock on behalf of the customer.

In this chapter, we'll see how to build a solution to provide timely information to retailers with the Simple Object Access Protocol (SOAP). SOAP supports Web-based remote procedure calls (RPC).

Obviously, SOAP is not specific to wholesalers. Many businesses would benefit from opening their information systems to some or all of their customers. For example, a manufacturer in a competitive industry might publish regular price updates; an airline can make flight information available online; a hotel can report free rooms; and an auction site can publish bids.

For completeness, SOAP also can be used in totally different contexts: Userland used XML-RPC (an early version of SOAP) in a distributed publishing application, which enabled the editor to interact with the Web site.

# Architecture

As you review your options, after the brainstorming, you find you essentially have three possibilities.

## A Web Site

The first option is to build a private Web site for retailers. After logging in to the site, retailers could check the availability of products.

The main argument in favor of this approach is that it is likely to be familiar to your developers. It would require connecting your Web server to the warehouse management application. You can find tools on the market (known as *application servers*) to help you build this solution.

The main issue with this solution is that it involves yet another Web site: To access stock data, the retailer must start his browser, log in to your site, and type his query. Your Web site is completely independent from the retailer's own inventory manager.

However, chances are that the retailer employees need to first search the product in their local warehouse. It's only when the product is not available locally that they will order from you.

Figure 9.1 illustrates this. Notice the two applications: the retailer's own stock manager and yours, which is Web accessible.

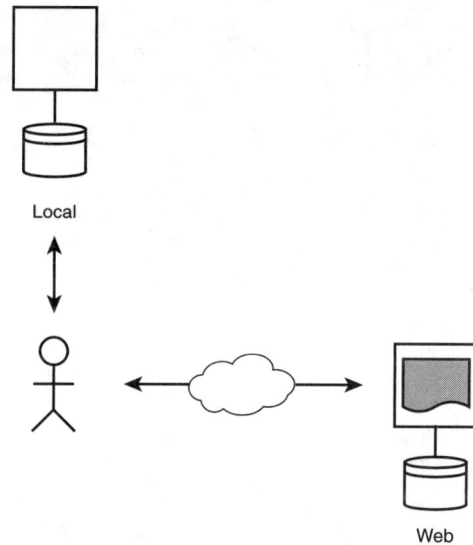

**Figure 9.1** The wholesaler Web site is independent from the retailer's stock manager.

In practice, companies are increasingly reluctant to train their clerical staff to access third-party Web sites. For the retailer's IT people, it's yet another application to learn and support. For the clerk, it's an annoyance to have to enter her search twice.

Finally, you should consider online retailers. An online retailer wants to publish as much information as possible on its own Web site. This setup forces them to redirect their customers to the wholesaler's Web site, which is seldom a good idea.

## Distributed Objects

Having established that a Web site does not properly serve your customers' needs, you'll strive to offer a more integrated solution.

Traditionally, to integrate applications running on different computers, you would use a distributed object architecture (middleware), such as OMG's CORBA, Microsoft's DCOM, or Java's RMI.

Essentially, the middleware wraps objects, such as Java or C++ objects, with a network layer. In this case, it would wrap the objects in your warehouse management application on a server.

This setup is illustrated in Figure 9.2. For the retailer, this is more attractive because he can integrate your data into his application. He has only one application to support.

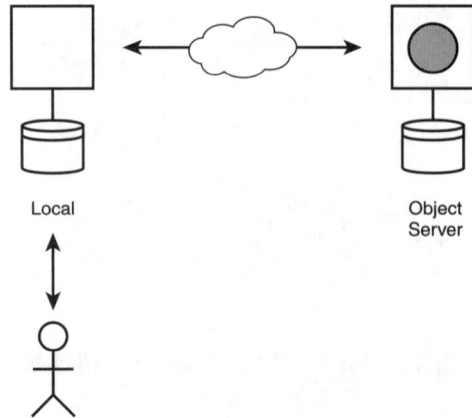

**Figure 9.2** Because objects are available on a server, the retailer can integrate them in his application.

However, this solution suffers from the following problems:

- CORBA, DCOM, and RMI have a reputation of being complex. I believe that if you give them the benefit of doubt, you'll find that most horror stories are unjustified but, still, it will be a tough sell.
- Distributed object architectures were designed primarily to work over local networks and are not optimized for the wider Internet.

One of the first practical problems is the use of firewalls. Most corporate firewalls accept only HTTP and SMTP traffic and will block CORBA and DCOM.

Furthermore, because it's an object server, you literally expose the guts of your application. The retailer can grab one of your application's objects and call its methods. This creates a very tight coupling between the two applications.

Who really wants to share her live application objects with outsiders? What happens if they inadvertently issue the wrong calls and crash your server? And we have not even touched on security.

Likewise, who wants to be responsible if problems occur with the retailer's application? He who publishes an object is responsible for its support. Do you really want to take over such a burden?

▶ **Warning**

To be fair to CORBA, DCOM, and RMI, I must mention that they provide mechanisms to alleviate these problems. For example, HTTP gateways are available to work around firewalls. Also, completely isolating your application from the objects on the server is possible.

Yet, it is when you have to deploy these advanced features that you find distributed object architectures can deserve their reputation for complexity!

## SOAP

Back to square one. At this point, you re-examine the Web site idea. Its main advantages were as follows:

- It is easy to set up because it uses technology with which you are already familiar.
- It is cheap to operate for the same reason.
- It has a proven track record for being deployed over the Internet.

The only problem is the integration issue. However, if you replace HTML with XML, you would have a format that can efficiently transport structured information and that enables integration. In essence, this is the idea behind SOAP.

SOAP is a protocol that formalizes how a Web client and Web browser can integrate using HTTP and XML. The most popular application of SOAP is XML-based remote procedure calls.

The SOAP approach is illustrated in Figure 9.3. As you can see, it combines the best of Figure 9.1 (reliance on Web protocols) with the best of Figure 9.2 (integrated applications).

Specifically, SOAP

- Works across firewalls because it runs over HTTP
- Is as easy to set up and manage as a Web site
- Is based on well-known technologies
- Is not limited to a local network but is designed for the wider Internet

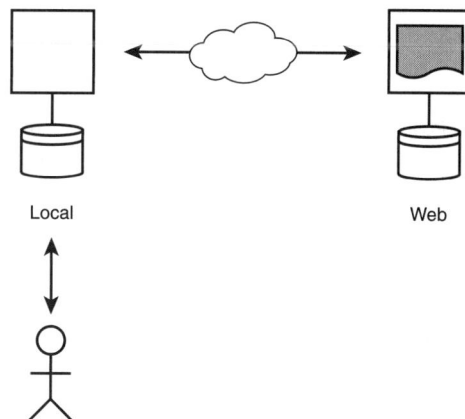

**Figure 9.3** SOAP offers the same benefits as an object server but over the Web.

However, there is no such thing as a free lunch. The price you pay for the flexibility is efficiency. SOAP is significantly slower than distributed object architectures for the following reasons:

- SOAP uses text-based messages that must be parsed on the receiving end and tend to be larger than binary protocols.
- SOAP relies on HTTP for communication, and HTTP is not the fastest protocol around.

**Note**

SOAP is another solution to implement a browser on autopilot, as introduced in Chapter 7. However, SOAP specifies what the request and response should look like.

# The SOAP Protocol

If you know HTTP and XML, you'll learn SOAP in minutes. Essentially, SOAP defines how a client should format its request and how the server should format its answer.

**Warning**

This discussion is based on SOAP 1.1, the latest version at the time of writing. At the time of writing, SOAP is not formally an Internet standard, but it appears that W3C might define its own XML-based RPC protocol. This new protocol would be based on the same principle as SOAP but might differ in the details.

I will post articles and news as the status of SOAP clarifies at www.marchal.com.

## SOAP Request

Listing 9.1 is a SOAP request. As you can see, it's an HTTP 1.1 POST request with an XML payload. The SOAP specification mandates the use of HTTP 1.1, POST, and XML. It also mandates the presence of the Content-Length and SOAPAction headers in the request.

SOAPAction is specific to SOAP. It is loosely defined in the specification as a URI identifying the intent of the request. However, it need not be the URL of the Web server (indeed, if you read the header, the request is for localhost/stockq, not http://www.psol.com/xmlns/stockq).

You should not worry too much about SOAPAction. It was introduced primarily to help firewalls separate SOAP traffic from regular Web requests.

Listing 9.1  **A SOAP Request**

```
POST /stockq HTTP/1.1
Host: localhost
Content-Type: text/xml
Content-Length: 422
SOAPAction: "http://www.psol.com/xmlns/stockq"

<?xml version='1.0'?>
<SOAP-ENV:Envelope
    xmlns:SOAP-ENV="http://schemas.xmlsoap.org/soap/envelope/">
    <SOAP-ENV:Body>
        <psol:getStock
            xmlns:psol='http://www.psol.com/xmlns/stockq'
            SOAP-ENV:encodingStyle='http://schemas.xmlsoap.org/soap/
⇒encoding/'>
            <manufacturer>Playfield</manufacturer>
            <sku>101</sku>
        </psol:getStock>
    </SOAP-ENV:Body>
</SOAP-ENV:Envelope>
```

The RPC is encoded as an XML document. SOAP defines the `SOAP-ENV:Envelope`, `SOAP-ENV:Body`, and `SOAP-ENV:Header` elements (in the `http://schemas.xmlsoap.org/soap/envelope/` namespace).

`SOAP-ENV:Envelope` must be the root of SOAP requests. `SOAP-ENV:Envelope` can contain a `SOAP-ENV:Header` and must contain a `SOAP-ENV:Body`. In Listing 9.1, the optional `SOAP-ENV:Header` is not present.

The `SOAP-ENV:Header` carries extensions to SOAP. Headers were introduced to manage transactions, payments, or authentication. So far, though, they are not used frequently.

The `SOAP-ENV:Body` contains the RPC data. The name of the RPC is encoded as an XML element: `psol:getStock` for the `getStock` RPC in Listing 9.1.

The parameters of the call are also encoded as elements. SOAP offers a default encoding for parameters, which Listing 9.1 uses. However, your application can use any encoding, provided it is declared in the `SOAP-ENV:encodingStyle` attribute. For example, SOAP for Java from IBM can encode parameters following the SOAP rules or XMI.

The SOAP encoding lists the parameters as XML elements whose names match the parameter names. In Listing 9.1, the two parameters are `manufacturer` and `sku`. Their values are `Playfield` and `101`.

> **Note**
>
> SOAP provides a mechanism to signal the type of the parameters. The specification states that values are always encoded as strings. For example, the integer fifty-three is represented by the string 53.
>
> SOAP defines an optional attribute (`xsi:type`) that you would use as follows:
>
> ```
> <manufacturer xsi:type="xsd:string">101</manufacturer>
> ```
>
> However, `xsi:type` is not required if the parameter supports only one type. In practice, you mainly use `xsi:type` for object parameters because, through inheritance and polymorphism, recognizing the actual parameter's type is not always easy.

## SOAP Response

When the server recognizes a SOAP request, it parses the payload and extracts the RPC name and its parameters. It executes the call and prepares a response, again as an XML document sent over HTTP.

Listing 9.2 is the response for the query in Listing 9.1. As you can see, it's a regular HTTP response with an XML payload.

Listing 9.2 **The SOAP Response**

```
HTTP/1.1 200 OK
Content-Type: text/xml
Content-Length: 555

<?xml version='1.0'?>
<SOAP-ENV:Envelope
    xmlns:SOAP-ENV="http://schemas.xmlsoap.org/soap/envelope/">
    <SOAP-ENV:Body>
        <psol:getStockResponse
            xmlns:psol='http://www.psol.com/xmlns/stockq'
            SOAP-ENV:encodingStyle='http://schemas.xmlsoap.org/soap/
➥encoding/'>
            <stockq>
                <manufacturer>Playfield</manufacturer>
                <sku>101</sku>
                <available>true</available>
                <level>10</level>
            </stockq>
        </psol:getStockResponse>
    </SOAP-ENV:Body>
</SOAP-ENV:Envelope>
```

You are now familiar with `SOAP-ENV:Envelope` and `SOAP-ENV:Body`. The body of the response is again an XML element, but the specification does not specify its name. It could be anything, even though the specification suggests you'd use the RPC name suffixed with `Response` (`psol:getStockResponse`).

The first element within the response is the return value (again, the specification does not enforce its name). In this example, the return value is a structure with four fields.

SOAP's rule to encode structures is that the names of the elements must match the names of the fields. So, in Listing 9.2, the four fields are `manufacturer`, `sku`, `available`, and `level`.

Although Listing 9.2 does not illustrate it, a response can include out parameters. They simply appear after the response element.

## SOAP Fault

As you have seen, in most cases, the content of `SOAP-ENV:Body` is defined by the application. However, SOAP defines one special element to report errors: `SOAP-ENV:Fault`. `SOAP-ENV:Fault` is a structure with four fields, the first two of which are mandatory:

- `faultcode`—Indicates the type of error (acceptable values are `SOAP-ENV:VersionMismatch`, `SOAP-ENV:MustUnderstand`, `SOAP-ENV:Client`, and `SOAP-ENV:Server`).
- `faultstring`—A human-readable description of the error.
- `faultfactor`—Used primarily when relaying SOAP messages (for example, when using a proxy). It is a URI that indicates on which relay the request failed.
- `detail`—Intended for application-specific errors.

Listing 9.3 is a response with an error. Note that SOAP mandates the use of the HTTP `500` return code.

Listing 9.3 **A SOAP Fault**

```
HTTP/1.1 500 Internal Server Error
Content-Type: text/xml
Content-Length: 333

<?xml version='1.0'?>
<SOAP-ENV:Envelope
    xmlns:SOAP-ENV="http://schemas.xmlsoap.org/soap/envelope/">
    <SOAP-ENV:Body>
        <SOAP-ENV:Fault>
            <faultcode>SOAP-ENV:VersionMismatch</faultcode>
            <faultstring>Unknown SOAP version</faultstring>
        </SOAP-ENV:Fault>
    </SOAP-ENV:Body>
</SOAP-ENV:Envelope>
```

# A SOAP Library

The two main approaches to implementing SOAP are as follows:

- Use a networking library that wraps Java objects in a SOAP network layer. This is similar to a CORBA broker: It takes Java objects and exposes them, as SOAP requests, on a Web server. The reference implementation from IBM (available from www.alphaworks.ibm.com) follows this approach.

- Treat SOAP requests as regular POST requests and write a servlet, or a JSP page, to handle them.

In this chapter, we'll use the second solution. At the time of writing, the SOAP libraries for Java are in the alpha stage and not suitable for inclusion in a book.

However, even if I had had the choice, I would have been inclined to treat SOAP requests as other Web requests. Remember, one of our goals is to build a flexible solution that does not depend directly on the specifics of a Java application.

In the remainder of the chapter, we will write the server to report product availability. We also will write a simple client to test and demonstrate the server. In so doing, we will cover both the wholesaler and the retailer situations.

As always, the focus is on XML, not on building the best stock management system. Indeed, as you will see, I have greatly simplified the inventory management!

## Architecture

Figure 9.4 shows the UML model for the client and the server.

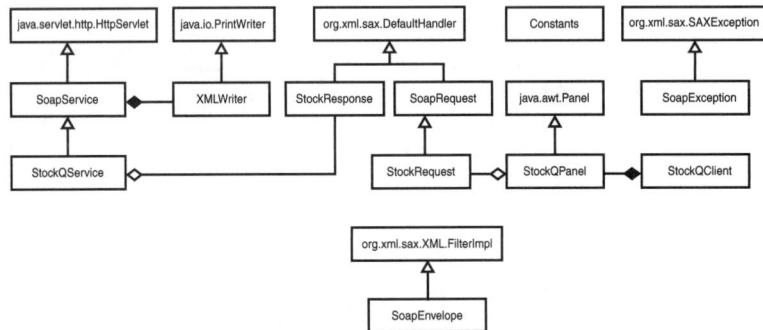

**Figure 9.4** The architecture of the client and the server.

The various classes in Figure 9.4 are

- SoapService—A servlet specialized to process SOAP requests.
- StockQService—The inventory management server.

- XMLWriter—A helper class to escape XML characters, such as &lt;.
- StockResponse—Parses getStock requests and prepares the responses.
- SoapRequest—Encapsulates the creation of a SOAP request.
- StockRequest—Inherits from SoapRequest and generates the getStock request.
- Constants—Holds various constants.
- StockQClient, StockQPanel—The inventory management client.
- SoapException—Encapsulates SOAP-ENV:Fault.
- SoapEnvelope—A SAX filter that parses the SOAP elements. Both SoapRequest and SoapService use it.

### SAX's XMLFilter

A filter is both an event *handler* and an event *source*: It intercepts events, performs some processing, and generates events of its own. In doing so, it also might remove or add events.

Filters are similar to AWT adapters. Typically you will use one or more filters to pre-process XML documents.

Figure 9.5 illustrates how this works. The document flows through a chain of filters where each filter transforms the document and passes the result to the next stage.

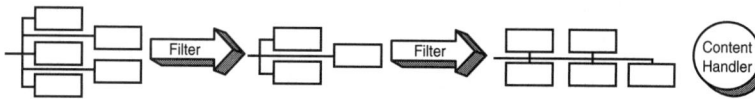

**Figure 9.5** Filters are chained to process XML documents.

Filters are typically used to recognize special vocabularies. For example, you can use filters that recognize XLink hyperlinks or use them to decode and validate digital signatures.

In this project, SoapEnvelope is a filter. It processes SOAP-defined elements, such as SOAP-ENV:Envelope and SOAP-ENV:Fault. This frees up the application-specific content handler to concentrate on application-specific elements, such as getProduct.

This supports code reuse (indeed, we use SoapEnvelope on the client and the server). It also isolates the SOAP protocol from the rest of the application, so if SOAP changes, updates will be limited to SoapEnvelope.

# The Stock Server

We'll start with the server. The server is connected to the warehouse database, accepts getStock RPC, and returns the latest status on product availability.

## SoapEnvelope

The first class we will look at, `SoapEnvelope`, is not specific to the server. This class is demonstrated in Listing 9.4.

Listing 9.4  *SoapEnvelope.java*

```
package com.psol.stockq;

import org.xml.sax.*;
import org.xml.sax.helpers.*;

public class SoapEnvelope
   extends XMLFilterImpl
{
   protected static final int NONE = 0,
                              ENVELOPE = 1,
                              HEADER = 2,
                              BODY = 3,
                              FAULT = 4,
                              FAULT_CODE = 5,
                              FAULT_STRING = 6;
   protected int status = NONE;
   protected static final String SOAP_URI =
      "http://schemas.xmlsoap.org/soap/envelope/";
   protected StringBuffer buffer = null;
   protected String[] data = null;

   public void startDocument()
      throws SAXException
   {
      status = NONE;
      getContentHandler().startDocument();
   }

   public void startElement(String namespaceURI,
                            String localName,
                            String rawName,
                            Attributes atts)
      throws SAXException
   {
      if(BODY == status)
         if(localName.equals("Fault") &&
            namespaceURI.equals(SOAP_URI))
         {
            status = FAULT;
            data = new String[2];
         }
         else
            getContentHandler().startElement(namespaceURI,
                                             localName,
                                             rawName,
```

Listing 9.4 **Continued**

```
                                                          atts);
      else if(localName.equals("Envelope") && NONE == status)
         if(namespaceURI.equals(SOAP_URI))
            status = ENVELOPE;
         else
            throw new SoapException("VersionMismatch",
                                    "Unknown SOAP version");
      else if(localName.equals("Body") &&
              namespaceURI.equals(SOAP_URI) &&
              ENVELOPE == status)
         status = BODY;
      else if(localName.equals("Header") &&
              namespaceURI.equals(SOAP_URI) &&
              ENVELOPE == status)
         status = HEADER;
      else if(status == HEADER)
      {
         // IMHO it really should be in the SOAP namespace
         String mu = atts.getValue("mustUnderstand");
         if(mu != null && mu.equals("1"))
            throw new SoapException("MustUnderstand",
                                    rawName + " unknown");
      }
      else if(localName.equals("faultcode") &&
              status == FAULT)
      {
         status = FAULT_CODE;
         buffer = new StringBuffer();
      }
      else if(localName.equals("faultstring") &&
              status == FAULT)
      {
         status = FAULT_STRING;
         buffer = new StringBuffer();
      }
   }

   public void endElement(String namespaceURI,
                          String localName,
                          String rawName)
      throws SAXException
   {
      if(BODY == status)
         getContentHandler().endElement(namespaceURI,
                                        localName,
                                        rawName);
      else if(localName.equals("Envelope") &&
              namespaceURI.equals(SOAP_URI) &&
              ENVELOPE == status)
         status = NONE;
```

Listing 9.4 **Continued**

```java
        else if(localName.equals("Body") &&
                namespaceURI.equals(SOAP_URI) &&
                BODY == status)
          status = ENVELOPE;
        else if(localName.equals("Header") &&
                namespaceURI.equals(SOAP_URI) &&
                HEADER == status)
          status = ENVELOPE;
        else if(localName.equals("Fault") &&
                namespaceURI.equals(SOAP_URI) &&
                status == FAULT)
          throw new SoapException(data[0],data[1]);
        else if(localName.equals("faultcode") &&
                status == FAULT_CODE)
        {
          status = FAULT;
          data[0] = buffer.toString();
          buffer = null;
        }
        else if(localName.equals("faultstring") &&
                status == FAULT_STRING)
        {
          status = FAULT;
          data[1] = buffer.toString();
          buffer = null;
        }
      }

      public void characters(char[] ch,int start,int len)
        throws SAXException
      {
        if(BODY == status)
          getContentHandler().characters(ch,start,len);
        else if(FAULT_CODE == status ||
                FAULT_STRING == status)
          buffer.append(ch,start,len);
      }

      public void skippedEntity(String name)
        throws SAXException
      {
        if(BODY == status)
          getContentHandler().skippedEntity(name);
      }

      public void ignorableWhitespace(char[] ch,
                                      int start,
                                      int len)
        throws SAXException
      {
```

Listing 9.4 **Continued**

```
            if(BODY == status)
                getContentHandler().ignorableWhitespace(ch,start,len);
        }

        public void processingInstruction(String target,String data)
            throws SAXException
        {
            if(BODY == status)
                getContentHandler().processingInstruction(target,data);
        }
    }
```

SoapEnvelope passes most events unmodified to its ContentHandler:

```
    public void startDocument()
        throws SAXException
    {
        status = NONE;
        getContentHandler().startDocument();
    }
```

The main methods are startElement() and endElement(). The filter intercepts events related to SOAP elements but passes other events unmodified.

SOAP-ENV:Header requires special attention. You will remember that header elements are not defined by SOAP. However, the header might influence how the server should process the request—for example, when a client makes a request within the context of a transaction, it might impact the server response. What happens if a server does not recognize the transaction elements?

SOAP suggests you label mandatory elements in the header with a mustUnderstand attribute. The server must either recognize the element or signal an error. The filter enforces this rule:

```
    else if(localName.equals("Header") &&
            namespaceURI.equals(SOAP_URI) &&
            ENVELOPE == status)
        status = HEADER;
    else if(status == HEADER)
    {
        // IMHO it really should be in the SOAP namespace
        String mu = atts.getValue("mustUnderstand");
        if(mu != null && mu.equals("1"))
            throw new SoapException("MustUnderstand",
                                    rawName + " unknown");
    }
```

The filter also enforces version control. SOAP uses namespaces for versioning. Elements not in the SOAP namespace indicate a new, incompatible version:

```
    else if(localName.equals("Envelope") && NONE == status)
        if(namespaceURI.equals(SOAP_URI))
```

```
            status = ENVELOPE;
        else
            throw new SoapException("VersionMismatch",
                                    "Unknown SOAP version");
```

## SoapService

SoapService, in Listing 9.5, inherits from a servlet to implement the SOAP protocol. Its descendants must worry about only the RPC.

Listing 9.5  *SoapService.java*

```
package com.psol.stockq;

import java.io.*;
import java.sql.*;
import org.xml.sax.*;
import javax.servlet.*;
import javax.servlet.http.*;
import org.xml.sax.helpers.*;

public abstract class SoapService
    extends HttpServlet
{
    public abstract void doSoap(XMLReader reader,
                                InputSource source,
                                XMLWriter writer)
        throws IOException, SoapException, SAXException;

    // to optimize, we could manage a pool of XMLReader

    public void doPost(HttpServletRequest request,
                       HttpServletResponse response)
        throws IOException
    {
        try
        {
            // check for SOAPAction, ignore its value
            // because the spec is unclear on what the server
            // should do with SOAPAction
            String soapAction = request.getHeader("SOAPAction");
            if(null == soapAction)
                throw new SoapException("Client",
                                        "Missing SOAPAction");
            XMLReader xmlReader =
                XMLReaderFactory.createXMLReader(
                                Constants.SAXPARSER);
            xmlReader.setFeature(Constants.SAXNAMESPACES,true);
            SoapEnvelope soapEnvelope = new SoapEnvelope();
            soapEnvelope.setParent(xmlReader);
```

Listing 9.5 **Continued**

```
        CharArrayWriter payload = new CharArrayWriter();
        payload.write("<?xml version='1.0'?>");
        payload.write("<SOAP-ENV:Envelope xmlns:SOAP-ENV='");
        payload.write(Constants.SOAPENV_URI);
        payload.write("'><SOAP-ENV:Body>");
        InputSource source =
          new InputSource(request.getReader());
        doSoap(soapEnvelope,source,new XMLWriter(payload));
        payload.write("</SOAP-ENV:Body></SOAP-ENV:Envelope>");

        Writer writer = response.getWriter();
        response.setContentType("text/xml");
        payload.writeTo(writer);
        writer.flush();
      }
      catch(SoapException e)
      {
        response.setStatus(
          HttpServletResponse.SC_INTERNAL_SERVER_ERROR);
        response.setContentType("text/xml");
        e.writeTo(new XMLWriter(response.getWriter()));
        response.getWriter().flush();
      }
      catch(SAXException e)
      {
        // when SAXException embeds another exception
        // it does a poor job at returning the embedded
        // exception message, so extract it
        response.setStatus(
          HttpServletResponse.SC_INTERNAL_SERVER_ERROR);
        response.setContentType("text/xml");
        Exception ex = e.getException() != null ?
                       e.getException() : e;
        new SoapException("Client",ex.getMessage()).
          writeTo(new XMLWriter(response.getWriter()));
        response.getWriter().flush();
      }
      catch(Exception e)
      {
        response.setStatus(
          HttpServletResponse.SC_INTERNAL_SERVER_ERROR);
        response.setContentType("text/xml");
        new SoapException("Server",e.getMessage()).
          writeTo(new XMLWriter(response.getWriter()));
        response.getWriter().flush();
      }
    }
  }
}
```

`SoapService` parses the envelope (through `SoapEnvelope`) but delegates processing of the request to its descendants (through a call to `doSoap()`). Likewise, it writes the SOAP envelope but lets its descendants write the response.

Notice how it creates a parser, turns on namespace processing, and activates the `SoapEnvelope` as an XML filter:

```
XMLReader xmlReader =
   XMLReaderFactory.createXMLReader(Constants.SAXPARSER);
xmlReader.setFeature(Constants.SAXNAMESPACES,true);
SoapEnvelope soapEnvelope = new SoapEnvelope();
soapEnvelope.setParent(xmlReader);
```

Next, it uses `SoapEnvelope` as if it were the parser itself:

```
doSoap(soapEnvelope,source,new XMLWriter(payload));
```

## XMLWriter

`XMLWriter`, in Listing 9.6, should look familiar. It provides a helper method to escape reserved characters (<, &, and more).

Listing 9.6  *XMLWriter.java*

```
package com.psol.stockq;

import java.io.*;

public class XMLWriter
   extends PrintWriter
{
   public XMLWriter(Writer writer)
   {
      super(writer);
   }

   public void escape(String s)
      throws IOException
   {
      for(int i = 0;i < s.length();i++)
      {
         char c = s.charAt(i);
         if(c == '<')
            write("&lt;");
         else if(c == '&')
            write("&amp;");
         else if(c == '\'')
            write("&apos;");
         else if(c == '"')
            write("&quot;");
         else if(c > '\u007f')
         {
```

Listing 9.6 **Continued**

```
            write("&#");
            write(Integer.toString);
            write(';');
        }
        else
            write;
    }
  }
}
```

## SoapException

SoapException, in Listing 9.7, stores the `faultcode` and `faultstring`. It also provides a convenient `writeTo()` method to write the fault in XML.

Listing 9.7 *SoapException.java*

```java
package com.psol.stockq;

import java.io.*;
import org.xml.sax.*;

public class SoapException
    extends SAXException
{
    protected String code;

    public SoapException(String code,String string)
    {
        super(string != null ? string : "Unknown error");
        this.code = code;
    }

    public String getCode()
    {
        return code;
    }

    public void writeTo(XMLWriter writer)
        throws IOException
    {
        writer.write("<?xml version='1.0'?>");
        writer.write("<SOAP-ENV:Envelope xmlns:SOAP-ENV='");
        writer.write(Constants.SOAPENV_URI);
        writer.write("'><SOAP-ENV:Body>");
        writer.write("<SOAP-ENV:Fault><faultcode>SOAP-ENV:");
        writer.escape(code);
        writer.write("</faultcode><faultstring>");
```

Listing 9.7 **Continued**

```
        writer.escape(getMessage());
        writer.write("</faultstring></SOAP-ENV:Fault>");
        writer.write("</SOAP-ENV:Body></SOAP-ENV:Envelope>");
    }
}
```

## Database

So far, we have looked at generic SOAP classes. To study the specifics of the stock server, we'll start with the database.

Again, because our focus is on XML, not stock management, I've kept the database simple. It contains a single table, `products`, which lists products and their availability (negative numbers indicate back orders). Products are identified by their manufacturer name and a product number (sku).

▶

### Warning

This chapter does not include a tool to update inventory levels. You will need to edit them through your database user interface.

However, it is probably not a good idea to let retailers remotely manipulate product availability! You want the database to reflect actual levels in the warehouse.

### StockResponse

StockResponse, in Listing 9.8, implements `ContentHandler`. Because it comes after a `SoapEnvelope` filter, it never sees the SOAP elements. As far as `StockResponse` is concerned, the root of the document is `getProduct`.

Listing 9.8 *StockResponse.java*

```
package com.psol.stockq;

import java.io.*;
import java.sql.*;
import org.xml.sax.*;
import org.xml.sax.helpers.*;

public class StockResponse
    extends DefaultHandler
{
    protected StringBuffer manufacturer = null,
                           sku = null;
```

Listing 9.8 **Continued**

```java
protected final static int NONE = 0,
                           GET_STOCK = 1,
                           MANUFACTURER = 2,
                           SKU = 3;
protected int status = NONE;

public void startDocument()
   throws SAXException
{
   status = NONE;
   manufacturer = null;
   sku = null;
}

public void startElement(String namespaceURI,
                         String localName,
                         String rawName,
                         Attributes atts)
   throws SAXException
{
   if(localName.equals("getStock") &&
      namespaceURI.equals(Constants.PSOL_URI) &&
      NONE == status)
      status = GET_STOCK;
   else if(rawName.equals("manufacturer") &&
           GET_STOCK == status &&
           null == manufacturer)
   {
      manufacturer = new StringBuffer();
      status = MANUFACTURER;
   }
   else if(rawName.equals("sku") &&
           GET_STOCK == status  &&
           null == sku)
   {
      sku = new StringBuffer();
      status = SKU;
   }
}

public void endElement(String namespaceURI,
                       String localName,
                       String rawName)
   throws SAXException
{
   if(localName.equals("getStock") &&
      namespaceURI.equals(Constants.PSOL_URI) &&
      GET_STOCK == status)
      status = NONE;
   else if(rawName.equals("manufacturer") &&
```

Listing 9.8 **Continued**

```
                    MANUFACTURER == status)
        status = GET_STOCK;
    else if(rawName.equals("sku") && SKU == status)
        status = GET_STOCK;
}

public void characters(char[] ch,int start,int len)
    throws SAXException
{
    if(SKU == status)
        sku.append(ch,start,len);
    else if(MANUFACTURER == status)
        manufacturer.append(ch,start,len);
}

public void writeResponse(Connection connection,
                          XMLWriter writer)
    throws SQLException, IOException, SoapException
{
    if(manufacturer == null || sku == null)
        throw new SoapException("Client",
                                "Missing manufacturer or sku");
    PreparedStatement stmt =
        connection.prepareStatement("select level " +
        "from products where manufacturer=? and sku=?");
    try
    {
        stmt.setString(1,manufacturer.toString());
        stmt.setString(2,sku.toString());
        ResultSet rs = stmt.executeQuery();
        try
        {
            writer.write("<psol:getStockResponse xmlns:psol='");
            writer.write(Constants.PSOL_URI);
            writer.write("' SOAP-ENV:encodingStyle='");
            writer.write(Constants.SOAPENCODING_URI);
            writer.write("'><stockq><manufacturer>");
            writer.write(manufacturer.toString());
            writer.write("</manufacturer><sku>");
            writer.write(sku.toString());
            writer.write("</sku><available>");
            if(rs.next())
            {

                writer.write("true</available><level>");
                writer.escape(rs.getString(1));
            }
            else
                writer.write("false</available><level>0");
            writer.write("</level></stockq>");
            writer.write("</psol:getStockResponse>");
```

Listing 9.8 **Continued**

```
        }
        finally
        {
            rs.close();
        }
    }
    finally
    {
        stmt.close();
    }
  }
}
```

`StockResponse` is also responsible for querying the database and writing the response in the `writeResponse()` method. Notice that in so doing, it ignores the SOAP envelope that will be added by `SoapService`:

```
public void writeResponse(Connection connection,
                          XMLWriter writer)
  throws SQLException, IOException, SoapException
{
  if(manufacturer == null || sku == null)
      throw new SoapException("Client",
                              "Missing manufacturer or sku");
  PreparedStatement stmt =
      connection.prepareStatement("select level " +
      "from products where manufacturer=? and sku=?");
  try
  {
      stmt.setString(1,manufacturer.toString());
      stmt.setString(2,sku.toString());
      ResultSet rs = stmt.executeQuery();
      try
      {
        writer.write("<psol:getStockResponse xmlns:psol='");
        writer.write(Constants.PSOL_URI);
        writer.write("' SOAP-ENV:encodingStyle='");
        writer.write(Constants.SOAPENCODING_URI);
        writer.write("'><stockq><manufacturer>");
        writer.write(manufacturer.toString());
        writer.write("</manufacturer><sku>");
        writer.write(sku.toString());
        writer.write("</sku><available>");
        if(rs.next())
        {
            writer.write("true</available><level>");
            writer.escape(rs.getString(1));
        }
        else
```

```
                  writer.write("false</available><level>0");
              writer.write("</level></stockq>");
              writer.write("</psol:getStockResponse>");
          }
          finally
          {
              rs.close();
          }
        }
        finally
        {
            stmt.close();
        }
    }
```

## StockQService

StockQService, in Listing 9.9, is the actual servlet. It parses SOAP requests and writes
the response through StockResponse.

Listing 9.9  *StockQService.java*

```java
package com.psol.stockq;

import java.io.*;
import java.sql.*;
import org.xml.sax.*;
import javax.servlet.*;

public class StockQService
    extends SoapService
{
    public void init()
        throws ServletException
    {
        try
        {
            Class.forName(getInitParameter("driver"));
        }
        catch(ClassNotFoundException e)
        {
            throw new ServletException(e);
        }
    }

    public void doSoap(XMLReader reader,
                       InputSource source,
                       XMLWriter writer)
        throws IOException, SoapException, SAXException
    {
```

Listing 9.9 **Continued**

```
    StockResponse response = new StockResponse();
    reader.setContentHandler(response);
    reader.parse(source);
    try
    {
        String url = getInitParameter("url"),
               username = getInitParameter("username"),
               password = getInitParameter("password");
        Connection connection =
            DriverManager.getConnection(url,username,password);
        try
        {
            response.writeResponse(connection,writer);
        }
        finally
        {
            connection.close();
        }
    }
    catch(SQLException e)
    {
        throw new SoapException("Server",
                                "SQL: " + e.getMessage());
    }
  }
}
```

**Warning**

For SOAP, a one-to-one mapping between servlets and RPCs is not available. A servlet can accept different RPCs: It should recognize them by their names.

# The Stock Client

This section presents a simple client. In practice, the wholesaler would not write the client. It would be left to the retailers to try to integrate the SOAP server in their existing applications. However, for completeness and to enable testing, we will write a simple SOAP client.

Figure 9.6 illustrates the stock client. As always, little effort has gone into the user interface so that the XML is more visible. The beauty of this client, however, is that it integrates the local (retailer) and remote (wholesaler) databases.

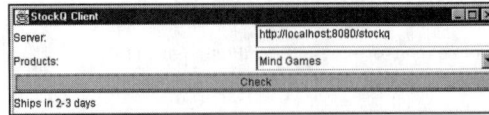

**Figure 9.6** The client provides an integrated view of the retailer and wholesaler databases.

The client application starts by looking in the local database. It is only if the product is not available locally that it connects to the wholesaler site and inquires about remote availability. The client interprets the results as follows:

- If the product is in stock locally, the client announces shipment within 24 hours.
- If the product is not available locally but is available from the wholesaler, the client reports shipment within 2–3 days.
- If the product is back-ordered both locally and at the wholesaler, the client announces shipment within 3–5 weeks.
- Finally, if the product is not available with the wholesaler, the client announces a special order.

### SoapRequest

SoapRequest, in Listing 9.10, implements the SOAP protocol for requests: It prepares the request, sends it over HTTP (as a POST request, ensuring it includes the required SOAPAction header), and uses SoapEnvelope to decode the response.

Listing 9.10 *SoapRequest.java*

```java
package com.psol.stockq;

import java.io.*;
import java.net.*;
import java.util.*;
import org.xml.sax.*;
import org.xml.sax.helpers.*;

public abstract class SoapRequest
    extends DefaultHandler
{
    protected String soapAction;

    public SoapRequest(String soapAction)
    {
        if(null == soapAction)
            soapAction = "\"\"";
        this.soapAction = '"' + soapAction + '"';
    }
```

Listing 9.10 **Continued**

```java
    public void invoke(URL server)
        throws IOException, SoapException, SAXException
    {
        HttpURLConnection conn =
            (HttpURLConnection)server.openConnection();
        conn.setDoOutput(true);
        conn.setDoInput(true);

        CharArrayWriter payload = new CharArrayWriter();
        payload.write("<?xml version='1.0'?>");
        payload.write("<SOAP-ENV:Envelope xmlns:SOAP-ENV='");
        payload.write(Constants.SOAPENV_URI);
        payload.write("'><SOAP-ENV:Body>");
        writeRequest(new XMLWriter(payload));
        payload.write("</SOAP-ENV:Body></SOAP-ENV:Envelope>");

        conn.setRequestProperty("Content-Length",
                                String.valueOf(payload.size()));
        conn.setRequestMethod("POST");
        conn.setFollowRedirects(true);
        conn.setRequestProperty("Content-Type","text/xml");
        conn.setRequestProperty("SOAPAction",
                                '"' + soapAction + '"');
        Writer writer =
            new OutputStreamWriter(conn.getOutputStream(),"UTF-8");
        payload.writeTo(writer);
        writer.flush();

        conn.connect();

        XMLReader xmlReader =
            XMLReaderFactory.createXMLReader(Constants.SAXPARSER);
        xmlReader.setFeature(Constants.SAXNAMESPACES,true);
        SoapEnvelope soapEnvelope = new SoapEnvelope();
        soapEnvelope.setParent(xmlReader);
        soapEnvelope.setContentHandler(this);
        InputSource is = new InputSource(conn.getInputStream());
        soapEnvelope.parse(is);
    }

    public abstract void writeRequest(XMLWriter writer)
        throws IOException;
}
```

Actual requests must inherit from `SoapRequest` and overwrite its `writeRequest()` method.

Note that `SoapRequest` inherits from `DefaultHandler` and registers itself as a
`ContentHandler` while parsing the response. Therefore, descendants should implement
`ContentHandler` to extract data they need:

```
XMLReader xmlReader =
    XMLReaderFactory.createXMLReader(Constants.SAXPARSER);
xmlReader.setFeature(Constants.SAXNAMESPACES,true);
SoapEnvelope soapEnvelope = new SoapEnvelope();
soapEnvelope.setParent(xmlReader);
soapEnvelope.setContentHandler(this);
InputSource is = new InputSource(conn.getInputStream());
soapEnvelope.parse(is);
```

### Warning

SoapRequest uses HttpURLConnection to execute the POST request. There is, however, one caveat in
using HttpURLConnection: If the server replies with a 500 code (for example, if a SOAP Fault has
occurred), HttpURLConnection throws an exception, and the application does not have a chance to
parse the Fault object.

This is a hotly debated issue with SOAP. SOAP mandates the use of HTTP return codes, but many proxies
and libraries already interpret these codes and might choose to discard the SOAP-ENV:Fault content.

## StockRequest

As its name implies, `StockRequest`, in Listing 9.11, enables `SoapRequest` to handle
stock requests.

Listing 9.11   *StockRequest.java*

```
package com.psol.stockq;

import java.io.*;
import java.awt.*;
import org.xml.sax.*;
import org.xml.sax.helpers.*;

public class StockRequest
    extends SoapRequest
{
    protected StringBuffer available = null,
                           level = null;
    protected String manufacturer = null,
                     sku = null,
                     responseTag = null,
                     responseNamespaceURI = null,
                     resultTag = null,
                     resultNamespaceURI = null;
    // ignore the manufacturer & sku
```

Listing 9.11 **Continued**

```
protected final static int NONE = 0,
                           RESPONSE = 1,
                           RESULT = 2,
                           AVAILABLE = 3,
                           LEVEL = 4;
protected int status = NONE;
protected Label message;

public StockRequest(Label message)
{
   super(Constants.PSOL_URI);
   this.message = message;
}

public void startDocument()
   throws SAXException
{
   status = NONE;
   available = null;
   level = null;
   manufacturer = null;
   sku = null;
   responseTag = null;
   resultTag = null;
}

public void startElement(String namespaceURI,
                         String localName,
                         String rawName,
                         Attributes atts)
   throws SAXException
{
   if(NONE == status)
   {
      status = RESPONSE;
      responseNamespaceURI = namespaceURI;
      responseTag = localName;
   }
   else if(RESPONSE == status &&
           null == resultTag)
   {
      resultNamespaceURI = namespaceURI;
      resultTag = localName;
      status = RESULT;
   }
   else if(RESULT == status &&
           rawName.equals("available") &&
           null == available)
   {
      status = AVAILABLE;
```

**Listing 9.11  Continued**

```
            available = new StringBuffer();
        }
        else if(RESULT == status &&
                rawName.equals("level") &&
                null == level)
        {
            status = LEVEL;
            level = new StringBuffer();
        }
    }

    public void endElement(String namespaceURI,
                           String localName,
                           String rawName)
        throws SAXException
    {
        if(namespaceURI.equals(resultNamespaceURI) &&
           localName.equals(resultTag) &&
           RESPONSE == status)
            status = NONE;
        else if(namespaceURI.equals(responseNamespaceURI) &&
                localName.equals(responseTag) &&
                RESULT == status)
        {
            status = RESPONSE;
            if(Boolean.valueOf(
                    available.toString()).booleanValue())
            {
                int lvl = Integer.parseInt(level.toString());
                if(lvl <= 0)
                    message.setText("Ships in 3-5 weeks");
                else
                    message.setText("Ships in 2-3 days");
            }
            else
                message.setText("Special order");
        }
        else if(rawName.equals("available") &&
                status == AVAILABLE)
            status = RESULT;
        else if(rawName.equals("level") &&
                status == LEVEL)
            status = RESULT;
    }

    public void characters(char[] ch,int start,int len)
        throws SAXException
    {
        if(AVAILABLE == status)
            available.append(ch,start,len);
```

Listing 9.11 **Continued**

```
        else if(LEVEL == status)
            level.append(ch,start,len);
    }

    public void setManufacturer(String manufacturer)
    {
        this.manufacturer = manufacturer;
    }

    public void setSku(String sku)
    {
        this.sku = sku;
    }

    public void writeRequest(XMLWriter writer)
        throws IOException
    {
        writer.write("<psol:getStock xmlns:psol='");
        writer.write(Constants.PSOL_URI);
        writer.write("' SOAP-ENV:encodingStyle='");
        writer.write(Constants.SOAPENCODING_URI);
        writer.write("'><manufacturer>");
        writer.escape(manufacturer);
        writer.write("</manufacturer><sku>");
        writer.escape(sku);
        writer.write("</sku></psol:getStock>");
    }
}
```

StockRequest parses getStockResponse. It does not worry about SoapEnvelope
because the filter has already taken care of these events.

Parsing the response is not as easy as parsing the request. The SOAP protocol specifies
that the names of the response and result elements are irrelevant—they could be anything. startElement() and endElement() must be careful not to make any assumptions
about them. In practice, startElement() uses variables to dynamically record the
names of the elements (an alternative would be to manage a stack):

```
public void startElement(String namespaceURI,
                         String localName,
                         String rawName,
                         Attributes atts)
    throws SAXException
{
    if(NONE == status)
    {
        status = RESPONSE;
        responseNamespaceURI = namespaceURI;
        responseTag = localName;
    }
```

```
    else if(RESPONSE == status &&
            null == resultTag)
    {
        resultNamespaceURI = namespaceURI;
        resultTag = localName;
        status = RESULT;
    }
    else if(RESULT == status &&
            rawName.equals("available") &&
            null == available)
    {
        status = AVAILABLE;
        available = new StringBuffer();
    }
    else if(RESULT == status &&
            rawName.equals("level") &&
            null == level)
    {
        status = LEVEL;
        level = new StringBuffer();
    }
}
```

`endElement()` analyzes the result and computes the expected shipment dates for the user. Note that this `ContentHandler` ignores the `manufacturer` and `sku` elements in the response:

```
    else if(namespaceURI.equals(responseNamespaceURI) &&
            localName.equals(responseTag) &&
            RESULT == status)
    {
        status = RESPONSE;
        if(Boolean.valueOf(
            available.toString()).booleanValue())
        {
            int lvl = Integer.parseInt(level.toString());
            if(lvl <= 0)
                message.setText("Ships in 3-5 weeks");
            else
                message.setText("Ships in 2-3 days");
        }
        else
            message.setText("Special order");
    }
```

## StockQPanel

`StockQPanel`, in Listing 9.12, supports the user interface for the client application.

Listing 9.12 *StockQPanel.java*

```java
package com.psol.stockq;

import java.io.*;
import java.sql.*;
import java.net.*;
import java.awt.*;
import org.xml.sax.*;
import java.awt.event.*;

public class StockQPanel
    extends Panel
{
    protected Connection connection;
    protected Choice products;
    protected TextComponent server;
    protected Label message;

    public StockQPanel(Connection connection)
        throws ClassNotFoundException, SQLException
    {
        this.connection = connection;
        setLayout(new BorderLayout());
        Panel topFields = new Panel();
        topFields.setLayout(new GridLayout(2,2));
        topFields.add(new Label("Server:"));
        server = new TextField("http://localhost:8080/stockq");
        topFields.add(server);
        topFields.add(new Label("Products:"));
        products = new Choice();
        topFields.add(products);
        Panel bottomFields = new Panel();
        bottomFields.setLayout(new GridLayout(2,1));
        Button check = new Button("Check");
        bottomFields.add(check);
        message = new Label("No product selected");
        bottomFields.add(message);
        add(topFields,"Center");
        add(bottomFields,"South");

        check.addActionListener(new ActionListener()
        {
            public void actionPerformed(ActionEvent evt)
            {
                checkStockLevel();
            }
        });
        Statement stmt = connection.createStatement();
        try
        {
            ResultSet rs = stmt.executeQuery(
```

Listing 9.12 **Continued**

```
                        "select name from products");
            try
            {
                while(rs.next())
                    products.addItem(rs.getString(1));
            }
            finally
            {
                rs.close();
            }
        }
        finally
        {
            stmt.close();
        }
    }

    public void checkStockLevel()
    {
        message.setText("Checking...");
        try
        {
            PreparedStatement stmt =
                connection.prepareStatement("select level, " +
                    "manufacturer, sku from products where name=?");
            try
            {
                stmt.setString(1,products.getSelectedItem());
                ResultSet rs = stmt.executeQuery();
                try
                {
                    if(rs.next())
                    {
                        if(rs.getInt(1) > 0)
                            message.setText("Ships in 24 hours");
                        else
                        {
                            URL url = new URL(server.getText());
                            StockRequest request =
                                new StockRequest(message);
                            request.setManufacturer(
                                rs.getString(2));
                            request.setSku(rs.getString(3));
                            request.invoke(url);
                        }
                    }
                }
                finally
                {
                    rs.close();
```

Listing 9.12 **Continued**

```
                }
            }
            finally
            {
                stmt.close();
            }
        }
        catch(SQLException e)
        {
            message.setText(e.getMessage());
        }
        catch(IOException e)
        {
            message.setText(e.getMessage());
        }
        catch(SoapException e)
        {
            message.setText(e.getCode() + ' ' +
                            e.getMessage());
        }
        catch(SAXException e)
        {
            Exception ex = null == e.getException() ?
                            e : e.getException();
            message.setText(e.getMessage());
        }
    }
}
```

checkStockLevel() packs all the fun. When the user clicks the button, it queries the
local database for the local stock level. If it finds that the product is in back order
locally, it sends a SOAP request to the wholesaler:

```
PreparedStatement stmt =
    connection.prepareStatement("select level, " +
        "manufacturer, sku from products where name=?");
try
{
    stmt.setString(1,products.getSelectedItem());
    ResultSet rs = stmt.executeQuery();
    try
    {
        if(rs.next())
        {
            if(rs.getInt(1) > 0)
                message.setText("Ships in 24 hours");
            else
            {
                URL url = new URL(server.getText());
```

```
                    StockRequest request = new StockRequest(message);
                    request.setManufacturer(rs.getString(2));
                    request.setSku(rs.getString(3));
                    request.invoke(url);
                }
            }
        }
        finally
        {
            rs.close();
        }
    }
    finally
    {
        stmt.close();
    }
}
```

## StockQClient

`StockQClient`, in Listing 9.13, is the `main()` method of the application. It opens a window, opens a connection to the local database, and adds the `StockQPanel` to the window.

Listing 9.13  *StockQClient.java*

```
package com.psol.stockq;

import java.io.*;
import java.net.*;
import java.sql.*;
import java.awt.*;
import java.util.*;
import org.xml.sax.*;
import java.awt.event.*;
import org.xml.sax.helpers.*;

public class StockQClient
{
    public final static void main(String args[])
        throws IOException, SoapException, SAXException,
               ClassNotFoundException, SQLException
    {
        Properties properties = new Properties();
        properties.load(new FileInputStream("./cfg/client.prp"));
        Class.forName(properties.getProperty("driver"));
        String url = properties.getProperty("url"),
               username = properties.getProperty("username"),
               password = properties.getProperty("password");
        Connection connection =
            DriverManager.getConnection(url,username,password);
```

Listing 9.13 **Continued**

```java
      try
      {
        Frame frame = new Frame();
        frame.add(new StockQPanel(connection));
        frame.pack();
        frame.setTitle("StockQ Client");
        frame.addWindowListener(new WindowAdapter()
        {
          public void windowClosing(WindowEvent evt)
          {
            System.exit(0);
          }
        });
        frame.show();
        try
        {
          Thread.currentThread().join();
        }
        catch(InterruptedException e)
          {}
      }
      finally
      {
        connection.close();
      }
    }
}
```

## Constants

Constants, in Listing 9.14, is a list of constants used throughout the project.

Listing 9.14 *Constants.java*

```java
package com.psol.stockq;

public class Constants
{
    public static final String PSOL_URI =
        "http://www.psol.com/xmlns/stockq";
    public static final String SOAPENV_URI =
        "http://schemas.xmlsoap.org/soap/envelope/";
    public static final String SOAPENCODING_URI =
        "http://schemas.xmlsoap.org/soap/encoding/";
    public static final String SAXPARSER =
        "org.apache.xerces.parsers.SAXParser";
    public static final String SAXNAMESPACES =
        "http://xml.org/sax/features/namespaces";
}
```

# Building and Running the Project

The StockQ project is available on the enclosed CD-ROM. Copy the project directory from the CD-ROM to your hard disk. Under Windows, start the server by double-clicking `server.bat`. Next, you can double-click `client.bat` and inquire about the availability of the various products.

▶

**Warning**

This project uses Jetty as its Web server. However, because it is based on servlets, it should be easy to adapt to Web servers. You can add servlet support to most Web servers with JRun.

The project on the CD-ROM includes databases for the client and the server, but if you need to re-create them, you can use Listings 9.15 and 9.16. Use Hypersonic SQL DatabaseManager to execute the script. To connect to the database, do the following:

- Select Hypersonic SQL Standalone.
- The URLs are `jdbc:HypersonicSQL:db/client` and `jdbc:HypersonicSQL:db/server`.

Listing 9.15 *client.sql*

```
CREATE TABLE products(name VARCHAR,manufacturer VARCHAR,sku
➥VARCHAR,level INTEGER);
INSERT INTO products(name,manufacturer,sku,level) VALUES
➥('Email Client','Emailaholic','100',10);
INSERT INTO products(name,manufacturer,sku,level) VALUES
➥('Email Server','Emailaholic','200',-1);
INSERT INTO products(name,manufacturer,sku,level) VALUES
➥('Arcade Games','Playfield','101',1);
INSERT INTO products(name,manufacturer,sku,level) VALUES
➥('Mind Games','Playfield','202',0);
INSERT INTO products(name,manufacturer,sku,level) VALUES
➥('Exclusive Games','Playfield','303',-1);
```

Listing 9.16 *server.sql*

```
CREATE TABLE products(manufacturer VARCHAR,sku VARCHAR,
➥level INTEGER);
INSERT INTO products(manufacturer,sku,level) VALUES
➥('Emailaholic','100',1000);
INSERT INTO products(manufacturer,sku,level) VALUES
➥('Emailaholic','200',-500);
INSERT INTO products(manufacturer,sku,level) VALUES
➥('Playfield','101',10);
INSERT INTO products(manufacturer,sku,level) VALUES
➥('Playfield','202',2);
```

> **Note**
> The project uses Hypersonic SQL for the database. Because Hypersonic SQL is a JDBC database, it should be easy to adapt it to other JDBC databases (including Access, Oracle, and SQL Server).

# Additional Resources

For some projects, you might want to turn to XML-RPC (www.xml-rpc.com). XML-RPC is simpler to implement but also less efficient than SOAP. In particular, XML-RPC requests are larger than SOAP requests.

However, because it was introduced before SOAP, XML-RPC has established a loyal user base. It is expected that SOAP will gradually replace XML-RPC. In fact, you will find that the developers of XML-RPC are among the editors of the SOAP protocol.

Another alternative to SOAP is WDDX from Allaire (www.wddx.org). WDDX specifies how to encode data structure to send requests between different languages, such as ColdFusion, Java, and JavaScript.

If you like SOAP but find it's too much work to implement it, you might want to use object libraries, which essentially hide the protocol from you. At the time of writing, you can choose between the following:

- SOAP for Java (the reference implementation from IBM), available from www.alphaworks.ibm.com
- The reference implementation from DevelopMentor, available from www.develop.com/SOAP

As has been discussed already, these libraries take a different approach and wrap Java objects in a SOAP layer. In that respect, they are closer to distributed object brokers. As we discussed, it might be seen as a blessing or a shortcoming, depending on the specifics of the project.

# 10
# Where to Now

THIS CHAPTER CONCLUDES THE SET of projects and solutions based on XML. I hope that, as you read through the solutions, you picked up valuable techniques, useful tips, and good ideas for your next project.

As explained in the Introduction, I deliberately organized this book as a set of solutions because I believe programmers learn more by studying listings and by sharing applications than by reviewing more theoretical lessons.

However, I recognize that one of the dangers of the hands-on, solution-oriented format is that, although this book covers a lot of ground, it is not always easy to see how things fit together. After many exercises and listings, I'd like to use this chapter to review the lessons we have learned.

Although this chapter is more abstract than the other chapters, I hope you will find it to be useful as you prepare to implement XML in your projects.

As you become more familiar with the techniques introduced in this book, I hope that you will see how your regular projects can benefit from XML.

If you are unsure about which is the best approach, remember that action always beats inaction: Flip through this book to find one or more examples that match your needs, reread the appropriate chapters, and copy the listings. You're on your way to success. Don't be afraid to make mistakes. You can learn a lot by reviewing your mistakes as well as those others make.

You will find that XML is a very flexible technology that works well for a wide range of problems. I wish you lots of success.

# XML As a File Format

As you know, XML is an extensible syntax. It does not define elements or attributes—it's up to you, the developer, to define them. One of the main issues for XML users is deciding on the vocabulary they need for their applications. In some cases, they can turn to standard vocabularies, such as RSS; in other cases, they will need to create their own.

I strongly believe that the best approach when deciding on a vocabulary for a given project is the following two-step process:

1. Survey the market for existing vocabularies that match your needs. (xml.org is an invaluable resource in that respect.)
2. Failing this, model your own vocabulary after existing file formats.

Unfortunately, XML is still young. After all, it was introduced only in 1998. Popular SGML DTDs, such as DocBook and HTML, have been ported to XML. XSLFO is also available, so if you are developing a publishing application, you will find good and stable vocabularies.

However, for other applications, chances are that no standard format exists yet. A lot of work is in progress to define XML vocabularies for applications as diverse as multimedia (SMIL and SVG), e-commerce (RosettaNet and ebXML), and content synchronization (SynchML), but the market has not decided on the winning formats yet.

Therefore, for the time being, you might be stuck with developing your own vocabulary. As you go through this process, I urge you to review existing file formats or legacy formats. Basing your new format on something already in existence is more efficient than starting from scratch. Legacy formats have accumulated tremendous experience and only a fool would want to ignore them.

However, you must walk a fine line between inspiration (not copying outright) and plagiarism. As you review legacy formats, use them for inspiration but don't feel bound by their limitations. Often, legacy formats have technical limitations that are no longer relevant with XML.

For example, in Chapters 5, "Export to Any Format," and 6, "Import from Any Format," I introduced an XML order that is inspired by a legacy order (EDIFACT). The XML order follows the same data model as the EDIFACT order with buyer, seller, and product lines. However, the similarities end there—the XML document takes advantage of XML, for example, by making the relationship between lines and products more explicit than in EDIFACT.

As you can see, I used EDIFACT for inspiration, but I didn't feel limited by EDIFACT's technical constraints.

To help you succeed, I urge you to use a modeling language, such as UML. In most cases, it is safer than trying to create a DTD from scratch—particularly if you are not yet experienced with XML.

The following are two serious advantages to going through a data model:

1. UML is well accepted and widely understood. This enables you to share your design with other programmers who might not be familiar with XML. Therefore, you can benefit from their experience.

2. The UML model is more abstract than the underlying XML vocabulary. The effort required to model at a higher level of abstraction guarantees that you will tend toward inspiration rather than plagiarism.

# Publishing Versus Data

Most people classify XML applications as either publishing or data applications. *Publishing* applications are related to Web publishing, printing, and email. *Data* applications deal with databases, application integration, and e-commerce.

This is a sound distinction at the modeling and architectural levels. You would not want to design an e-commerce solution in the same way you would design a publishing solution.

Yet, at the technical level, the distinction blurs. In fact, I have often found that to benefit from XML, you must think creatively, outside the two boxes.

Let's look at a few examples. Chapter 3, "Electronic Forms," presents an XML editor, which is a publishing tool. However, it is used in a forms-based application, and forms are typically classified as database applications. So, Chapter 3 uses a publishing tool in a non-publishing context…with great success.

Another example is XSLT. XSLT is a style sheet language—originally a publishing technology. Yet, as Chapter 7, "Write an e-Commerce Server," demonstrates, it works very well for data applications such as e-commerce.

Conversely, Chapter 8, "Organize Teamwork Between Developers and Designers," uses a data solution (servlets) for a publishing application (Web site publishing).

This is what I mean by thinking outside the two boxes. Knowing whether you are building a publishing or data application is useful, but these distinctions do not necessarily hold at the technical level.

In my experience, the maximum benefits are often derived at the edges—when you take a solution that was originally developed in one context and apply it in the other context.

To me, this is what makes XML powerful and attractive. It is a flexible technology that works well across a broad range of applications.

## Flexible, Generic Tools

This leads me to generic and flexible tools. As a programmer, what makes XML attractive to me is the ample supply of quality tools.

This book covers three important tools with which any XML programmer should be familiar:

- **The XSLT processor**—XSLT is a very effective scripting language that you need to master if you are serious about XML programming. As Chapters 5 and 6 demonstrate, XSLT easily can be extended with new elements, functions, or formatters.
- **The XML parser**—Chapter 3 uses a DOM parser, but the other chapters rely on a SAX parser. A DOM parser is ideal if the application manipulates XML documents (such as an editor). SAX is the best choice for other applications. In other words, SAX is appropriate when the application has its own object structure.
- **The XML editor**—I found that many developers neglect the XML editor. However, a good editor is an ideal starting point for a data-entry application.

## e-Commerce

e-Commerce is one of my pet topics. In 1997, with three colleagues, I founded the XML/EDI Group (www.xmledi.com). We believed that an open, extensible, standard format was required for business-to-business e-commerce.

I have debated this point at length in various forums (one of the most recent examples is at www.pineapplesoft.com/newsletter/20000601_ecommerce.html). Let me try to summarize it for you.

One of the fundamental laws of a capitalist economy is that the transparent market, one in which every player has access to all product and pricing information, is the ideal market. The transparent market will, over time, converge toward the best pricing for the best products with the best level of services.

That's the economic theory, at least. In practice, creating transparent markets is very difficult. The stock market and, possibly, eBay are the best approximations in existence. Yet, the theory is useful in guiding our actions. For example, anti-trust laws are derived directly from this theory.

When it comes to the Internet, you can read this law in many interesting ways, and XML is one of the most interesting readings. The Internet has proven such a fertile soil for the development of e-commerce and the so-called new economy because it is a good basis on which to build a relatively transparent market.

To achieve a transparent market, it is essential that every actor, no matter how big or small it is, no matter which operating system it uses, and no matter which accounting package it has installed, can participate.

In the consumer space, HTML fits the bill. HTML is a neutral format that enables buyers and sellers to meet and conduct business activities electronically.

However, because HTML is a formatting language, it is appropriate only for low volumes of transactions. As we saw in Chapter 5, to handle larger volumes (as required in business-to-business e-commerce), HTML is not appropriate. Instead we need a more structured format, such as XML.

I'm often asked, "Why XML? Why not [insert a format name here]?" One of the reasons is that XML is a standard. It is not only a formal standard maintained by the W3C but, more importantly, it is an industry standard. It is used and adopted by most e-commerce players.

The second reason is that it is an open standard. As discussed before, it is crucial that every business—no matter how small or how exotic their operating systems—can participate. If you are curious, I am running Windows, but it does not mean I don't want to do business with Linux, Mac, and Palm users.

Furthermore, the solution must be cheap. Expensive solutions are accessible only to large businesses. To reach a more transparent market, a cheap solution is necessary—a solution that is affordable for large and small businesses.

Frankly, at the time of writing, we're not there yet. Chapter 7 is an e-commerce application, and, although it is not complex, it remains costly to build and costly to deploy.

However, I am confident that we will witness the same evolution as we have in the consumer arena. Until 1996 or 1997, if you had come to me and inquired about building an online shop, I would have fired up my programmer's editor and written one for you. Few businesses could afford it, though.

In 1997, I would have sold you a product. I don't remember the exact figures, but depending on the options, the cost was between $3,500 and $10,000. That was still expensive.

Today, most ISPs offer shopping carts for $50–$200 per month. In addition, HTML editors, such as NetObjects, enable you to edit and manage your shop from your desktop.

At the time of writing, XML is similar to what HTML was like in 1996. It requires a lot of custom programming, but the first generation of products (the expensive ones) is appearing on the market.

I would be surprised if prices don't go down. In a couple of years, most ISPs will offer an XML-based e-commerce module as part of their standard package. At that point, we'll have a more transparent market.

I hope this book succeeded in teaching you how to write applications for this new market.

## XML Elements

*Elements* are the basis of XML documents. Indeed, an XML document is essentially a tree of elements. Elements are made of the following:

- A name
- An optional content
- An optional list of attributes

The following is a `library` element made up of two `loan` elements. Each `loan` in turn contains a `member` and a `title` element. `loan` elements have a `date` attribute, whereas `member` and `title` contain text:

```
<library>
   <loan date="2000-03-27">
      <member>Jack Smith</member>
      <title>XML by Example</title>
   </loan>
   <loan date="2000-03-12">
      <member>John Doe</member>
      <title>Applied XML Solutions</title>
   </loan>
</library>
```

Unlike HTML, no element is predefined by XML. It is up to you, the developer, to create tags that are meaningful in your application.

## Element Name

The element name must start with a Unicode letter, followed by zero or more Unicode letters or digits. Also, spaces are not allowed. Names are case sensitive and cannot start with the three letters XML (upper- or lowercase).

In the document, the element name appears within tags (start tag and end tag). The tags surrounds the content, as in

```
<title>Applied XML Solutions</title>
```

## Content

If an element has no content, it is said to be empty. Non-empty elements contain text, other elements, or a combination of both. In other words, elements can nest to form a tree.

Empty elements have a simplified syntax where the slash (/) from the end tag migrates at the end of the start tag:

```
<book isbn='0-672-32054-1'/>
```

## Attribute

An *attribute* is made up of a name and a value attached to an element. Attribute names follow the same rules as element names.

Attributes appear in the element's start tag. The element name and its value are separated by an equal sign, and the value is located between single or double quotes. For example

```
<book isbn='0-672-32054-1'/>
```

or

```
<loan date="2000-03-12">
   <member>John Doe</member>
   <title>Applied XML Solutions</title>
</loan>
```

## Predefined Attributes

Two attributes are predefined by the XML standard:

- xml:lang, which is the content language
- xml:space, which indicates that spaces must be preserved in the content of the element

# XML Document

In its simplest form, an XML document is one (and only one) element. This top-level element is called the *root*. However, because an element can contain other elements, the document can be large and complex.

The only rule to remember is that the document cannot have more than one root. The following is a valid XML document:

```
<set>
   <book isbn='0-672-32054-1'/>
   <book isbn='0-7897-2215-1'/>
</set>
```

## XML Declaration

The document can start with an optional XML declaration. The declaration has a number of attributes to specify:

- The version of XML in use (at this time 1.0). This attribute is required.
- The character set encoding in use (if not using a standard Unicode encoding such as UTF-8 or UTF-16). This attribute is optional.
- Whether the document is standalone; in other words, whether the XML parser must read an external file (such as the external DTD subset) to properly decode it. This attribute is optional.

The following document has a declaration with optional encoding and standalone attributes:

```
<?xml version="1.0" encoding="ISO-8859-1" standalone="yes"?>
<set>
   <book isbn='0-672-32054-1'/>
   <book isbn='0-7897-2242-9'/>
</set>
```

## Document Type Declaration

An optional model can be associated to the document, such as a Document Type Definition (DTD), or another model, such as the forthcoming XML Schema. The document references the model in the document type declaration (not to be confused with the DTD):

```
<?xml version="1.0"?>
<!DOCTYPE set SYSTEM "http://www.psol.com/axs/bookset.dtd">
<set>
   <book isbn='0-672-32054-1'/>
   <book isbn='0-7897-2242-9'/>
</set>
```

The document type declaration can be any of the following:

- SYSTEM, pointing to a system identifier (a file or an URI)
- PUBLIC, including a so-called public identifier of the form
  -//Pineapplesoft//Book Set//EN
- A copy of the model between square brackets
- A combination of the above

# Entities

The content of an element can include entities. An *entity* is shorthand for a piece of text. Entities are declared in the DTD (see the previous section) and have a name and a content. In addition, entities are inserted in the document between the & and ; characters.

Assuming the entity axs was declared with the content Applied XML Solutions, the parser will resolve

```
<title>&axs;</title>
```

as

```
<title>Applied XML Solutions</title>
```

## Predefined Entities

XML predefines a small number of entities to escape special characters:

- &lt;—Stands for <
- &amp;—Stands for &
- &gt;—Stands for >
- &apos;—Stands for '
- &quot;—Stands for "

## Character Entities

XML also defines character entities. A *character entity* references a single Unicode character. They are typically used to call characters that are not legal in the current encoding.

The name of character entities has the form *#number*, where *number* is the Unicode code for the character. For example, © is Unicode character 169, so

```
<notice>&#169; 2000, Pineapplesoft</notice>
```

is equivalent to

```
<notice>© 2000, Pineapplesoft</notice>
```

# Namespaces

Because XML is extensible, anybody or any organization can draft its own tags. This raises the risk that two different organizations or people will use the same tag with different meanings.

The namespace mechanism is a small extension to XML to clearly label the owner of a tag. The mechanism builds on the familiar URIs (URLs and URNs).

For example, the following uses the element `title` as defined in the context of name-space `http://www.psol.com/axs/library`. The namespace is declared (with the `xmlns` attribute) and bound to a prefix (`psol`).

```
<psol:title xmlns:psol="http://www.psol.com/axs/library">
➥Applied XML Solutions</psol:title>
```

Although simple, namespace is the source of much confusion so let's debunk two of the most common errors:

- The URI is only an identifier; it doesn't need to point to a description of the element.

- The prefix is used only as a shorthand for the URI because the URIs are typically large and include characters not valid for XML names.

It is probably easier if you forget the prefix and think of the document as

```
<http://www.psol.com/axs/library:title>Applied XML Solutions
➥</http://www.psol.com/axs/library:title>
```

In practice, however, this would be verbose and the element name would include illegal characters (such as /). Hence the prefix mechanism.

# Parser Reference

THIS APPENDIX IS A REFERENCE of the main SAX2 API for Java. The definitive reference is at www.megginson.com/SAX. The SAX2 distribution includes SAX1 as deprecated classes, interfaces, and methods. This appendix concentrates on SAX2 only.

Unless otherwise noted, these classes and interfaces reside in the `org.xml.sax` package.

## XMLReader

`XMLReader` is the main interface to the parser. The application must create an instance of `XMLReader` and register the appropriate event handlers with it.

### Registering Event Handlers

The following methods are used to register event handlers:

- `void setContentHandler(ContentHandler handler)/ContentHandler getContentHandler()`—Register a `ContentHandler`.
- `void setDTDHandler(DTDHandler handler)/DTDHandler getDTDHandler()`—Register a `DTDHandler`.

- void setErrorHandler(ErrorHandler handler)/ErrorHandler getErrorHandler()—Register an ErrorHandler.
- void setEntityResolver(EntityResolver resolver)/EntityResolver getEntityResolver()—Register an EntityResolver.

## Parsing

The following are the two parse() methods:

- void parse(InputSource input)—Parses an XML document identified by an InputSource.
- void parse(String systemId)—Parses an XML document from a system identifier (typically a URI).

## Features and Properties

XMLReader also offers methods to parsing options:

- void setFeature(String name,boolean value)/boolean getFeature(String name)—Set a feature; a feature has a Boolean value and is identified by a name.
- void setProperty(String name,Object value)/Object getProperty(String name)—Set a property; a property has an object value and is identified by a name.

Similar to namespaces, feature and property names are URIs. This limits the risk that two developers would define conflicting features or properties with the same name.

Parser developers are free to implement their own features and properties. The SAX2 specification defines the following standard features. The first two features are mandatory for SAX2 parsers:

- http://xml.org/sax/features/namespaces—When true, the parser must process namespaces. When false, the parser is free to process them as it sees fit.
- http://xml.org/sax/features/namespace-prefixes—When true, the parser must report the original prefixed names and attributes used for namespace declarations.
- http://xml.org/sax/features/string-interning—When true, all names are internalized strings. When false, strings are internalized as the parser sees fit.
- http://xml.org/sax/features/validation—Turns on and off validation errors.
- http://xml.org/sax/features/external-general-entities—Controls the inclusion of external general entities.
- http://xml.org/sax/features/external-parameter-entities—Controls the inclusion of external parameter entities.

The specification also defines the following standard properties. Parsers do not have to recognize them:

- `http://xml.org/sax/properties/dom-node`—This read-only property returns the current DOM node (or root for iteration, when not parsing) if this is a DOM iterator.
- `http://xml.org/sax/properties/xml-string`—This read-only property returns the literal string of characters that was the source for the current event.

# ContentHandler

The `ContentHandler` interface defines the events for the content of the document. To register for content-related events, applications must implement this interface. The events are as follows:

- `void setDocumentLocator(Locator locator)`—Optionally called by the parser before any other event to pass a locator to the event handler
- `void startDocument()/void endDocument()`—Start/end of document
- `void startPrefixMapping(String prefix,String uri)/void endPrefixMapping(String prefix)`—Start/end of scope for prefix mapping when processing namespaces
- `void startElement(String namespaceURI,String localName,String qName, Attributes atts)/void endElement(String namespaceURI,String localName, String qName)`—Start/end of element
- `void characters(char[] ch,int start,int length)`—Character data
- `void ignorableWhitespace(char ] ch,int start,int length)`—Ignorable whitespaces, as defined by the XML recommendation
- `void processingInstruction(String target, String data)`—Processing instruction
- `void skippedEntity(String name)`—Skipped entity

# DTDHandler

The `DTDHandler` interface defines events for a minimalist processing of DTD. The two events are as follows:

- `void notationDecl(String name, String publicId,String systemId)`—Notation declaration
- `void unparsedEntityDecl(String name,String publicId,String systemId, String notationName)`—Unparsed entity declaration

**Tip**

For more comprehensive information on the DTD, turn to the DeclHandler interface in the org.xml.sax.ext package. However, this is a SAX2 extension and not every parser recognizes it.

# ErrorHandler

The ErrorHandler interface receives notifications of errors. It defines three methods to match the three levels of errors in the XML recommendation:

- void warning(SAXParseException exception)—A warning
- void error(SAXParseException exception)—A recoverable error
- void fatalError(SAXParseException exception)—A non-recoverable error

# EntityResolver

Few applications will need to implement the EntityResolver interface. EntityResolver enables the application to resolve external entities—for example, by loading the entity from a database. By default, the parser resolves most external entities as URIs.

The interface defines only one method:

- InputSource resolveEntity(String publicId,String systemId)—Enables the application to return the appropriate InputSource for this entity

# InputSource

The parser uses this class to read entities. In most cases, the application creates an InputSource with one of its four constructors. The constructors with InputStream and Reader are particularly useful:

- InputSource()—Default constructor.
- InputSource(InputStream byteStream)—The source is an InputStream.
- InputSource(Reader characterStream)—The source is a character reader.
- InputSource(String systemId)—The source is a URI that the parser must resolve.

InputSource also defines the following methods. They read the entity:

- void setByteStream(InputStream byteStream)/InputStream getByteStream()—Get the InputStream for this input source

- `void setCharacterStream(Reader characterStream)/Reader getCharacterStream()`—Get the reader for this input source
- `void setEncoding(String encoding)/String getEncoding()`—Get the character encoding for the `InputStream` or URI
- `void setPublicId(String publicId)/String getPublicId()`—Get the public identifier for this entity
- `void setSystemId(String systemId)/String getSystemId()`—Get the system identifier for this entity

## Attributes

This interface, used by `startElement()`, enables the application to access the element attributes. The various methods are as follows:

- `int getLength()`—Returns the number of attributes in the list
- `String getValue(int index)/String getValue(String qName)/String getValue(String uri, String localName)`—Return the attribute's value by index or by XML 1.0 qualified name, respectively
- `String getType(int index)/String getType(java.lang.String qName)/String getType(String uri,String localName)`—Return the attribute's type by index, by XML 1.0 qualified name, or by namespace, respectively
- `String getQName(int index)`—Returns the attribute XML 1.0 qualified name by index
- `String getURI(int index)`—Returns the attribute's namespace URI by index
- `String getLocalName(int index)`—Returns the attribute local name by index
- `int getIndex(String qName)/int getIndex(String uri,String localPart)`—Return the index of an attribute from XML 1.0 qualified name or by using its namespace, respectively

**Warning**

Beware that `Attributes` is valid only during the call to `startElement()`. If you need to store `Attributes` for later processing, make a copy with `org.xml.sax.helpers.AttributeImpl`.

## Locator

The SAX parser uses an instance of `Locator` to provide location information (line and column). The four methods are as follows:

- `int getColumnNumber()`—The column where the current event ends
- `int getLineNumber()`—The line where the current event ends

- `String getPublicId()`—The public identifier for the current event
- `String getSystemId()`—The system identifier for the current event

## Exceptions

SAX2 also defines the following exceptions:

- `SAXException`—A generic exception
- `SAXParseException`—Indicates a parsing error
- `SAXNotRecognizedException`—Thrown by `getFeature/setFeature/ getProperty/setProperty` to indicate an unknown feature or property
- `SAXNotSupportedException`—Thrown by `getFeature/setFeature/ getProperty/setProperty` to indicate a feature or property that is known but not supported

## XMLFilter

`XMLFilter` extends `XMLReader` with two methods:

- `XMLReader getParent()`—Gets the parent reader
- `void setParent(XMLReader parent)`—Sets the parent reader

An `XMLFilter` is similar to an `XMLReader`, but it obtains its events from another `XMLReader`. Typically, the `XMLFilter` filters some or all of the events.

**Tip**

`XMLFilterImpl`, in the `org.xml.sax.helpers` package, is convenient when implementing filters. The class forwards the events from its parents to the appropriate event handlers. Your application needs to override only those events it must filter.

## XMLReaderFactory

`XMLReaderFactory` helps create `XMLReader`. This class is in the `org.xml.sax.helpers` package. It defines two static methods:

- `static XMLReader createXMLReader()`—Creates an XML reader using the value of the `org.xml.sax.driver` system property as the parser classname
- `static XMLReader createXMLReader(String className)`—Creates an XML reader from a classname

# DefaultHandler

This class provides default implementations for events in the `ContentHandler`, `DTDHandler`, `EntityResolver`, and `ErrorHandler` interfaces.

This is convenient when your application needs to register with only a few events. It derives from `DefaultHandler` instead of implementing the original interface.

This class is in the `org.xml.sax.helpers` package.

# XSLT Reference

T HIS APPENDIX SUMMARIZES THE MOST commonly used XSLT aspects. It does not pretend to be a complete reference, but a reference to the most commonly used XSLT elements and functions.

## Style Sheet

An XSLT style sheet is an XML document. Its root element is an `xsl:stylesheet` where the `xsl` prefix is bound to `http://www.w3.org/1999/XSL/Transform`. Its main attribute is `version`, which, for the time being, must have the value `"1.0"`:

```
<xsl:stylesheet
   version="1.0"
   xmlns:xsl=" http://www.w3.org/1999/XSL/Transform">
   <!-- content deleted -->
</xsl:stylesheet>
```

## Output

One of the first elements within `xsl:stylesheet` should be `xsl:output`. `xsl:output` specifies how the processor should write the output. Note that the processor may elect to ignore this recommendation:

```
<xsl:output method="xml"/>
```

The most commonly used attributes are as follows:

- method—Its value can be xml, html, text, or another name. The method selects the formatter; for example, xml follows the XML syntax (<BR/>), whereas html follows the HTML syntax (<BR>).
- encoding—Controls the XML encoding; for example, UTF-8, UTF-16, ISO-8859-1, and so on.
- media-type—Is the MIME type of the result; for example, text/xml, application/xml, text/plain, and so on.
- omit-xml-declaration—Controls whether the processor should output an XML declaration. The value is either yes or no.

# Templates

The bulk of a style sheet is a list of templates (xsl:template). The templates describe the various steps in the transformation. Most templates match an XPath (see the section "XPath" later in this chapter). The template content describes the corresponding output:

```
<xsl:template match="Title">
   <H1><xsl:apply-templates/></H1>
</xsl:template>
```

## Priority and Mode

The priority and mode attributes control which template is used when two or more templates match the same name. priority boosts or lowers a template's priority:

```
<xsl:template match="Title" priority="-1">
   <H1><xsl:apply-templates/></H1>
</xsl:template>
```

mode allows an element to be processed several times by various templates:

```
<xsl:template match="Title" mode="toc">
   <H1><xsl:apply-templates mode="toc"/></H1>
</xsl:template>
```

## Named Templates

Named templates are similar to functions: They can be invoked by their names (a name attribute) and accept parameters:

```
<xsl:template name="label-it">
   <xsl:param name="label"/>
   <xsl:value-of select="$label">: <xsl:apply-templates/>
</xsl:template>
```

Named templates are called through an xsl:call-template element. xsl:call-template applies the template to the current node:

```
<xsl:call-template name="label-it">
   <xsl:with-param name="">Title</xsl:with-param>
</xsl:call-template>
```

# Template Content

The content of the template specifies what output it will generate. Typically, the template contains a mixture of text, XML elements, and XSL instructions.

Two styles for writing templates exist. A template can be input directed or output controlled. The two modes are not exclusive; in fact, many style sheets effectively combine the two.

## Input Directed

These templates are guided by the input document. Essentially, the processor recursively walks the input document, selects a template that matches the current node, and applies it.

The `xsl:apply-templates` element moves one level down in the input document, kicking in the recursion:

```
<xsl:template match="Title">
   <H1><xsl:apply-templates/></H1>
</xsl:template>
```

The `select` and `mode` attributes control how the processor walks the input tree. For more information about `mode`, see the section "Priority and Mode" earlier in the chapter. `select` is an XPath that controls which nodes the processor visits next:

```
<xsl:template match="Body">
   <H1><xsl:apply-templates select="Section/Title"/></H1>
</xsl:template>
```

## Output Controlled

When the output is regular and well defined, it is more efficient to use `xsl:for-each` in combination with `xsl:value-of` elements:

```
<xsl:template match="Body">
   <xsl:for-each select="Title">
      <H1><xsl:value-of select="."/></H1>
   </xsl:for-each>
</xsl:template>
```

## XML Elements

To generate XML elements in the output document, insert them in a template:

```
<xsl:template match="Date">
   <PODate><xsl:apply-templates/></PODate>
</xsl:template>
```

Alternatively, a style sheet can compute elements with `xsl:element`, which can compute the element name from the style sheet:

```
<xsl:template match="Field">
   <xsl:element name="{@id}">
      <xsl:apply-templates/>
   </xsl:element>
</xsl:template>
```

### Tip

The `xsl:namespace-alias` enables you to transform namespaces between the input and output documents. It is typically used for style sheets that need to output elements in the XSL namespace:

```
<xsl:stylesheet
   version="1.0"
   xmlns:xsl="http://www.w3.org/1999/XSL/Transform"
   xmlns:alias="http://www.psol.com/XSL/Alias">

<xsl:namespace-alias stylesheet-prefix="alias"
                        result-prefix="xsl"/>

<!-- templates deleted-->

</xsl:stylesheet>
```

## XML Attributes

Likewise, to generate attributes in the output document, insert them in the template:

```
<xsl:template match="Date">
   <PODate format="ISO"><xsl:apply-templates/></PODate>
</xsl:template>
```

If the value of the attribute is an XPath, you must enclose it in curly brackets:

```
<xsl:template match="Date">
   <PODate format="{Format}"><xsl:apply-templates/></PODate>
</xsl:template>
```

On the other hand, a style sheet can compute elements with `xsl:attribute`, which computes the attribute name or value from the style sheet:

```
<xsl:template match="Date">
   <PODate><xsl:attribute name="format"/>
      <xsl:call-template name="get-format"/>
   </xsl:attribute></PODate>
</xsl:template>
```

## Text

In most cases, to output text, you type it in the template. However, to gain better control on how the processor interprets whitespaces, you should mark up the text with an `xsl:text` element:

```
<xsl:template match="Date">
   <xsl:text>Date: </xsl:text>
   <xsl:value-of select=".">
</xsl:template>
```

**Tip**

To insert entities in the output—particularly HTML entities such as  —write the following:

```
<xsl:text disable-output-escaping="yes"> </xsl:text>
```

# XPath

XPath select elements in the source XML document. The paths are very similar to paths on a file system. Elements are separated by the / character. A single / points to the root of the document. The *, ., and .. characters behave as you would expect (all nodes, current node, and node parent). Here are some absolute paths, starting from the root of the document:

```
/
/Body/Title
/Body/attribute::*
/Body/Section/Para/Image
```

The following, on the other hand, are some relative paths, starting from the current node:

```
.
Title
Invoice/Date
../Code
```

The / separator selects only direct descendants, whereas the // separator selects all descendants:

```
//Para
Body//Image
```

To select attributes, prefix them with the @ character:

```
Total/Amount/@Currency
@xml:lang
```

For the text content of a node, use the text() function:

```
Para/text()
```

Use predicates to restrict the path to elements that meet a certain condition. Predicates appear between square brackets after the element to which they apply:

```
/Body/Para[2]
Invoice/Product[@type="book"]/Code
Section[Status="Draft" and Editor="PZ"]
```

## Axes

XPath uses axes to control how the processor walks the tree. By default, the processor uses the `child` axis, but you can select any axis by prefixing the element with the axis name followed by `::`. Axes are used for advanced style sheets when you need fine control over which nodes will be selected:

```
child::Para
Section/following::Footnote
```

The most useful axes are as follows:

- `following` and `preceding`—Contain the nodes that are after or before the current node, excluding descendants, attributes, and namespace nodes.
- `following-sibling` and `preceding-sibling`—Contain the following or preceding siblings of the current node.
- `attribute`—Contains the attributes of the current node.
- `namespace`—Contains the namespace nodes of the context node.
- `self`—Contains the context node itself.
- `descendant-or-self` and `ancestor-or-self`—Contain the current node and its descendant or ancestor nodes.

### Note

The `..`, `//`, and `@` characters are shorthand for the `parent`, `descendant-or-self`, and `attribute` axes.

# Combining Style Sheets

Two solutions to combine two or more style sheets are available: inclusion or importing. Style sheet *inclusion*, through `xsl:include`, appends the templates of the included style sheet in the current style sheet. If a template is defined in both style sheets, a duplicate definition results:

```
<xsl:include href="common.xsl"/>
```

*Importing* is more sophisticated. Similar to inclusion, it appends templates from the imported style sheet in the current one. However, the current style sheet can redefine some (or all, although it is less useful) of the imported templates. The redefined templates take precedence over the imported ones:

```
<xsl:import href="common.xsl"/>
```

Templates that override imported templates can call the original definition with `xsl:apply-imports`:

```
<xsl:template match="Title">
  <FONT COLOR="black">
    <xsl:apply-imports/>
  </FONT>
</xsl:template>
```

# Parameters and Variables

Style sheets and templates can use *parameters* and *variables*. Both are names bound to a value. The difference is that a parameter only binds a default value, which can be overridden by the caller:

```
<xsl:variable name="amount" select="/Invoice/Total"/>
<xsl:param name="label">Date: </xsl:param>
```

The value of the variable or parameter is accessible in XPath by prefixing the name with a dollar sign ($):

```
$date/Currency
$label
```

# Tests and Conditions

`xsl:if` offers the equivalent of an `if` statement. The content of `xsl:if` is generated if the test is true:

```
<xsl:if test="not(position()=last())"> | </xsl:if>
```

`xsl:choose` is the equivalent of the Java `switch` statement. It selects one among a number of possible alternatives:

```
<xsl:choose>
    <xsl:when test="Currency='USD'">Dollars</xsl:when>
    <xsl:when test="Currency='EUR'">Euros</xsl:when>
    <xsl:when test="Currency='BEF'">Belgian Francs</xsl:when>
    <xsl:when test="Currency='CAD'">Canadian Dollars</xsl:when>
</xsl:choose>
```

> **Tip**
>
> There is no direct equivalent for the if/then/else statement in XSLT, but it can be simulated as follows:
>
> ```
> <xsl:choose/>
>     <xsl:when test="Confidential='true'">
>        <B>For Your Eyes Only</B>
>     </xsl:when>
>     <xsl:otherwise><B>You Can Circulate</B></xsl:otherwise>
> </xsl:choose>
> ```

# Functions

XPath and XSLT define many functions. Most of these functions take an XPath for a parameter. However, when called with no parameter, they apply to the current node:

```
position("//Product")
position()
```

The following are the most useful functions:

- `position()`—Returns the position of the expression evaluation context.
- `last()`—Returns the position of the last node from the expression evaluation context.
- `count()`—Returns the number of nodes from the expression evaluation context.
- `string()`—Converts its parameter to a string.
- `substring()`—Returns a substring of the first argument.
- `not()`—Performs a logical not.
- `format-number()`—Converts its first argument to a string using a format pattern.
- `generate-id()`—Returns a string that uniquely identifies the current node. If the function is called again on the same node, it will return the same ID.

# Copying

`xsl:copy` creates a copy of the current node in the output document. The identity transformation is written as follows:

```
<xsl:template match="@*|node()">
   <xsl:copy>
      <xsl:apply-templates select="@*|node()"/>
   </xsl:copy>
</xsl:template>
```

# Extensions

It is possible to extend XSLT with new elements and new functions. However, extensions must be introduced in a special namespace. For elements, the extension namespace must be registered with either the `extension-element-prefixes` of `xsl:stylesheet` or an `xsl:extension-element-prefixes` attribute attached to an element:

```
<xsl:stylesheet
    xmlns:xsl="http://www.w3.org/1999/XSL/Transform"
    xmlns:axslt="http://xml.apache.org/xslt"
    xmlns:psol="http://www.psol.com/xsledi/extensions"
    extension-element-prefixes="psol"
    version="1.0">
    <!-- deleted -->
</xsl;stylesheet>
```

Extension functions must also be declared in a special namespace, although it doesn't need to be registered with `xsl:extension-element-prefixes` or a similar attribute. A function with a namespace prefix is an extension function:

```
psol:query-db($name)
```

### Warning

XSLT does not specify how to link extension elements and functions with Java code. This is left to the processor writer.

# Index

## Symbols

## A

## B

# C

## Q–R

# Y-Z

# Licensing Agreement

**Read This Before Opening the Software**

By opening this package, you are agreeing to be bound by the following agreement:

You may not copy or redistribute the entire CD-ROM as a whole. Copying and redistribution of individual software programs on the CD-ROM is governed by terms set by the licensors or individual copyright holders.

The installer and code from the author is copyrighted by the publisher and the author.

This software is sold as is, without warranty of any kind, either expressed or implied, including but not limited to the implied warranties of merchantability and fitness for a particular purpose. Neither the publisher nor its dealers or distributors assumes any liability for any alleged or actual damages arising from the use of this program. (Some states do not allow for the exclusion of implied warranties, so the exclusion may not apply to you.)

*NOTE:* This CD-ROM uses long and mixed-case filenames requiring the use of a protected-mode CD-ROM driver.